Spawning Militancy:
Pakistan a Home Ground for Terror

Spawning Militancy-Pakistan A Home Ground for Terror

Col. Indrajeet Singh (Retd.)

Gaurav Book Centre Pvt. Ltd.
NEW DELHI-110002

Publisher
GAURAV BOOK CENTRE PVT LTD
4832/24, Prahlad Lane,S-207 Ansari
Road, Daryaganj, Delhi-110002
Ph.: 43570976, 23278261
Email: gauravbookcentre@gmail.com

Edition: 2015

ISBN: 978-93-83316-32-8

Laser Typesetting
JEE-VEE Graphics, Delhi

Price: 1295/-

Printed
Neeta Press, Delhi

Contents

Preface

The Pakistan military claims it has successfully destroyed terrorist infrastructure in NWA. Indeed, militant hideouts, storage houses for armaments, training sites, as well as factories producing explosive devices have all been targeted. However, this belies the fact that the modus operandi of militants is evolving, and there has been a failure to adopt the policies and strategies aimed at de-radicalization and reintegration of IDPs and non-combatant militants. Failure to do so will mean that Operation Zarb-e-Azb will only prove a quick fix and not a long lasting solution to the menace of militancy in Pakistan.

The War in North-West Pakistan is an armed conflict between the Pakistan Armed Forces and armed religious groups such as the Tehrik-i-Taliban Pakistan (TTP), Lashkar-e-Islam, TSNM, Arab and Central Asian militants including Al-Qaeda, regional armed movements and elements of organized crime. The armed conflict began in 2004 when tensions, rooted in the Pakistan Army's search for Al Qaeda fighters in Pakistan's mountainous Waziristan area (in the Federally Administered Tribal Areas), escalated into armed resistance. Pakistan's actions were presented as Pakistan's role in the War on Terror in the international War on Terrorism. Clashes erupted between Pakistani army troops and Arab and Central Asian militia forces. The foreign militants were joined by Pakistani non-military veterans of the War in Afghanistan (2001–present) which subsequently established the Tehrik-i-Taliban Pakistan and other militia organizations such as Lashkar-e-Islam. The Tehreek-e-Nafaz-e-Shariat-e-Mohammadi (TSNM) established in 1992 allied with the Tehrik-i-Taliban Pakistan and Lashkar-e-Islam.

The post-9/11 War on Terrorism in Pakistan has had two principal elements: the government's battle with jihad groups banned after 9/11, and the U.S. pursuit of Al-Qaeda, usually (but not always) in coordination with Pakistani forces.

This book is a modest attempt to discuss all these issues.

—*Editor*

1

Terrorism in Pakistan

Terrorism in Pakistan has been a problem in recent years, and has been attributed to the government allying itself with the United States in the global "war on terror". Currently, the biggest threat to the state and citizens of Pakistan stems from the politically motivated killing of civilians and police officials, possibly attributed to General Zia ul-Haq's controversial "Islamization" policies in the 1980s.

His tenure saw Pakistan's involvement in Soviet-Afghan War, which led to greater influx of ideologically driven Afghan Arabs in the tribal areas and an increase in guns and drugs. The state and its Inter-Services Intelligence, in alliance with the CIA, encouraged the "mujahideen" to fight a proxy war against the Soviet Union; most of the mujahideen were never disarmed after the war. Some of these groups were later activated under the behest of the state in the form of Lashkar-e-Taiba, Harkat-ul-Mujahideen and others were encouraged like Taliban to achieve state's agenda in the Kashmir conflict and Afghanistan. The same groups are now taking on the state itself. From the summer of 2007 to late 2009, more than 5,500 people were killed in suicide and other attacks on civilians. The attacks have been attributed to a number of causes: sectarian violence between Sunni and Shia Muslims; the easy availability of guns and explosives of a "kalishnikov culture" and influx of ideologically driven "Afghan Arabs" based in or near Pakistan, originating from and the subsequent war against the Afghan communists in the 1980s which blew back into Pakistan; Islamist insurgent groups and forces such as the Taliban and Lashkar-e-Taiba; Pakistan's thousands of fundamentalist madrassas which are thought by some to provide training for little except jihad; secessionists movements - the most significant of which is the Balochistan liberation movement - blamed on regionalism problematic in a country with Pakistan's diverse cultures, languages, traditions and customs.

Causes

Two of the main causal factors contributing to terrorism in Pakistan are sectarian/religious violence, the active support of the Pakistani state in nurturing terrorist proxies for perceived strategic ends. After imposition of martial law in 1956 Pakistan's political situation suddenly changed and entered into dictator type of national behaviour at different levels either civil servants, the army (the most involved people), political forces and British Indian Land Lords. The British originally didn't consider Pakistan as an independent state. Other causes, such as political rivalry and business disputes, also take their toll. It is estimated that more than 4,000 people have died in Pakistan in the past 25 years due to sectarian strife.

Pre-1980

The onset of partition of British India, saw massive killing of Hindus and Sikhs by Muslims, mainly because Hindus & Sikhs rejected the creation of Pakistan. This resulted in migration of half of the Muslim population from current Indian region to the geographical regions of what was to be Pakistan. The mass genocide type killing of Hindus by Muslims was initiated in Calcutta and Bengal by the call for direct action by Mohammed Ali Jinnah in 1945-46 during Muslim League rule in Bengal. It was done to create condition for partition. The first rioting in Punjab in 1947 was in the west Punjab area dominated by Muslims. So, the killing of Hindus and Sikhs was done first by Muslims in Muslim dominated areas.

In the late 1960s, Pakistani government faced a rebellion in eastern wing of the country and its struggle with its western counter-part over resources and political power and the eventual

Bangladesh Liberation War changed the dynamics of the country, and led the Pakistani state to "deal harshly with Hindus and Muslims" in East Pakistan. Bangladeshi authorities controversially claim that three million people were killed,. A further eight to ten million people fled the country to seek safety in India.

Aid to Mujahideen and Arab Afghans

Terrorism in Pakistan since the 1980s began primarily with to the Soviet-Afghan War, and the subsequent war against Afghan communists that continued for at least a decade. The war brought numerous fighters from all over the world to South Asia in the name of jihad. These fighters, known as mujahideen, carried out insurgent activities inside the country well after the war officially ended.

The sectarian violence plaguing the country presently is also said to originate in the controversial Islamic policies of General Muhammad Zia ul-Haq initiated during his tenure from 1977 to 1988. These policies gave immense power to religious figures in the country, who in turn spread intolerant religious dogmas among the masses.

Post Afghan War

At the end of the Afghan War, between 1990 and 1996, the Pakistani establishment continued to organize, support and nurture the Mujahideen groups. The idea was to use these groups for proxy warfare in Indian Kashmir and to support the doctrine of "strategic depth" in Afghanistan through the use of the Taliban. The 9/11 attacks brought this strategy of Pakistan under increased international scrutiny.

WAR ON TERRORISM IN PAKISTAN

The post-9/11 War on Terrorism in Pakistan has had two principal elements: the government's battle with jihad groups banned after 9/11, and the U.S. pursuit of Al-Qaeda, usually (but not always) in coordination with Pakistani forces.

In 2004, the Pakistani army launched a pursuit of Al-Qaeda members in the mountainous area of Waziristan on the Afghan border, although sceptics question the sincerity of this pursuit. Clashes there erupted into a low-level conflict with Islamic militants and local tribesmen, sparking the Waziristan War. A short-lived truce known as the Waziristan accord was brokered in September 2006.

PAKISTAN'S ROLE IN THE WAR ON TERROR

Pakistan's role in the War for Terror was initiated by the September 11 attacks in the United States in 2001 on the World Trade Center and the Pentagon. These acts were a new manifestation of terrorism, which altogether changed the political psyche of the world. The problem of terrorism, which had been confined to small groups and few states, was changed to a global menace.

The Saudi born Zayn al-Abidn Muhammed Hasayn Abu Zubaydah was arrested by Pakistani officials during a series of joint U.S. and Pakistan raids during the week of March 23, 2002. During the raid the suspect was shot three times while trying to escape capture by military personnel. Zubaydah is said to be a high-ranking al-Qaeda official with the title of operations chief and in charge of running al-Qaeda training camps.

Later that year on September 11, 2002, Ramzi Binalshibh was arrested in Pakistan after a three-hour gunfight with police forces. Binalshibh is known to have shared a room with Mohammad Atta in Hamburg, Germany and to be a financial backer of al-Qaeda operations. It is said Binalshibh was supposed to be another hijacker, however the U.S. Citizenship and Immigration Services rejected his visa application three times, leaving him to the role of financier. The trail of money transferred by Binalshibh from Germany to the United States links both Mohammad Atta and Zacarias Moussaoui.

On March 1, 2003, Khalid Shaikh Mohammed was arrested during CIA-led raids on the suburb of Rawalpindi, nine miles outside of the Pakistani capital of Islamabad. Mohammed at the time of his capture was the third highest ranking official in al-Qaeda and had been directly in charge of the planning for the September 11 attacks.

Escaping capture the week before during a previous raid, the Pakistani government was able to use information gathered from other suspects captured to locate and detain Mohammed. Mohammed was indicted in 1996 by the United States government for links to the Oplan Bojinka, a plot to bomb a series of U.S. civilian airliners.

Other events Mohammed has been linked to include: ordering the killing of Wall Street Journal reporter Daniel Pearl, the USS Cole bombing, Richard Reid's attempt to blow up a civilian airliner with a shoe bomb, and the terrorist attack at the El Ghriba synagogue in Djerba, Tunisia. Khalid Shaikh Mohammed has described himself as the head of the al-Qaeda military committee. Amidst all this, in 2006, Pakistan was accused by NATO commanding officers of aiding and abetting the Taliban in Afghanistan; but NATO later admitted that there was no known evidence against the ISI or Pakistani government of sponsoring terrorism. However in 2007, allegations of ISI secretly making bounty payments up to CDN$ 1,900 (Pakistani rupees. 1 lakh) for each NATO personnel killed surfaced. The Afghan government also accuses the ISI of providing help to militants including protection to the recently killed Mullah Dadullah, Taliban's senior military commander, a charge denied by the Pakistani government. India, meanwhile continues to accuse Pakistan's Inter-Services Intelligence of planning several terrorist attacks in Kashmir and elsewhere in the Indian republic, including the July 11, 2006 Mumbai train bombings, which Pakistan attributes it to "homegrown" insurgencies.

Many other countries like Afghanistan and the UK have also accused Pakistan of State-sponsored terrorism and financing terrorism. The upswing in American military activity in Pakistan and neighboring Afghanistan corresponded with a great increase in American military aid to the Pakistan government. In the three years before the attacks of September 11, Pakistan received approximately $9 million in American military aid. In the three years after, the number increased to $4.2 billion, making it the country with the maximum funding post 9/11.

Such a huge inflow of funds has raised concerns that these funds were given without any accountability, as the end uses not being documented, and that large portions were used to suppress civilians' human rights and to purchase weapons to contain domestic problems like the Balochistan unrest.

Waziristan

In 2004 the Pakistani Army launched a campaign in the Federally Administered Tribal Areas of Pakistan's Waziristan region, sending in 80,000 troops. The goal of the conflict was to remove the al-Qaeda and Taliban forces in the region.

After the fall of the Taliban regime many members of the Taliban resistance fled to the Northern border region of Afghanistan and Pakistan where the Pakistani army had previously little control. With the logistics and air support of the United States, the Pakistani Army captured or killed numerous al-Qaeda operatives such as Khalid Shaikh Mohammed, wanted for his involvement in the USS Cole bombing, Oplan Bojinka plot and the killing of Wall Street Journal reporter Daniel Pearl.

However, the Taliban resistance still operates in the Federally Administered Tribal Areas under the control of Haji Omar.

TRAINING GROUND FOR EUROPEAN MILITANTS

In 2009, a politically instable Pakistan emerged as a new global hub for anti-West militancy, but, because of the constant threat of US attacks, recruits were reportedly more likely to spend their time under instruction and in training than carrying out assertive action. In his report on the matter, focusing on an alarming influx of European extremists, *Reuters* security correspondent William Maclean wrote,

Long a favored destination of British militants of Pakistani descent, Pakistan's northwestern tribal areas are now attracting Arabs and Europeans of Arab ancestry who three years ago would probably have gone to Iraq to fight U.S. forces.

With the Iraq war apparently winding down, security sources say, the lure for these young men is to fight U.S. forces in neighboring Afghanistan or to gain the skills to carry out attacks back home in the Middle East, Africa or the West. One consequence: Western armies in Afghanistan increasingly face the possibility of having to fight their own compatriots. He added that the matter was likely to surface in a meeting on May 6 between United States President Barack Obama, Pakistani President Asif Ali Zardari and Afghan President Hamid Karzai, the first-mentioned looking to bring an end to the employment of Pakistan's tribal zones as a launching pad for al Qaeda activity around the world.

Background

The events of September 11 impacted international polices and the regional situation within Pakistan necessitated change to its internal policies. Pakistan found that it had no risk-free options: all polices were full of danger and risk of varying degrees. The test was to adopt such a policy and course of action that could minimize the risk and offered the best possible option in the given circumstances.

Geo-strategic location of Pakistan and links with Taliban administration absolved Pakistan to remain unaffected immediately after the attack. Moreover Pakistan was among the three countries, which recognized the Taliban government. Any effort of US and World coalition against Taliban could not have been succeeded without active cooperation of Pakistan. After declaring Al-Qaeda and Osama bin Laden as a prime suspect U.S. President George W. Bush said,

"Every nation in every region now has a decision to make. Either you are with us or with the terrorists."

The Taliban were asked to hand over Osama and close down bases of his Al-Qaeda network or face the consequences. The rest of the world was told that there could not be any neutral party in the war against terrorism. Pakistan, due to its strategic importance and close relation with the Taliban regime, was asked to cooperate.

Military President Pervez Musharraf, was told to either abandon the support of Taliban or be prepared to be treated like the Taliban. The military government, due to Pakistan's compulsions or concerns, Pakistan security and stability from external threat, the revival of economy, its nuclear and missile assets and Kashmir cause decided to join US led coalition on war against terrorism.

So once again, under another military ruler, Pakistan became front line state.

Actions

After joining the war on terrorism and abandoning its Taliban policy Pakistan opted for a very crucial and challenging task. Though Musharaf tried skilfully to manage the political dissent inside the country, it so far has found it very hard to manage law and order situation in the country. Pakistan has played a vital role in the war against terrorism. It has been a key ally in this war and suffered a lot. Despite its enormous efforts in war against terrorism, Pakistan has been criticized by the US. It is a fact that US cannot win without Pakistan's help, as 75 present of US/NATO supplies pass through Pakistan and the country has deployed more than 120,000 of its troops in tribal areas. It has lost more than three thousand soldiers in the war against terrorism. Pakistan has established 1500 checkpoints along the border with Afghanistan, and is the only US ally which has captured or killed more than 700 Al-Qaeda members. Despite all these efforts Pakistan has been blamed for not doing enough.

EFFECTS OF PAKISTAN'S ROLE IN THE WAR

On the International Stage

Pakistan's role in war against terrorism significantly improved her international status. Scholars argue that, US would leave Pakistan after gaining her objectives in war against terrorism. After joining the war on terror Pakistan gained billions of dollars of economic and military aid and also made some gains diplomatically but has lost its control over Afghan affairs.

Within Pakistan

After September 11 and US invasion in Afghanistan there has been a dramatic rise in domestic terrorism, extremism and sectarianism in Pakistan. Pakistan is in the grip of regular suicide bombings, and has suffered high levels of civilian and military casualties as a result. Baluchistan and Tribal area issues are other implications for Pakistan, with US drones attacks in tribal areas being a real source of concern for Pakistani citizens. The US so far has carried out number of attacks in Pakistani territory. These attacks have led to deterioration of the security situation in tribal areas and the rest of the North-West Frontier Province. In Pakistan there is a growing resentment among people against these attacks on Pakistani soil.

Western Involvement in Terrorism Inside Pakistan

On July 8, 2010, Pasha categorically stated that foreign powers are involved in terrorist activities inside Pakistan. He said, ""The foreign powers are involved in terrorism and destabilization of the country." During a briefing in the National Security Committee session headed by Senator Raza Rabbani, DG ISI Ahmed Shuja Pasha said that the western powers are involved in the terror activities inside the country.

"The US policy against terrorism is under consideration and the changes will be brought with time in accordance with the national interest," he said. This is not new claim inside Pakistan, many Pakistani political commentators have been speaking publicly about this phenomenon. It is alleged that terrorist activities inside Pakistan were actively carried out by the CIA, the RAW and the MOSSAD for different purposes. Chief among those, is changing the public perception of the War on Terror in the favor of the United States. There are confirmed reports that to achieve its objectives the CIA hired the services of at least a dozen Afghan warlords inside Afghanistan and provided through them arms and finances to militants in FATA and Swat to carry out murders and devastation in the country. It was like a double-edged sword not only to get the Army launch attacks against Taliban on Pakistani side of the border but also to give a message to the ISI that the CIA can use the Pakistani Taliban against their own security forces. Thousands of people have been killed in Pakistan due to terror attacks since the beginning of war on terror.

Future Concerns

There is no doubt that a military campaign is necessary against extremists in the country but it must be supported by social, economic and political change with political reforms being at the top of agenda. The future of Pakistan's role in the war against terrorism is dependent on its political and economic ties with the US. Pakistan is a part of global war on terrorism and was not only defending itself, but also protecting the entire world form the catastrophe of terrorism and extremism, therefore, needs strategic partnership with the rest of the world to foster peace and stability in the region, promote economic stability and address energy needs.

WAR IN NORTH-WEST PAKISTAN

The War in North-West Pakistan is an armed conflict between the Pakistan Armed Forces and armed religious groups such as the Tehrik-i-Taliban Pakistan (TTP), Lashkar-e-Islam, TSNM, Arab and Central Asian militants including Al-Qaeda, regional armed movements and elements of organized crime. The armed conflict began in 2004 when tensions, rooted in the Pakistan Army's search for Al Qaeda fighters in Pakistan's mountainous Waziristan area (in the Federally Administered Tribal Areas), escalated into armed resistance. Pakistan's actions were presented as Pakistan's role in the War on Terror in the international War on Terrorism. Clashes erupted between Pakistani army troops and Arab and Central Asian militia forces. The foreign militants were joined by Pakistani non-military veterans of the War in Afghanistan (2001–present) which subsequently established the Tehrik-i-Taliban Pakistan and other militia organizations such as Lashkar-e-Islam. The Tehreek-e-Nafaz-e-Shariat-e-Mohammadi (TSNM) established in 1992 allied with the Tehrik-i-Taliban Pakistan and Lashkar-e-Islam.

Background

December 2003: Waziri attempts on President Musharraf's life. In December 2003, two assassination attempts against President Pervez Musharraf were traced to Waziristan. The government responded by intensifying military pressure on the area, however the fighting was costly and government forces would sustain heavy casualties throughout 2004 and into early 2005 when the government switched to a tactic of negotiation instead of direct conflict.

2004: Fighting Breaks Out

On March 16, 2004, the bloody mountainous battle between Pakistan Army and the combined Taliban and Al-Qaeda fighters was insued. Both the International and National media speculated that Pakistan Armed Forces had surrounded the *"High Value Target"* in the mountainous region, possibly Al-Qaeda's Second-in-Command Ayman al-Zawahiri. The battle was concluded as the Army had captured the entire mountainous region, and captured hundreds of Al-Qaeda fighters. However, the Army was failed to captured Ayman al-Zawahiri as he was either later escaped or he was never among the fighters.

Peace Deals

In April 2004, the Government of Pakistan signed the first of three peace agreements with militants in South Waziristan. It was signed with militia commander Nek Muhammad Wazir, but was immediately abrogated once Nek Muhammad was killed by American Hellfire missile in June 2004. The second was signed in February 2005 with Nek's successor Baitullah Mehsud, which brought relative calm in the South Waziristan region. This deal will be later mimicked in the neighboring North Waziristan territory in September 2006 as the third and final truce between the government and the militants. However, all of these truces would not have a substantial effect in reducing bloodshed. The later two deals were officially broken in August 2007 with the Lal Masjid siege, which raised the suicide attacks on Pakistani forces tenfold throughout the country.

2005-2006

On May 4, 2005, Pakistani commandos captured Abu Faraj al-Libbi after a raid outside the town of Mardan, 30 miles northeast of Peshawar. Abu Farraj al-Libbi was a high ranking al-Qaeda official, rumored to be third after Osama bin Laden and Ayman al-Zawahiri. Al-Libbi replaced Khalid Shaikh Mohammed after his arrest in March 2003 in connection with the September 11th attacks. The Pakistani government arrested al-Libbi and held him on charges in relation to being a chief planner in two assassination attempts on the life of President Pervez Musharraf in December 2003.

On January 13, 2006, the U.S. launched an airstrike on the village of Damadola. The attack occurred in the Bajaur tribal area, about 7 km (4.3 mi) from the Afghan border, and killed at least 18 people. The attack again targeted Ayman al-Zawahiri, but later evidence suggests he was not there.

June 2006: Ceasefire

On June 21, 2006, pro-Tehrik-i-Taliban Pakistan militants in the Bannu region of North Waziristan stated they shot down a Bell military helicopter that was reported to have crashed. The government denied missile fire as the cause, stating it was due to technical faults. The helicopter had taken off from a base camp in Bannu at around 7am for Miramshah and crashed 15 minutes later into the Baran Dam in the Mohmandkhel area on Wednesday morning. Four soldiers were killed including Captain Shams (pilot), Captain Faisal (co-pilot), Lance Naik Ikram and sepoy Altaf, while three other, Sardar Ali, Waseem Abbas and Mohammad Arshad, were rescued. On the same day militants killed an inspector and two constables on a road connecting Bannu and the main town of Miranshah. On June 21, 2006, Afghan Taliban leader Sirajuddin Haqqani issued a decree that it was not (Afghan) Taliban policy to fight the Pakistan Army. However, the Tehrik-i-Taliban Pakistan intentionally did not circulate the decree in North Waziristan thereby keeping pressure on the government.

September 2006: Waziristan Peace Accord Signed

On September 5, 2006, the Waziristan Accord, an agreement between tribal leaders and the Pakistani government was signed in Miranshah, North Waziristan. to end all fighting. The agreement includes the following provisions:

- The Pakistani Army will help reconstruct infrastructure in tribal areas of North and South Waziristan.
- The Pakistani Military will not tolerate any assistance to intruders in North Waziristan, and will monitor actions in the region.

- The Pakistan government is to compensate tribal leaders for the loss of life and property of innocent tribesmen.
- "Foreigners" (informally understood to be foreign jihadists) are not allowed to use Pakistani territory for any terrorist activity anywhere in the world.
- 2,500 foreigners who were originally held on suspicion of having links to the Taliban were to be detained for necessary action against them.

The agreement, dubbed the Waziristan accord, has been viewed by some political commentators as a success for Pakistan. Further details of the agreement, as well as comments on the agreement made by US, Pakistani, and Taliban spokesmen is available in the Waziristan accord article.

October 2006: The Madrassa Air Strike

On October 30, 2006, the Pakistani army conducted an air strike against a madrassa in the Bajaur region bordering Afghanistan. The madrassa was destroyed killing 70 to 80 people. In retaliation for the attack the militants conducted a suicide bombing on an army camp on November 8, 2006, killing 42 Pakistani soldiers and wounding 20.

2007

In March, Pakistan signed a peace treaty with Faqir Mohammed, the main militant leader in Bajaur. Militant groups now held three districts in the Federally Administered Tribal Areas: South Waziristan, North Waziristan and Bajaur Agency.

Waziri-Uzbek Tensions

Reportedly, the fighting sparked by the killing of Saiful Adil, an al-Qaeda-linked Arab, blamed on the Uzbeks by Maulavi Nazir, described as a top pro-Taliban militant commander in the region. According to the other version, fighting started after Mullah Nazir, whom the government says has come over to its side, ordered the Uzbek followers of Tohir Yo'ldosh, formerly a close confidant of Osama bin Laden, to disarm. It was also preceded by the clashes between the IMU and a pro-government tribal leader in Azam

Warsak, in which 17 to 19 people died before a ceasefire was announced.

Defeat of the Islamic Movement of Uzbekistan

Local militants allied to the tribesmen were reported attacking and seizing the IMU's private jail in Azam Warsak. The Pakistan Army said it did not intend to step in, but witnesses say government artillery fired on the Uzbek bunkers they set up to fight the tribesmen. Heavy fighting resumed on March 29, ending a week-long ceasefire between tribal fighters and foreign militants. According to initial reports, tribesmen attacked a checkpoint manned by Uzbek militants and captured two of them. The clashes also left one tribal fighter dead and three wounded. The following day, a senior Pakistani official announced that 52 people were killed during the past two days, 45 of them Uzbeks and the rest tribesmen. One of Maulvi Nazir's aides put the death toll at 35 Uzbeks and 10 tribal fighters. However, residents in the area said that the death toll on both sides was inflated. The conflict further escalated on April 2 when a council of elders declared jihad against foreign militants and started to raise an army of tribesmen. According to Pakistani security officials, heavy fighting concentrated in the village of Doza Ghundai left more than 60 people dead, including 50 foreigners, 10 tribal fighters and one Pakistani soldier. He also said that "dozens" of Uzbeks had surrendered to tribal forces and that many bunkers used by militants were seized or destroyed. On April 12, 2007 the army general in charge of South Waziristan said that tribal fighters had cleared the Uzbeks out of the valleys surrounding Wana and the foreign militants had been pushed back into the mountains on the Afghan border. Four days later, the local tribesmen has urged Islamabad to resume control of law and order in the area.

Lal Masjid siege

On July 3, 2007, the militant supporters of Lal Masjid and Pakistani security forces clashed in Islamabad after the students from the mosque attacked a nearby government ministry building with stones. Their resultant faceoff with the military escalated, despite the intervention of then-ruling Pakistan Muslim League

(Q) leaders Chaudhry Shujaat Hussain and Muhammad Ijaz-ul-Haq. The Pakistani security forces immediately put up a siege around the mosque complex which lasted until July 11 and resulted in 108 deaths. This represented the main catalyst for the conflict and eventual breakdown of the truce that existed between Pakistan and the Pakistani Taliban groups. Already during the siege there were several attacks in Waziristan in retaliation for the siege.

Truce in Waziristan Broken

As the siege in Islamabad ensued, several attacks on Pakistani troops in Waziristan were reported. On July 14, 2007, a suicide bomber attacked a Pakistani Army convoy killing 25 soldiers and wounding 54. On July 15, 2007, two suicide bombers attacked another Pakistani Army convoy killing 16 soldiers and 5 civilians and wounding another 47 people. And in a separate incident a fourth suicide bomber attacked a police headquarters killing 28 police officers and recruits and wounding 35 people. The assault on the Red Mosque prompted rebels along the border with Afghanistan to scrap the controversial Waziristan Accord with the government.

The new war in Waziristan

The Army moved large concentration of troops into Waziristan and engaged in fierce clashes with militants in which at least 100 militants were killed including wanted terrorist and former Guantanamo Bay detainee, Abdullah Mehsud. The militants also struck back by attacking Army convoys, security check points and sending suicide bombers killing dozens of soldiers and police and over 100 civilians. In one month of fighting during the period from July 24 to August 24, 2007, 250 militants and 60 soldiers were killed. On September 2, 2007, just a few dozen militants led by Baitullah Mehsud managed to ambush a 17-vehicle army convoy and captured an estimated 247 soldiers without a shot being fired, an event that shocked the nation. Several officers were among the captured.

After the army returned to Waziristan, they garrisoned the areas and set up check-points, but the militants hit hard. In mid-

September the Tehrik-i-Taliban Pakistan and other forces attacked a number of Pakistani army outposts all across North and South Waziristan. This resulted in some of the heaviest fighting of the war. Following the Lal Masjid Siege, On September 12, 2007, the first outpost was attacked and overrun by the militants resulting in the capture of 12 Pakistani soldiers.

The next day on September 13, 2007, a suicide bomber in Tarbela Ghazi attacked a Pakistani army base, destroying the main mess hall and killing 20 members of the Karrar commando group; Pakistan's most elite army unit. A series of attacks ensued and by September 20, 2007 a total of five Pakistani Army military outposts had been overrun and more than 25 soldiers captured. More than 65 soldiers were either killed or captured and almost 100 wounded. A little over two weeks later, the Army responded with helicopter gunships, jet fighters and ground troops. They hit militant positions near the town of Mir Ali. In heavy fighting over four days, 257 people were killed, including 175 militants, 47 soldiers and 35 civilians.

Battle of Swat Valley

By the end of October fighting erupted in the Swat district of the Khyber Pakhtunkhwa province, with a large Tehreek-e-Nafaz-e-Shariat-e-Mohammadi force, under the command of Maulana Fazlullah, trying to impose Sharia law. Around 3,000 paramilitary soldiers were sent to confront them. After almost a week of heavy fighting the battle came to a standstill with both sides suffering heavy casualties. Then on November 1 and November 3, 220 paramilitary soldiers and policemen surrendered or deserted after a military position on a hill-top and two police stations were overrun.

This left the Tehreek-e-Nafaz-e-Shariat-e-Mohammadi (TNSM) in control of most of the Swat district. The fighting in Swat is the first serious insurgent threat from militia forces in what is known as a settled area of Pakistan. Forces loyal to Maulana Fazlullah, including some foreign fighters, after taking control of a series of small towns and villages, tried to implement strict Islamic law in November 2007. In mid-November the regular army was deployed with the help of helicopter gunships to crush the uprising. The Pakistan Army deployed over 2,500 men. By the beginning of December the fighting had ended and the Army recaptured Swat. Almost 400 of Maulana Fazlullah's fighters were dead along with 15 Pakistani soldiers and 20 civilians in the military offensive. Despite the victory by the Pakistani army, TNSM militants slowly re-entered Swat over the coming months and started engaging security forces in battles that lasted throughout 2008. By early February 2009, the whole district was in Pakistan Army Control.

The Rawalpindi Attacks

On September 3, two suicide bombers targeted a military intelligence (ISI) bus and a line of cars carrying ISI officers. The bus attack killed a large number of Defence Ministry workers and the other attack killed an Army colonel. In all 31 people, 19 soldiers and 12 civilians, were killed. Over two months later on November 24, one of the targets was a military intelligence bus. Almost everyone on the bus was killed. The other bomber blew up at a military checkpoint. 35 people were killed, almost all military.

State of Emergency

The 2007 Pakistani state of emergency was declared by Pervez Musharraf on 2007-11-03 and lasted until 2007-12-15. During this time the constitution of the country was suspended. This action and its responses are generally related to the controversies surrounding the re-election of Musharraf during the presidential election that had occurred on 2007-10-06, and also was claimed by the government to be the reaction to the actions by militants in Waziristan.

Benazir Bhutto's Assassination

On December 27, 2007, Pakistani opposition leader Benazir Bhutto was killed upon leaving a political rally for the Pakistan Peoples Party (PPP) in Rawalpindi, Pakistan. A suicidal assassin reportedly fired shots in Bhutto's direction just prior to detonating an explosive pellet-laden vest, killing approximately 24 people and wounding many more. Musharraf and the army blamed the attack on Al-Qaida, but the following day a statement by Baitullah

Mehsud was sent to the media saying that he and Al-Qaida had no involvement in the murder of the former Prime Minister, he briefed that these were the crimes of Musharraf and the army.

The killing was followed by a wave of violence across the country that left 58 people dead, including four police officers. Most of the violence was directed at Musharraf and the pro-Musharraf political party, Pakistan Muslim League (Q). The public chanted slogans against the army and Musharraf: "Musharraf Dog", "General is a murderer", "uniform (army) wearing murderers", etc. Bhutto had previously survived an assassination attempt made on her life during her homecoming which left 139 people dead and hundreds wounded.

2008: More fighting in South Waziristan

In January 2008, militants overran Sararogha Fort, and may have overrun a fort in Ladah as well. Both forts are in South Waziristan, and were held by the Pakistani army. On February 25, 2008, a suicide bomber struck in the garrison-town of Rawalpindi killing Pakistani Lt. Gen. Mushtaq Baig along with two more soldiers and five civilians. Baig was the highest-level military official to be assassinated since Pakistan joined the war on terror.

Operation Zalzala

A full-fledged security operation called 'Zalzala' (*earthquake*) by Pakistan Army's 14th Infantry Division in January to flush out Baitullah Mehsud's Tehrik-i-Taliban Pakistan militants from the area. Until then the area was infested with militants, with some villagers providing them support and shelter. Many militants were killed during the operation, and within three days the security forces were in full control of the area. The army later captured a few other villages and small towns to put the squeeze on Baitullah Mehsud. However, the operation led to a huge displacement of local population. According to 14 Division GOC Maj Gen Tariq Khan, about 200,000 people, including men, women and children, were displaced. Khalid Aziz, former NWFP chief secretary and expert on tribal affairs, said the displacement was "one of the biggest in tribal history" adding that human cost of the conflict in Waziristan "has gone unrecorded."

Peace agreement

On February 7, 2008, the Tehrik-i-Taliban Pakistan (TTP) led by Baitullah Mehsud offered a truce and peace negotiations resulting in a suspension of violence. On May 21, 2008 Pakistan signed a peace agreement with the Tehrik-i-Taliban Pakistan (TTP). Despite the agreement sporadic fighting continued until late June and escalated with the takeover of the town of Jandola on June 24, by the militants. 22 pro-government tribal fighters were captured and executed by the TTP at that time. On June 28, 2008, Pakistan's Army started an offensive against militia fighters in Khyber, codenamed *Operation Sirat-e-Mustaqeem*. The military took control of a key town and demolished an insurgent group's building. 1 militant was reportedly killed while 2 soldiers died in Swat valley. The operation was halted in early July.

On July 19, 2008, clashes erupted between the Tehrik-i-Taliban Pakistan and a faction of pro-government Taliban militants. 10-15 of the pro-government fighters were killed and another 120 were captured. Among the captured were two commanders who were tried under "Islamic" law by the Taliban and then executed. On July 21, 2008, heavy fighting in Baluchistan killed 32 militants, 9 soldiers and 2 civilians. More than two dozen militants were captured and a large weapons cache was found. Between July 28 and August 4, 2008, heavy fighting flared up in the northwestern Swat valley leaving 94 militants and 22 soldiers and policemen dead. Another 28 civilians were also killed.

Bajaur Offensive Starts

Heavy fighting erupted on August 6, 2008, in the Loisam area of Bajaur district. Loisam lies on the strategically important road leading towards the main northwestern city of Peshawar. The fighting started when hundreds of militants poured into the area attacking government forces. After four days of fighting on August 10 the military withdrew from the area. 100 militants and 9 soldiers were confirmed killed and another 55 soldiers were missing, at least three dozen of them captured by the militants. While the fighting was going on in Bajaur, in the Buner area of Khyber-Pakhtunkhwa militants killed at least nine policemen in an attack on a check post. The checkpoint was then abandoned, and the local Pakistani forces withdrew to Khar, the main town of Bajaur Agency. There were reports that the town of Khar was then besieged by tribal militants. On August 21, 2008, in response to the military offensive in Bajaur, two suicide bombers attacked the Pakistan Ordnance Factories in Wah while workers were changing shifts. The attack killed at least 70 people.

Tribesmen Declare War Against the Militants

By the beginning of September 2008, Pakistani tribal elders began organising a private army of approximately 30,000 tribesmen to fight the militias. A lashkar, or private army, composed of Pakistani tribesmen, began torching the houses of militia commanders in Bajaur, near the Afghan border, vowing to fight them until they are expelled. This included the house of a local militant commander named Naimatullah, who had occupied several government schools and converted them into seminaries. A tribal elder named Malik Munsib Khan, who heads the lashkar, said that tribesmen would continue their struggle until the militants were expelled from the area, adding that anyone found sheltering militants would be fined one million rupees and their houses will be torched. The tribesmen also torched two important centres of the militants in the area and gained control of most of the tehsil.

The main reasons for this was that the operations that were taking place in the Federally Administered Tribal Areas had displaced some 300,000 people while dozens of citizens have been killed in clashes between the militants and military. Since the start of Pakistan's war against the militants some 150,000 tribesmen have sided with them.

US Support and Aid for Pakistani Tribesmen

Recent American military proposals outlines an intensified effort to enlist tribal leaders in the frontier areas of Pakistan in the fight against Al Qaeda, the Afghan Taliban and Pakistani militia groups, as part of a broader effort to bolster Pakistani forces against militancy in the region. The proposal is modeled in part on a similar effort by American forces in Iraq that has been hailed as a great success in fighting foreign insurgents there. But it raises the question of whether such partnerships can be forged without a significant American military presence in Pakistan. And it is unclear whether enough support can be found among the tribes. Small numbers of United States military personnel have served as advisers to the Pakistani Army in the tribal areas, giving planning advice and helping to integrate American intelligence. Under this new approach, the number of advisers would increase. American officials said these security improvements complemented a package of assistance from the Agency for International Development and the State Department for the seven districts of the tribal areas that amounted to $750 million over five years, and would involve work in education, health and other sectors. The State Department's Bureau of International Narcotics and Law Enforcement Affairs is also assisting the Frontier Corps with financing for counternarcotics work.

Islamabad Marriott Hotel Bombing

On September 23, 2008, the Pakistani Army, backed by helicopter gunships and artillery killed more than 60 insurgents in northwest Pakistan in offensives as the response to the Islamabad Marriott Hotel bombing over the weekend at the Marriott hotel in the capital Islamabad that killed 53 people. In the nearby Bajur tribal region, the Army killed at least 10 militants, according to government officials. The Bajur operations, which the army says has left more than 700 suspected militants dead, has won praise from U.S. officials.

Renewed Bajaur Offensive

Pakistani President Asif Ali Zardari publicly vowed revenge in response to the Islamabad Marriott Hotel bombing. By September 26, 2008, Pakistani troops had successfully conducted and completed a major offensive in the Bajaur and the Tang Khata regions of the Federally Administered Tribal Areas, codenamed *Operation Sherdil*. Pakistani troops had killed over 1,000 militants in a huge offensive, a day after President Asif Ali Zardari lashed out at US forces over a clash on the Afghan border.

Tariq Khan, Inspector General of the Paramilitary Frontier Corps, mentioned to journalists that since the beginning of the Bajaur operations, there were up to 2,000 militant fighters including hundreds of foreigners who were fighting with the soldiers and the security forces. The overall death toll was over 1,000 militants and also adding that 27 Pakistani soldiers had also been killed with 111 soldiers seriously wounded. Five top Al-Qaeda and militia commanders were among those killed in a month-long operation in Bajaur. Of the five militant commanders killed, four appeared to be foreigners: Egyptian Abu Saeed Al-Masri; Abu Suleiman, an Arab; an Uzbek commander named Mullah Mansoor; and an Afghan commander called Manaras. The fifth was a Pakistani commander named only Abdullah, a son of ageing hardline leader Maulvi Faqir Mohammad who is based in Bajaur and has close ties to Al-Qaeda second-in-command Ayman al-Zawahiri.

Between October 22 and October 24, security forces engaged in another push against militants in the restive Bajaur and Khyber tribal regions. Air strikes were carried out in the Nawagai and Mamond sub-districts of Bajaur Agency. The troops destroyed several centres of militants at Charmang, Chinar and Zorbandar and had inflicted heavy losses on them. Gunship helicopters shelled in Charming, Cheenar, Kohiand Babarha areas of Nawagai and Mamund Tehsil of Bajaur agency, destroying various underground hideouts and bunkers of militants. The security forces had also taken control of different areas of Loisam, a militant headquarters, and advanced towards other areas for complete control.

Intensified U.S. Strikes

Since the end of August 2008, the United States had stepped up its attacks in the Federally Administered Tribal Areas. On September 3 a commando attack took place in a village near the Afghan border in South Waziristan, and there have been 3 strikes from unmanned drones in North Waziristan, culminating on the morning of September 8, 2008, when a United States Air Force drone aircraft fired a number of missiles at a "guest house for militants arriving in North Waziristan", which unsuccessfully targeted Jalaluddin Haqqani, killed 23 people.

On September 25, 2008, following exchanges of gunfire between US and Pakistani forces on the frontier, President Zardari told the United Nations that Pakistan would not tolerate violations of its sovereignty, even by its allies. The incident happened after two US military helicopters came under fire from the Pakistani side, a US military spokesman said, insisting that they had been about a mile and a half inside Afghanistan.

President Zardari told the United Nations, "Just as we will not let Pakistani's territory to be used by terrorists for attacks against our people and our neighbours, we cannot allow our territory and our sovereignty to be violated by our friends," he said, without citing the United States or the border flareup.

Militants Targeting of Tribesmen

On October 10, 2008, Islamic militants beheaded four kidnapped pro-government tribal elders in the Charmang area of Bajaur on Friday. The militants had killed them because the elders had been pro-government.

On October 11, 2008, a suicide bomber struck an anti-Militant gathering of tribal elders, just as they had decided to form a lashkar (tribal militia), killing at least 110 anti-Taliban tribesmen and wounding 125 others. The suicide bomber drove his car into the gathering itself and blew himself up. The attack on the tribal council took place in Orakzai, normally a relatively quiet corner of the nation's restive tribal areas.

Fighting for the NATO Supply Lines

On October 19, 2008, the Pakistan Army was locked in a fierce battle with militants to keep open the fuel and arms supply routes to British and American forces in Afghanistan. For months, militants had been trying to either attack or seal off the supply routes. The army claimed that Mohammad Tariq Alfridi, the militant commander, had seized terrain around the mile-long Kohat tunnel, south of Peshawar, three times since January. He had coordinated suicide bomb attacks and rocket strikes against convoys emerging from it. Maulvi Omar, a Tehrik-i-Taliban Pakistan spokesman, said that his fighters would lay down their arms if the Pakistan Army ceased fighting. The Pakistan Army ignored his offer. The battle for the tunnel began at the start of the year when Tehrik-i-Taliban fighters seized five trucks carrying weapons and ammunition. They held the tunnel for a week before they were driven out in fierce fighting with the Army. Since then, Tariq and his men have returned several times to attack convoys. The army launched its latest onslaught after a suicide bomb attack at one of its bases near the tunnel six weeks ago. Five people were killed and 45 were injured, including 35 soldiers, when a pickup truck packed with explosives was driven into a checkpoint.

On November 11, 2008, militants attacked two convoys at the Khyber Pass capturing 13 trucks which were headed for Afghanistan. One convoy was from the United Nations World Food Programme and was carrying wheat. The second was intended for NATO troops and one of the captured trucks was carrying with it two U.S. military Humvees, which were also seized. On December 8, 2008, militants torched more than 160 vehicles destined for US-led troops in Afghanistan. The militants attacked the Portward Logistic Terminal in the northern city of Peshawar at around 02:30 AM, destroying its gate with a rocket-propelled grenade and shooting dead a guard. They then set fire to about 100 vehicles, including 70 Humvees, which shipping documents showed were being shipped to the US-led coalition forces and the Afghan National Army. At the same time, militants torched about 60 more vehicles at the nearby Faisal depot, which like Portward is on the ring road around Peshawar, where convoys typically stop before heading for the Khyber Pass.

2009

On February 3, 2009, militants blew up a bridge at the Khyber Pass, temporarily cutting a major supply line for Western troops in Afghanistan. After the attack supplies along the route had been halted "for the time being", according to NATO.

Swat Ceasefire

Pakistan agreed to impose Sharia law and suspend military operations in the scenic Swat Valley. The decision is troubling for the United States, which believes that it will embolden militants who are fighting US-led troops in Afghanistan and want to impose Islamic law across nuclear-armed Pakistan. US officials believe that it will now provide another safe haven for the militants within 80 miles of Islamabad, the Pakistani capital, as well as a corridor between the Afghan border and the disputed region of Kashmir. Pakistani officials said that it was the only way to pacify a fierce Islamist insurgency and avoid more civilian casualties in Swat – whose ski resort and mountain scenery once made it a popular tourist destination. Amir Haider Khan Hoti, the chief minister for the Khyber Pakhtunkhwa province, announced the government's decision after a meeting with militant leaders in the provincial capital, Peshawar. He said that local authorities would impose Islamic law across Malakand region, which includes Swat. Officials said that Asif Ali Zardari, the Pakistani President, would sign off on the deal once peace had been restored. The agreement came the day after the militants in Swat said that it would observe a ten-day ceasefire in support of the peace process. Pakistani officials say that the laws allow Muslim clerics to advise judges, but do not outlaw female education, music or other activities once banned by the Afghan Taliban in Afghanistan.

Defeat of the Militants in Bajaur

On March 1, 2009, the Pakistan Army finally defeated Bajaur militants and foreign militants in Bajaur, which is a strategically important region on the Afghan border. Major-General Tariq Khan, who was commanding the military operations in five of the seven agencies, said his Army and the Frontier Corps had killed most militants in Bajaur, the smallest of the agencies but a major infiltration route into Afghanistan, after a six-month offensive. By the time the six-month long battle in Bajaur was over, the Pakistan Army killed over 1,500 militants while losing 97 of their own soldiers and another 404 soldiers seriously injured.

Militant Counter-attack

On March 30, militia commandos struck in Lahore. They attacked the Munawan Police Academy killing and taking hostage police cadets. A siege was under way for about eight hours after the militants had barricaded themselves in the academy. Eventually police forces managed to retake the compound. 18 people were killed in the attack: eight policemen, eight militants and two civilians. At least 95 policemen were wounded and 10 were taken hostage before being rescued. Four gunmen were captured by the police. On April 4, a suicide bomber attacked a military camp in Islamabad killing eight soldiers. Less than 24 hours later on April 5, two more suicide attacks occurred. One bomber targeted a market on the border with Afghanistan killing 17 people and the other attacked a mosque in Chakwal, in the eastern Pakistani province of Punjab, killing 26 more civilians. The next day, the leader of the Tehrik-i-Taliban Pakistan, Baitullah Mehsud, promised that there were to be two suicide attacks per week in the country until the Pakistani army withdraws from the border region and the United States stops its missile attacks by unmaned drones on militant bases.

Militants Violate Swat Deal

In March 2009, many Pakistanis were horrified when a videotape surfaced that showed miliant enforcers publicly whipping a 17-year-old girl in Swat accused of having an affair. The girl had not committed fornication or adultery but was flogged simply because she refused her brother's demand to marry someone of his choosing. Protests broke out all over Pakistan to demonstrate against the flogging. Raja Zafar ul-Haq, a well-respected Pakistani Islamic scholar and political activist said this summary punishment of flogging simply for refusing a marriage proposal was totally un-Islamic and had nothing to do with Sharia. He went on to say that Prophet Muhammad had strictly forbidden the practice of forced marriages and in this case, the girl had not done anything wrong by refusing a marriage proposal.

A five-member team appointed by the Supreme Court investigated the video's origins, and concluded that it had been faked, raising questions at Pakistani intelligence agencies. In Buner, the Taliban continued their criminal activities when residents said Taliban fighters had been stealing cattle for meat, stealing other livestock, berating men without beards and recruiting teenagers into their ranks. The Taliban also began to steal vehicles belonging to government officials and ransacked the offices of some local non-government organisations for no apparent reason. 12 schoolchildren were killed by a bomb contained in a football.

Second Battle of Swat

On April 26, 2009, the Pakistani Army started Operation Black Thunderstorm, with the aim of retaking Buner, Lower Dir, Swat and Shangla districts from the Pakistani Taliban after the militants took control of the area since the start of the year.

The operation largely cleared the Lower Dir district of militia forces by April 28 and Buner by May 5. On May 5, operations started to retake Swat and later on Shangla. Fighting in Swat was particularly fierce since the Taliban threw away their insurgent tactics and the army their counter-insurgency tactics. Both sides favoured more conventional frontline warfare as a means of fighting each other. By May 14, the military was only six kilometers south of Mingora, the milita-held capital city of Swat, and preparations for all-out street fighting was under way.

On May 23, the battle for Mingora started and by May 27, 70 percent of the city was cleared of militants. On May 30, the Pakistani military had taken back the city of Mingora from the Pakistani Taliban, calling it a significant victory in its offensive against the militants.

However, some sporadic fighting was still continuing on the city's outskirts. In all, according to the military, 128 soldiers and more than 1,475 militants were killed and 317 soldiers were wounded during operation Black Thunderstorm. 95 soldiers and policemen were captured by the militants, 18 of them were rescued while the fate of the others remained undetermined. 114 militants were captured, including some local commanders. At least 23 of the militants killed were foreigners.

Sporadic fighting throughout Swat continued up until mid-June. On June 14, the operation was declared over and the military had regained control of the region. Only small pockets of Taliban resistance remained and the military started mopping up operations.

This led to a refugee crisis, and by August 22, 1.6 million of 2.3 million have returned home according to UN estimates.

Blockade of South Waziristan

On June 16, 2009, in the aftermath of the successful victory and recapture of the entire Swat valley, the Pakistan Army began a massive troop build-up along the southern and eastern borders of South Waziristan. Pakistan was now taking the fight to Mehsud's mountainous stronghold, ordering an expansion of its current offensive against Tehrik-i-Taliban Pakistan fighters in the Swat valley. On Sunday night, denouncing Mehsud as "the root cause of all evils," Owais Ghani, the governor of the Khyber Pakhtunkhwa, said the government has called on the army to launch a "full-fledged" military operation to eliminate Mehsud and his estimated 20,000 men.

The crucial battle may prove to be the most difficult that Pakistan's military has faced on its soil in recent years. Islamabad's decision to launch the offensive against Mehsud signals a deepening of Pakistani resolve against the militants. The army has targeted the Tehrik-i-Taliban Pakistan leader on three separate occasions — in 2004, 2005 and 2008 — but walked away each time after signing ruinous "peace deals" that have only served to embolden Mehsud. But the military appears more determined this time. It also enjoys the backing of a government that has gained public support as the recent wave of terrorist attacks has heightened revulsion against the Taliban.

Killing of Baitullah Mehsud

The leader of Tehrik-i-Taliban Pakistan, Baitullah Mehsud, was killed in a drone attack in early August 2009. This was later confirmed by captured chief spokesman Maulvi Umar. He was replaced by Hakimullah Mehsud.

Militant October–November 2009 Counter-offensive

In early October 2009, the Tehrik-i-Taliban Pakistan started a string of attacks in cities across Pakistan. The goal of the attacks was to show that the militants were still a united fighting force following the death of their leader and to disrupt a planned military offensive into South Waziristan. Places targeted include the U.N. World Food Program offices in Islamabad, Khyber bazaar in Peshawar, Army General Headquarters in Rawalpindi, a market in Shangla, security establishments in Lahore, police stations in Kohat and Peshawar, the International Islamic University in Islamabad, and Pakistan Air Force Complex in Kamra.

The month ended with a car bombing of Meena Bazaar, Peshawar killing 118 civilians. The army then began a ground offensive in South Waziristan. November saw suicide bombings of the Army's National Bank of Pakistan in Rawalpindi, a market in Charsadda and six bombings of Peshawar including the regional headquarters of the ISI and the Judicial Complex.

South Waziristan Offensive

On October 17, the Pakistani Army launched a large-scale offensive in South Waziristan involving 28,000 troops advancing across South Waziristan from three directions.

On October 19, the first town to fall to the Army was Kotkai, the birthplace of the Pakistani Taliban leader Hakimullah Mehsud. However, the next day, the Tehrik-i-Taliban Pakistan re-took the town from the military.

Troops had thrust into Kotkai only to be hit by a determined counteroffensive that killed seven soldiers, including an army major, and wounded seven more. Still, the Army managed to take the town once again on October 24, after days of bombardments.

On October 29, the town of Kaniguram, which was under the control of Uzbek fighters from the Islamic Movement of Uzbekistan, was surrounded. And on November 2, Kaniguram was taken.

On November 1, the towns of Sararogha and Makin were surrounded, and fighting for Sararogha started on November 3. The fighting there lasted until November 17, when the town finally fell to the military. The same day, the town of Laddah was also captured by the Army and street fighting commenced in Makin. Both Sararogha and Laddah were devastated in the fighting. By November 21, more than 570 militants and 76 soldiers were killed in the offensive.

On December 12, 2009, the Pakistan army declared victory in South Waziristan.

2010

Orakzai and Kurram Offensive

In an offensive in Bajaur by Frontier Corps, a militants' stronghold village Damadola was captured and cleared by February 6, 2010. Bajaur was declared conflict free zone by April 20. On March 23, 2010, the Pakistan army launched an offensive to clear Orakzai. Officials also announced a future offensive in North Waziristan. The week prior the Pakistan military killed approximately 150 militants in fighting in the region. It is expected that all tribal areas would be cleared by June 2010. June 3, Pakistani authorities announced a victory over the insurgents in Orakzai and Kurram.

Casualties

2,637 security forces members and 12,847 militants were killed between January 2003, and November 12, 2009, according to government sources.

On February 18, 2010, the Pakistani military confirmed that since September 11, 2001, 2,351 soldiers have been killed in the war and another 6,512 have been wounded. Also, there have been 21,672 civilian casualties (at least 7,598 of these were killed). The military stated that 17,742 militants have been killed or captured. Among these, by November 2007, were 488 foreign extremists killed, 24 others arrested and 324 injured. An additional 220 policemen were killed in fighting in 2007 and 2008. Before all-out fighting broke out in 2003, independent news sources reported only four incidents of deaths of Pakistani security forces members in 2001 and 2002, in which a total of 20 soldiers and policemen were killed. The independent South Asia Terrorism Portal website has estimated that at least 1,865 soldiers and policemen were killed between 2003 and 2008. The Pak Institute For Peace Studies has estimated that 1,185 soldiers and policemen were killed in 2009.

Also, at least 857 soldiers and policemen have been reported captured by the militants since the start of the war, with at least 558 of them being released.

Mr. Naushad Ali Khan Superintendent of Research and Analysis, NWFP Police in his article *Suicide and terrorist attacks and police actions in NWFP, Pakistan* has provided details of different activities of the terrorists during 2008. Accordingly 483 cases were registered with 533 deaths and 1290 injured. Similarly 29 suicidal cases were registered that resulted in the death of 247 persons while 695 persons sustained injuries. During the same period 83 attempts of terrorism were foiled by the NWFP Police. The full article can be viewed on the official website of Pakistan Society of Criminology.

United States Role

Until July 2009 the conflict, as well as terrorism in Pakistan, had cost Pakistan $35 billion. According to US Congress and the Pakistani media, Pakistan has received about $18 billion from the United States for the logistical support it provided for the counter-terrorism operations from 2001 to 2010, and for its own military operation mainly in Waziristan and other tribal areas along the Durand line. The Bush administration also offered an additional $3 billion five-year aid package to Pakistan for becoming a frontline ally in its 'war on terror'. Annual instalments of $600 million each split evenly between military and economic aid, began in 2005.

In 2009, President Barack Obama pledged to continue supporting Pakistan and has said Pakistan would be provided economic aid of $1.5 billion dollars each year for the next five years. Unfolding a new US strategy to defeat Taliban and Al-Qaeda, Obama said Pakistan must be a 'stronger partner' in destroying Al-Qaeda safe havens. In addition, President Obama has also planned to propose an extra $2.8 billion dollars in aid for the Pakistani military to intensify the US-led war on terror along the Pakistan-Afghanistan border. The military aid would be in addition to the civilian aid of $1.5 billion dollars a year for the next five years from 2009 onwards.

In his autobiography, President Musharraf wrote that the United States had paid millions of dollars to the Pakistan government as bounty money for capturing al-Qaeda operators from tribal areas bordering Afghanistan. About 359 of them were handed over to the US for prosecution. Pakistan has bought 1,000 laser-guided bomb kits and 18 F-16 fighter jets from USA, to attack militants.

Amongst Pakistanis opinion about the role of the US is generally negative. Incidents of terrorism cause rage and anger against the terrorist organizations but they also cause frustration with the United States. According to Pew Global Polls only 17% of Pakistanis have a positive view of the US and only 11% it as a useful partner in the war on terror.

CLEARING UP PAKISTAN'S COUNTERTERRORISM FEAT

The Afghan government's dissatisfaction and now increasingly the American polity's displeasure with Pakistan's performance in counterterrorism operations are conditioned considerably by the perception of Pakistan's unwillingness to crack down on terrorism comprehensively. This is a serious and, in actuality, complex charge. By all accounts, President Musharraf himself is strongly committed to purging both al- Qaeda and the Taliban.

The imperatives of eliminating al- Qaeda are obvious: Pakistan was never directly a sponsor of this group in Afghanistan, and destroying its network remains the sine qua non of the lucrative Pakistani counterterrorism partnership with the United States. Musharraf also remains personally opposed to the political philosophy represented by the Taliban.

He has repeatedly identified the "talibanization" of Pakistan as the most pressing threat facing his state, but whether this translates into a decision to physically apprehend or eradicate the Taliban cadres, and especially their leadership, is less clear. Drawing a distinction between "diehard militants and fanatics," who "reject reconciliation and peace" and accordingly must be targeted even though they are hard to find, and the larger Taliban cadres, "most of [whom] may be ignorant and misguided" but "are a part of

Afghan society," Musharraf has urged Kabul, Washington, and the larger international community to begin instead a campaign of reconciliation with the Taliban focused on "winning [their] hearts and minds." Musharraf's attitude toward the Taliban thus remains complex and multifaceted: he clearly detests their worldview, referring to talibanization as a species of extremism that "represents a state of mind and requires [a] more comprehensive, long- term strategy where military action must be combined with a political approach and socioeconomic development." He is also opposed to what he calls "terrorist elements and foreign militants" within the movement, which he acknowledges "must be dealt with a strong hand." Musharraf argues, however, for peacefully integrating the Taliban's rank and file into civil society, a judgment that is premised heavily on the belief that these elements are merely misguided miscreants rather than implacable foes.

The nucleus of military officials around Musharraf appears to reflect his own sinuosity. While all senior Pakistani military officers are agreed that the al- Qaeda presence in the FATA must be eliminated, there is a considerable diversity of views in regard to the Taliban. Although many feel that the optimal outcome for Pakistan would be simply a Taliban that progressively lose their effectiveness and support and thereby fade into obscurity— a finale that would spare Pakistanis the distasteful obligation of having to turn their guns against their old clients— others are conflicted about these reactionaries for different reasons.

To begin with, many officers are disenchanted by Washington's approach to managing the larger issues associated with Afghanistan's political reconstitution. Since the emergency loya jirga held in 2002 and the subsequent Afghan presidential election of 2004, these officials have been dismayed by what they perceive as the U.S. partiality toward the Durrani Pashtuns, who have traditionally been the privileged political elite in Afghan society (and from whose ranks, through the Popalzai tribe, emerged President Hamid Karzai). The calculated neglect of the Ghilzai Pashtuns— who are primarily rural and uneducated peasantry and who constituted a critical source of manpower for the Taliban cause— grates on many Pakistani national security managers not only because they believe that the continuing alienation of the Ghilzai feeds the Taliban ranks but also because it represents an enduring and deliberate disregard of their own clients in intra-Afghan politics. This latter consideration is significant because it has the effect of portraying Islamabad as feckless and incapable of influencing U.S. policy in directions more helpful to its friends despite Pakistan's large investments in the U.S. war on terror.

When these concerns are added to other strategic calculations about protecting the Taliban as a hedge against either the failure of the Karzai regime in Kabul or the dreaded prospect of increasing Indian influence in Afghanistan, the senior leadership of the Pakistani military— as well as President Musharraf— believe they have good enough reasons to avoid targeting the Taliban comprehensively in the manner sought by both Kabul and Washington. The dangers of a heightened and targeted anti- Ghilzai campaign leading to a political mobilization that renews the demand for an independent "Pakhtunistan" further exacerbate the fears of senior Pakistani military officials. Because the status of the Durand Line separating Afghanistan and Pakistan is still formally contested by Kabul, any provocation that results in strengthening the political dimensions of Pashtun solidarity among the tribes living on both sides of this boundary is viewed immediately as a potential threat to the territorial integrity of Pakistan. With the vivisection of 1971 indelibly emblazoned in the consciousness of the Pakistani military, senior commanders are extremely reluctant to embark on any military operations that would aggravate the local Pashtun tribes in the FATA and provoke them into making common territorial cause with their confreres on the other side of the border against the Pakistani state.

While ambivalence about the Taliban at senior levels in the Pakistani military thus has both strategic and self- interested dimensions, other more prosaic, but tactically important, considerations also play a role. Recognizing that the Taliban are essentially Ghilzai Pashtuns with deep consanguineal ties to the tribes that have dominated the FATA for centuries, many Pakistani commanders are afraid that any continued large- scale military presence in the area, especially if exemplified by massed infantry operations of the kind mounted in 2002–2004, will only further inflame tribal sensitivities and diminish cooperation between tribal leaders and the armed forces, a cooperation that is absolutely necessary if the armed forces are to successfully apprehend the "terrorist elements and foreign militants" located in their midst.

Although such embitterment has already occurred with problematic consequences for the success of antiterrorism operations, the leadership of the Pakistani military remains continually fearful that any added aggravation could lead to even greater tribal support for terrorist groups closeted in the area and a systematic denial of access to the military units tasked for operations therein. That such contingencies already appear to have materialized in the FATA suggests that the reluctance of senior Pakistani military leaders to violently engage the Taliban will be reinforced even further.

The most problematic elements within the Pakistani state, however, are probably the ISID officers in the field who were tasked with managing the liaison relationship with the Taliban over the years. Some simply feel loyalty to their old clients. Others are content to exploit their leadership's own ambivalence about the Taliban. And some others are prepared to disregard leadership directives that enjoin interdicting the Taliban for either nationalist, ideological, or personal reasons— if they believe they can get away with it. Whatever the cause, the field operatives of the ISID are widely perceived in Afghanistan and in the United States as being less than fully committed to targeting the Taliban leadership in the manner required for the success of counterterrorism operations in the FATA and beyond.

At first sight, this is indeed a curious phenomenon because nothing in the organizational structure of the ISID suggests that it is either an autonomous or a rogue entity. The reportedly 10,000-strong ISID is staffed primarily by Pakistani military officers who are assigned to the service on deputation for a fixed period of time, and its leadership reports to the chief of army staff. The pay, promotions, and operations of the directorate are also regulated by military rules and procedures, and by all accounts the Pakistan Army is a professional and bureaucratically efficient organization.

Consequently, the notion that ISID officers might be undermining policies pursued by the corporate leadership of the Pakistan Army appears counterintuitive at first sight and cannot be reconciled with the image of the Pakistan Army as a tightly centralized organization unless due credit is given to three realities.

To begin with, the ISID, similar to many other intelligence organizations worldwide, has considerable operational latitude because of the nature of its activities in the covert realm: this includes access to financing "off the books," recruitment of agents from diverse sources to include those with unsavory backgrounds, and the systematic use of retired case officers who can conduct officially permitted operations while still providing the state with plausible deniability.

Further, the implementation of many ISID operations is typically regulated by "directive control" as opposed to "detailed control," where field officers have the flexibility to accomplish strategic goals without having to secure prior approval of every particular from their superiors.

And, finally, because ISID is simultaneously an external intelligence organization as well as a coercive instrument for implementing the preferences of military authoritarianism in Pakistan, Musharraf's management of this organization historically was manifested primarily through the promulgation of broadly defined policies, which were then implemented by a chain of subordinates who acted upon their understanding of his strategic intent and which simultaneously served to protect him from detailed knowledge of what may frequently have been highly troublesome activities. Given these realities, the pervasive belief about ISID unreliability in the war against terror, and particularly against the Taliban, can be accounted for— despite the otherwise professional character of the Pakistan Army— only by one or more of the following hypotheses:

- That, despite their public claims, President Musharraf and his corps commanders are not yet committed to a policy of eliminating the Taliban and especially its leadership, root and branch; consequently, Musharraf and his commanders have not directed their military and intelligence services to systematically implement such a strategy.

- That, although President Musharraf and his corps commanders have settled on a strategy of eliminating the Taliban in principle, the operational predicates of this policy insofar as they apply to the leadership and other high-value targets have not yet been specified deliberately, thus permitting line- level officers to use their discretion when it comes to supporting or undermining particular counterterrorism operations.
- That, although President Musharraf and his corps commanders have settled on a strategy of eliminating the Taliban, to include its leadership and other "diehard militants," the large size and complex bureaucratic structure of the ISID permit its field officers, and especially the retired case officers still on its active payroll, to covertly ignore or violate leadership directives in many instances for nationalist, ideological, or personal reasons without fear of immediate retribution.

Whatever the real explanation for ISID recalcitrance may be—and the truth probably implicates a complex admixture of factors—the fact remains that the Pakistani campaign against the Taliban, and particularly its leadership, remains hobbled by convolution and hesitation. During the past several years, this has resulted in a deepening entrenchment of the Taliban and their sympathizers throughout the seven administrative agencies of the FATA and a growing expansion of their influence in the Tank, Dera Ismail Khan, and Swat Valley areas of the North West Frontier Province of Pakistan. Since October 2007, for instance, the idyllic mountain region of Swat, barely 90 miles from Islamabad, has been occupied by self- styled "Pakistani Taliban" forces led by Maulana Qazi Fazlullah and his Tehrik- e- Nafaz- e- Shariate- Muhammad (Movement for the Enforcement of Islamic Laws) shaheen (fighters), who may be present in the area in greater than brigade strength. This development suggests not only that the Taliban movement and its sympathizers have moved beyond the traditionally stateless regions close to the Durand Line and into more settled areas within Pakistan but also, and more ominously, that what began as localized terrorist operations now threatens to evolve into a mature insurgency with the militant opposition able to eject government forces from a given territory, hold ground against state opposition, and coerce any local opponents into cooperating in order to sustain the newly secured safe haven.

This intensifying talibanization in the sensitive areas of the North West Frontier Province has had diverse effects, including increased tensions with and between the traditional tribes resulting in both growing intertribal conflicts as well as bolder attacks on the Pakistan Army and paramilitary units in the region.

In one dramatic encounter, more than three hundred Frontier Corps infantry men were taken hostage by local militants in August 2007 in South Waziristan, to be freed only after President Musharraf ignominiously released more than two dozen previously jailed Islamists, including Mullah Obaidullah Akhund, the highest-ranking Taliban official captured by the Pakistani military. On occasion, the tribal dissatisfaction with local talibanization, and particularly with some of the groups that support it, has been all to the good as, for example, when indigenous tribes in the Azam Warsak area of South Waziristan, supported by Pakistani military forces, attacked and expelled numerous Uzbeks belonging to the Islamic Movement of Uzbekistan— a constituent of Osama bin Laden's International Islamic Front— who had settled in that locale. Unfortunately, such successful cleansing operations have been all too few. The main consequence of talibanization in the FATA instead has been, as one observer put it, to "provide more opportunities to the ISI[D] to indirectly support some Taliban commanders sympathetic to Pakistan's objectives" in the ongoing war in Afghanistan.

The growing talibanization in the FATA and beyond has in fact resulted in the creation of a secure sanctuary for a variety of terrorist groups now conducting anticoalition military operations in Afghanistan. The evidence suggests that Taliban presence is strongest in the Helmand, Kandahar, Zabol, and Oruzgan provinces in southern Afghanistan and is either significant or conspicuous in Paktika, Khowst, Nangarhar, Konar, and Nuristan provinces in eastern Afghanistan. In these areas, the Taliban have been able to deploy and sustain a large number of armed fighters in situ, which has permitted the movement to effectively displace the Afghan state by usurping its traditional functions such as maintaining law and order; extracting resources through taxation; administering justice through various adjudicative mechanisms backed by local militias; and dispensing welfare through the maintenance of schools, provision of social services, and the oversight of economic activities.

Performing these statal functions is possible because the Taliban undoubtedly continue to derive support from the Ghilzai Pashtuns in Afghanistan; however, their record of increasingly ruthless retribution against any uncooperative tribal leaders does not hurt either. In this context, the Taliban's ability to sustain the strong coercive presence they currently have in the southern and eastern Afghan provinces is enhanced considerably by their access to the safe haven in the FATA whence they can draw a large number of fighters, procure diverse kinds of ordnance and combat equipment, and tap into different streams of financial resources (including, but not restricted to, the zakat, the Islamic tithe) for the prosecution of the ongoing jihad against the Karzai regime and the foreign forces now present in Afghanistan. As one respected analysis has noted, "using [the sanctuary provided by the FATA] to regroup, reorganize and rearm," Taliban and other foreign militants, including al- Qaeda sympathizers, "are launching increasingly severe cross- border attacks on Afghan and international military personnel, with the support and active involvement of Pakistani militants." The fruits of this activity are witnessed in the deteriorating security situation in Afghanistan.

Since the successful presidential election in October 2004—an event that received the full support of the international community and heralded hope for a new Afghanistan— the Taliban insurgency has metastasized in scale, intensity, and fury. By 2006, the level of violence had increased dramatically, and previous operations that had been centered on assassinations, ambushes, and isolated hit- and- run attacks were now supplemented by more ominous tactics involving beheadings and suicide bombings, which historically have been utterly alien to Afghan culture. Equally problematic has been the employment of ever more sophisticated improvised explosive devices, rockets, missiles, and man- portable air defense weapons, many of which continue to be fabricated in the arms foundries in the FATA but are now also increasingly supplied by al- Qaeda and foreign powers such as Iran.

Even more remarkably, Taliban military operations have gradually evolved from singular covert attacks mounted by tiny groups to more complex, set- piece military operations undertaken by larger units, often involving attempts to seize and hold territory against superior forces, and employing more diverse and sophisticated crew- served weaponry, including indirect fire systems such as mortars and unguided rockets, as supplements to the traditionally ubiquitous personal firearms and direct- fire weapons.

The strategic objectives of these new modes of warfare have also become more complex. Rather than simply harassing the new Afghan government, which seemed to be the original intention, the current military activities of the Taliban are accompanied by sophisticated forms of information operations. Betraying evidence of lessons learned from their al- Qaeda accomplices, Taliban operatives use a variety of techniques ranging from sending crude low-technology "night letters" often conveying threats to specific individuals, to circulating DVDs and videotapes containing political propaganda, to exploiting more advanced technology such as radio, television, mobile and satellite telephony, and the Internet.

In general, all these technologies are used to signal to the Afghan tribes that the return of the Taliban to power in Kabul is inevitable— despite whatever tactical losses might be suffered at the hands of NATO forces in the interim— and that resistance or neutrality is therefore futile. As one analysis pointed out, even if this campaign does not persuade the Afghan people, "[t]he Taliban's own hearts and minds activities are now prolonging and exacerbating an already difficult insurgency problem for the Afghan Government and the International Security Assistance Force (ISAF) in the south of the country."

Finally, and perhaps most important, both the Taliban's information and its actual war-fighting operations have moved beyond simple terrorist attacks aimed at disrupting the Afghan government toward more ambitious objectives revolving around the progressive domination of territory. Focused today primarily on NATO's Regional Command (South) for both symbolic and strategic reasons, the Taliban leadership appears intent on slowly seizing critical areas, district by district, through a strategy of covert infiltration in the Helmand, Kandahar, Oruzgan, and Zabol provinces as a prelude to wresting control of the city of Kandahar, which is intended to become the base for first dominating the South and eventually all of Afghanistan itself. If this evolution gradually succeeds, the Taliban insurgency in southeastern Afghanistan will have successfully metamorphosed from a guerrilla operation into something resembling a more conventional civil war with grave advantages to the militants in their struggle against the Karzai government in Kabul.

Although the safe havens in the FATA and the ability to derive local Ghilzai support in the southern and eastern Afghan provinces (by providing the benefits of security, justice, and even development) have thus enabled a dramatic transformation in both the character of the ongoing Afghan war and the fortunes of the Taliban as an insurgent organization, a particularly dangerous consequence— especially from a U.S. perspective— has been the enhanced prospects for survival they have offered al- Qaeda. There is little doubt today that the survival of the Taliban sanctuary in the FATA (to include the talibanization of the wider area more generally) has been singularly responsible for the continuing regeneration of al- Qaeda as an organization because it has permitted the leadership and the operatives of this terrorist group, who are relatively smaller in number, to safely "dissolve" into a larger geosocial environment that is either hospitable to them directly or that protects them by disguising their presence amid a larger pool of Taliban adherents.

The al- Qaeda leadership, which is believed to be currently ensconced somewhere in the Bajaur Agency of the FATA, has further enhanced its immunity to interdiction by pursuing what appears to be a subtle strategy toward its Taliban hosts. Recognizing that the Taliban's Pashtun cadres remain the original denizens of the FATA and the adjacent areas in eastern and southern Afghanistan, al- Qaeda's overseers have been careful to tread lightly: despite their independent access to significant streams of foreign resources, they do not seem to have levied any excessive demands in terms of either hospitality or security, nor have they used their superior access to advanced military- technical capabilities worldwide to attempt any "takeover" of the Taliban movement. Rather, they appear to understand that an independent Pashtun insurgency that answers to no one but its own indigenous leadership stands the best chance of not only regaining control in Afghanistan but also securing the continued support of the tribal elements in the FATA, which in turn only better conduces to al-Qaeda's survival over the long term.

Al- Qaeda leaders thus have repeatedly endorsed the Pashtun leadership of the Taliban, centered on Mullah Omar's coterie, on many an occasion publicly, beginning in 2002 when Osama bin Laden conferred on Mullah Omar the title of Emir Al- Momineen (Leader of the Faithful). The increasing sophistication of the Taliban's military operations, the new integration of suicide attacks into its modus operandi, and its increasing emphasis on information operations for a group that historically despised the modern media also indicate that al- Qaeda elements continue to assist Taliban forces with at least technology and training, and possibly financial assistance, as partial recompense for the refuge they receive in the FATA as they continue to bide their time awaiting the reestablishment of Taliban control in Afghanistan. Pakistan's failure to target the Taliban and especially its leadership since 2001 has, therefore, had several deleterious consequences.

To begin with, it has resulted in the creation of a safe haven for various terrorist elements in the FATA, whence the Taliban war against the Karzai regime can be prosecuted and the al- Qaeda leadership protected and regenerated as it plans more catastrophic attacks on the West and on the United States in particular. It has also permitted the Taliban to nurture their indigenous bases of support within southern and eastern Afghanistan itself, whence they can slowly evolve into a tumorous state within a state. Further, it has bred a cancerous nest of violent extremism inside Pakistan resulting in the rise of new Islamist militant groups, sometimes labeled the Pakistani Taliban, that are either sympathetic to or affiliated with al- Qaeda and committed to waging a holy war against the Pakistani government, the liberal elements in Pakistani politics, as well as other foreign adversaries such as India, Israel, and the United States. The invigoration of these indigenous radical outfits has in the process produced a new generation of foot soldiers available to different extremist entities throughout the country and strengthened the social bases of support for the otherwise marginal Islamist parties in Pakistani politics. Finally, it has added to the already long and intractable list of problems confronting Pakistan as it struggles to transform itself into a moderate and successful Muslim state: in particular, it has condemned the Pakistani leadership, including acknowledged moderate leaders like Musharraf, to prosecute antiterrorism operations under highly disadvantageous conditions and in an area that by history and tradition has long been lawless, has been bereft of any concentrated state penetration, and that had no regular military presence worth the name until recently, yet is dominated by those very groups that have strong ethnic and increasingly ideological ties to the same terrorist elements sought by the Pakistani state.

If the foregoing discussion amplifies how Pakistan's counterterrorism performance has been structurally compromised by motivational and institutional problems, this is by no means the whole story. An equally important source of inadequacy has been the operational complexity of the counterterrorism operations themselves and Pakistan's myriad weaknesses in coping with these challenges. These difficulties— three of which are illustrated in the discussion that follows— only complicate the challenges caused by the larger problem of whether Pakistan believes eliminating the Taliban decisively is in its national interest.

First, Pakistan's inability to secure the tactical intelligence required for successful counterterrorism operations against key Taliban and al- Qaeda elements in the FATA has now become painfully obvious. Although the ISID and the army's director general of military intelligence have primary responsibility for the collection of targeting intelligence in the FATA, their ability to carry out these tasks has been severely hampered in recent times. In part, this is undoubtedly because many Pakistani intelligence officers are simply sympathetic to radical Islamist elements who have been their clients for many years. Even when this is not the case, however, state intelligence activities have been hindered by the peculiarities of the political structures in the FATA and the corrosive changes that have been occurring therein.

It is often insufficiently recognized that, although the tribal areas are physically located within Pakistani territory, they are not governed by either Pakistani laws and regulations or the political institutions normally associated with national politics. In fact, the relationship between these tribal areas and the Pakistani state is regulated not by any common laws but by formal treaties between the resident tribes and the federal government in Islamabad. The existence of such treaties exemplifies what two analysts have rightly labeled "the anomaly of [the] FATA": it signifies that the link between the tribes and the Pakistani government resembles one that exists between coordinate, and not superordinate and subordinate, political entities. This is further corroborated by the fact that these treaties not only guarantee the tribes' immunity to the codified laws and regulations that govern political life in the rest of Pakistan but also bestow on them exclusive responsibility for the management of their own internal affairs. With the exception of the Frontier Crimes Regulation, a written document more than a century old that elaborates the principle of settling disputes through arbitration by tribal jirgas, most of the governing rules in the FATA are essentially unwritten, being based on a combination of rewaj (tribal customs) and Sharia (Islamic law).

The foundation of maintaining order and authority in such a system, which is anchored in custom, tradition, and legal practices going back to the British Raj, lay in the inculcation of harmonious relations between the political agent— a mid- level civil servant with sweeping powers who, although deputed by the governor of the North West Frontier Province as the highest- ranking official representative in each tribal agency, was ultimately responsible to the federal government in Islamabad— and the tribal maliks, or elders, who managed tribal affairs day to day and who until 1996 were the only individuals permitted to vote in elections for Pakistan's National Assembly. The ties between the agents and the maliks were critical to the production of good intelligence: the agents disbursed the resources provided by Islamabad to acquire the information required to keep the government up to date about developments along the frontier, and the maliks used the subventions provided to buttress their own influence, access, and standing with the tribes they supervised.

Although it was possible to alter this traditional structure of management in the FATA, successive authoritarian regimes in Islamabad eschewed that alternative because the system of direct control through the political agent invariably appeared more attractive to Pakistan Army leaders who were innately uncomfortable with the idea of democratic alternatives involving the introduction of universal adult suffrage, the development of representative institutions, and the presence of civilian political parties in local politics. As a result, the traditional governing mechanisms, centered on the interactions between agents and maliks against the backdrop of the privileges encoded in the old treaties, were only reinforced by Islamabad despite the fact that the bonds between these agents and maliks had became increasingly discredited because of the widespread corruption and politicization that came to characterize their relationship. As a result over time, the tribes along the frontier no longer looked up to their own maliks as selfless leaders or to the political agents as fair representatives of a federal government that sought to advance their welfare.

By the time the 1980s set in, the anti- Soviet jihad brought about a further— and deadlier— acceleration of this crisis. Egged on by the initiatives of Pakistan's Islamist president, Zia ul- Haq, the FATA witnessed a steady social transformation that resulted in the traditional authorities— the political agents and the maliks— being slowly supplanted by new religious leaders, the maulvis, who viewed issues of political loyalty primarily through religious or ideological lenses. The progressive demise of the old social order thus made the long- standing Pakistani human intelligence collection apparatus dramatically ineffective as the radicalized maulvis, viewing the protection of the Taliban and al- Qaeda cadres in the FATA as a politico- religious obligation, appear determined to deny the Pakistani state the necessary information required to apprehend these targets. The widespread outcry in the frontier areas against the U.S. war in Iraq, coupled with the growing perception that Musharraf's prosecution of counterterrorism operations represents illegitimate support for a U.S. administration involved in a global anti- Muslim crusade, has only strengthened the determination of the maulvis and the new Islamists, who have filled the "power vacuum" caused by the demise of the agent-malik relationship in the FATA, to protect the terrorist targets sought by Pakistan and the United States.

The limitations of Pakistani technical intelligence capabilities in the context of counter terrorism operations also do not help matters any. As a matter of fact, Pakistan does have an impressive array of national intelligence collection capabilities.

These systems, which are focused primarily on gathering signals and communications intelligence (SIGINT and COMINT), are largely under ISID control although the actual intercept operations are conducted by inter- services signals units that employ technical personnel drawn from the army's Corps of Signals, the air force, and the navy. For the most part, however, strategic SIGINT and COMINT collection in Pakistan— the intercept, analysis, and dissemination of electronic signatures and communications waveforms— is disproportionately oriented toward targeting India. Islamabad's most sophisticated assets, accordingly, focus on the detection, direction finding, surveillance, and intercept of the high frequency (HF), very high frequency (VHF), ultra high frequency (UHF), and satellite bandwidths used by Indian diplomatic and military communications.

These resources, together with the tactical SIGINT and COMINT systems possessed at the corps level in the Pakistan Army, make Islamabad certainly capable of monitoring the communication devices used by the Taliban and al- Qaeda, because these in fact most likely resemble those supplied by the ISID to various Kashmiri terrorist groups and recovered over the years by the Indian military. The insurgency in Kashmir revealed that Pakistani-supported terrorist groups in South Asia, including those operating in Afghanistan, generally use HF radio, satellite telephony, and cellular phones for long- range connectivity, with commercially available line- of- sight VHF and UHF radios produced by companies such as Yeasu, Kenwood, and I- Com for their operational and tactical communications.

Targeting the communications traffic generated through these systems, however, requires Pakistan's national and tactical collection assets to be systematically tasked for this purpose, but both Indian and Afghan military intelligence officials believe that New Delhi continues to remain a higher- priority target for Pakistani technical collection in comparison with either the Taliban or al-Qaeda. Even when this is not the case, however, Pakistani surveillance systems may continue to be ineffective in the counterterrorism mission for many reasons.

If Taliban and al- Qaeda operatives use low- power devices sporadically for tactical communications, the short range and random nature of these transmissions may defeat even a technically competent operator if no surveillance devices are in proximity to the threat. Further, sophisticated technologies such as frequency hopping, portable encrypted, or digital burst radios, many of which are available commercially, can be used to elude even skilled surveillance especially if the monitoring systems are not available or are not dedicated full- time to the mission.

Finally, the increased use of the Internet by Taliban and al-Qaeda operatives, including their growing use of encryption software, makes it hard for the ISID to monitor such communications systematically because, in the absence of prior cueing, high- speed computation married to sophisticated search algorithms would be required if the relatively large volume of Internet traffic, even within an otherwise relatively low tele- density state like Pakistan, is to be successfully monitored. It is simply not clear whether Pakistan possesses such capabilities.

In principle, U.S. advantages here could serve to compensate, but the growing appreciation of the capabilities of U.S. assets has resulted in these opposition forces— both Taliban and al- Qaeda— increasingly relying on more primitive but more secure means of communication, such as "snail mail" and human couriers, for their operational planning.

This workaround, in turn, denies both Pakistan and the United States the kind of targeting data that might otherwise have become available through technical intelligence.

Recognizing these problems, Pakistan has begun the arduous task of rebuilding both its technical and its human intelligence collection assets in the FATA. The latter capabilities are indeed the most critical, but these also take the longest to mature and to yield their fruit. A long- term Pakistan Army presence in the FATA amid conditions of relative peace is, therefore, an essential precondition for Islamabad to be able to develop and consolidate an effective human intelligence network.

The $750 million U.S. assistance program to the FATA, if properly directed, could help considerably in advancing this goal of local stability; but the complicated and time- consuming nature of this endeavor, the uncertainty about the program's effective implementation, and Washington's failure to condition the availability of these funds on Islamabad's implementation of political reforms in the tribal regions— to include, inter alia, the drastic revision of the Frontier Crimes Regulation; the elimination of the political agent as part of the larger process of integrating the FATA into Pakistan's North West Frontier Province under the full jurisdiction of the provincial and national legislatures and the judicial system; and the withdrawal of restrictions on political parties operating in the FATA with an eye to introducing conventional political institutions— imply that neither the United States nor Pakistan ought to expect quick breakthroughs in their efforts "to build confidence and trust between the Government of Pakistan (GOP) and [the] FATA tribal communities" leading to the demolition of the al- Qaeda and Taliban networks that have regenerated in this area over the last few years.

Second, the arrival of the Pakistan Army in strength in the FATA has resulted in social disruptions that have undermined its counterterrorism effectiveness. Although the insertion of the Army's XI Corps and the SSG battalions into the autonomous areas was a brave and necessary decision of the part of General Musharraf, it has nonetheless eroded the delicate compact that previously existed between the FATA and the Pakistani state. The resulting alienation and resentment on the part of the indigenous population have been reflected in significant counterterrorism problems. The Pakistan Army— which draws its cadres largely from outside the FATA and is primarily non- Pashtun in composition— is a highly professional force, but its maneuver units have often been stymied by their inability to secure the cooperation of the local populace, which views it today as an unwelcome intruder. The army's SSG is very effective in tactical counterterrorism operations but, being an elite unit, is far too diminutive to make a difference at the theater level.

The Frontier Corps, which is composed primarily of tribal levies and is the resident paramilitary force, could be potentially the most effective element, but it is often compromised by its close ties with the local inhabitants. Riddled with sympathizers, inadequately motivated, suspicious of both Islamabad's and Washington's intentions, poorly trained and equipped for counterterrorism operations, yet present in strength throughout the FATA, the Frontier Corps (along with its other local siblings such as the Frontier Constabulary, the tribal police [khassadars], and tribal militias [lashkars]) represents the perfect exemplar of the structural challenge facing Pakistan's counterterrorism effort: its best local units, the ones that share affinities with the tribes they patrol and consequently the forces likely to secure potentially the most useful intelligence, are also the fighting elements least able or willing to cope with the battle-hardened terrorists they are deployed against.

Unfortunately, the infantry elements of the Pakistan Army that have been pressed into the fight have their own problems as well. Unlike the Indian Army, which thanks to two decades of combating Pakistani- supported subconventional conflict now has considerable counter terrorism skills, the infantry battalions of Pakistan's XI Corps are configured primarily as strategic reserves for possible conventional warfare against India. Counterterrorism operations are not their forte, and, while they have done a decent job of learning by doing, they still betray a proclivity for operational responses that while sensible against a conventional adversary are less than effective (and, perhaps, even counterproductive) when dealing with irregular forces: large unit deployments, intense (and sometimes indiscriminate) employment of fire, and sledgehammer cordon- and- search tactics.

While the attrition strategies of the Pakistani military have been criticized by many for their detrimental consequences, it must be recognized that these are not always attributable to the "self- proclaimed invincibility of the [Pakistani] armed forces." Rather, the hostile terrain in which counterterrorism operations are conducted and the unexpectedly heavy firepower that Taliban and al- Qaeda terrorists have mustered in the past have been the two factors most responsible for the military's recourse to the relatively coarse counterterrorism tactics that are invariably derided.

It is not difficult to sympathize with Islamabad's predicament. For starters, the topography of the FATA is incredibly inhospitable as far as counterterrorism operations are concerned. The general geography of the area is characterized by harsh, rugged, and inaccessible mountainous terrain with steep slopes being the rule rather than the exception. The crest elevations in the region vary from 3,600 meters to 4,700 meters in the Khyber, Kurram, and Orakzai agencies of the central FATA, dropping somewhat to between 1,500 meters and 3,400 meters in the southern agencies of North and South Waziristan. These mountain ranges running roughly from northeast to southwest function as a complex barrier that breaks up the terrain into numerous tiny basins or valleys that are dotted with minuscule settlements surviving either through livestock grazing, subsistence agriculture, or petty trade. The size of these settlements is generally very small, ranging from literally a few dozen people in some instances to a few thousand at most in the largest hamlets.

The lines of communication between these outposts are invariably tenuous, extending along the ridgelines of the adjacent mountains or traversing them through numerous passes, tracks, and trails, many of which support only pedestrian traffic or pack animals. Because many of these routes are intestinal and insignificant, they are often known only to the locals who, along with smugglers, drug runners, and arms peddlers, have exploited these conduits in the natural terrain to carry out their business undisturbed for centuries. These terrain features produce three significant operational consequences that have great impact on the conduct of military operations.

First, the isolation of the hamlets amid craggy geophysical features and the small sizes of the populations sheltered within them make it virtually impossible for outsiders to monitor any personnel movement to or from these locations, especially if the transit occurs on foot, by animal, or by isolated vehicular traffic (where possible). This is especially true if the movement concerned occurs in adverse weather or at night. Second, the consanguineal character of the tribal populations living in these areas implies that strangers cannot travel within the area without being readily detected, and safe passage in such circumstances usually occurs only when the local inhabitants are persuaded about the alien's peaceful intentions through some form of attestation by individuals known to the resident tribes. Third, the distances between the populated outposts can be significant given the absence of paved or metaled roads and, consequently, quick movement across the terrain invariably requires either strenuous marches on foot on or off established paths (depending on circumstances) or the use of animals, accompanied by guides in most cases. In several locations vehicular traffic is in fact possible, but, because such movement invariably hews to well- established roads and pathways, covert entry and exit through such access routes is generally difficult.

This concatenation of features abundantly explains why Pakistani counterterrorism operations have often run into tactical difficulties requiring recourse to "excessive" force. The isolated setting of many FATA settlements where terrorist cadres find refuge essentially prevents the Pakistani pursuers of the terrorists from being able to approach these locales clandestinely. Even small commando units operating on foot are susceptible to premature detection by the locals, and the munitions and weapons required to be carried over the harsh terrain and along the great distances within the region often tax the abilities of even the fittest infantry units, which must conserve their strength for the arduous military action at the end of their insertion. This consideration invariably mandates traveling on established tracks and paths, but even off- track approaches do not provide any assurance that the attacking force will be able to close in on its target undetected.

Because the risk of compromise is consistently high, many terrorist refugees have been able to simply escape at the first warning of military units moving en route to their hideouts. Early engagements with the Taliban and al- Qaeda cadres who chose to remain bivouacked also revealed— often to the surprise of their attackers— just how heavily armed they were; in fact, the character of their military equipment could often make the difference in whether they chose to escape or stand their ground and fight. Whenever they settled upon fighting, their employment of heavy weapons was invariably made doubly effective by the natural advantages accruing to the defense especially in mountainous terrain— gains that were further magnified by the clever use of stealthy tactics, the cunning utilization of the surrounding topography, the erection of effective positional defenses, and the exploitation of the timely warning provided by the local inhabitants.

The persistence of such challenges compelled the Pakistani military to seek operational work- arounds that offered some chance of success. The solution that proved most attractive in many circumstances was to forgo tactical surprise, which might have ensued from the exclusive use of small units relying entirely on covert foot penetration, in favor of larger operations that sought to exploit tactical superiority through the employment of heliborne elements for both the transportation of substantial strike teams to some location in proximity to their designated target and for the firepower required in support of the actual assault. Because the final engagement in such situations usually involved a heavily armed and a partially or fully alerted adversary— if the latter had not already escaped— the attacking Pakistani combat teams were often forced to employ even heavier weapons than might have been originally intended, including mortars, antitank recoilless rifles and guided missiles, field artillery, helicopter- and aircraft-fired cannon and unguided rockets, and occasionally even general-purpose bombs delivered by tactical aircraft. The lessons offered by such engagements since 2002 are stark and clear: unless the tribal populations residing in the FATA are sympathetic to the government and are willing to either warn the army of the militants' presence in their midst or desist from alerting the terrorists to the military's anticipated arrival in their hamlets, counterterrorism missions will either fail or be condemned to rely on even greater applications of brute force for their success.

The inevitable, but unintended, consequence of implementing such solutions has been significant collateral damage among civilians in the tribal areas. The residents, in response, have reacted to these losses by mounting violent attacks on, and repeated seizures of, Pakistani troops and paramilitary forces deployed in the area. The more extremist outfits, to include al-Qaeda elements, have sought to exact their revenge by undertaking lethal suicide attacks against Pakistani military and intelligence personnel both within the FATA and deep inside the nation's heartland in an effort to compel President Musharraf to terminate his counterterrorism operations conclusively. These continuing attacks on Pakistani military personnel have, by many anecdotal accounts, lowered morale within the frontline units now operating inside the FATA and caused increased desertions, suicides, and frequent discharge applications. Not surprisingly then, these developments have induced deepened soul- searching on the part of local commanders who wonder about the strategic wisdom of the ongoing war on terror and question the benefits specifically accruing to Pakistan. The growing antagonism caused by the collateral damage associated with U.S. military strikes from the Afghan side of the FATA has not helped make the Pakistan Army's problems any easier in this regard.

Throughout Pakistani society in general, there is a growing weariness with the counterterrorism operations presently being waged on the country's soil. Recent polling, for example, suggests only weak support for using force against Islamic militants operating within Pakistan, and most respondents overwhelmingly oppose allowing outside forces to combat al-Qaeda on their national territory. A survey recently conducted by the Program on International Policy Attitudes at the University of Maryland in collaboration with the U.S. Institute of Peace found that just 44 percent of urban Pakistanis favored sending the Pakistan Army to the tribal areas to "pursue and capture al Qaeda fighters," and only 48 percent would allow the Pakistan Army to act against "Taliban insurgents who have crossed over from Afghanistan." In general, the survey concludes that "Pakistanis reject overwhelmingly the idea of permitting foreign troops to attack al-Qaeda on Pakistani territory. Four out of five (80 percent) say their government should not allow U.S. or other foreign troops to enter Pakistan to pursue and capture al Qaeda fighters," and three out of four (77 percent) oppose allowing foreign troops to attack Taliban insurgents based in Pakistan. Other polls reveal similar levels of disenchantment with the U.S.-supported campaign against terrorism. One report summarized it: ... despite their own concerns about terrorism, Pakistanis overwhelmingly oppose U.S.led efforts to fight terrorism— six- in- ten (59%) oppose America's anti- terror campaign, while only 13% back it. Like many other Muslim publics throughout Asia, the Middle East, and elsewhere, Pakistanis also oppose other key facets of U.S. foreign policy. Three- quarters (76%) say the U.S. should remove its troops from Iraq, and a similar proportion (75%) believe the U.S. and NATO should withdraw from Afghanistan, which shares a 1,500 mile border with Pakistan.

But Pakistanis are not just worried about the use of U.S. force in neighboring countries. They also fear they could become a target. More than seven- in- ten (72%) are very or somewhat worried that the U.S. could become a military threat to their country. And 64% name the U.S. as one of the countries posing the greatest potential threat to Pakistan, more than even long-standing arch- rival India (45%), with whom Pakistan has fought three major wars in the last sixty years.

Musharraf has attempted to cope with this increasing national weariness and to circumvent the problems caused by his army's operations, minimize its casualties, and soothe the roiling political environment in the tribal areas by episodic strategies of appeasement built around so- called peace accords with the pro-Taliban locals in South and North Waziristan. Under these accords, the indigenous residents were tasked with preventing cross- border movements of terrorists into Afghanistan and further attacks on Pakistani civilian and military targets. They were also to ensure either the ejection or the surrender of all foreigners, meaning the non–South Asian cadres loyal to al- Qaeda, from the FATA in exchange for which the Pakistan Army would withdraw to its barracks, suspend its combat operations against the terrorists, and defer to the tribes in regard to resolving disputes relating to the status of particular individuals.

Musharraf's understandable objective in pursuing such a solution was to restore the status quo ante— hold the tribes responsible for maintaining peace and security as they had done traditionally— but it was a strategy that was doomed to failure because it did not appreciate the extent of radicalization in the FATA and the tribes' new determination to protect their al-Qaeda and Taliban cortege against the Pakistani government and the United States, which were viewed as the greater threats. Thus, although several tribal groups have sought to cooperate with the government in rooting out the radicals in their midst, the more extremist entities, not surprisingly, used the breathing space provided by the accords to recruit, train, and rearm the terrorists in anticipation of a heightened and continuing campaign in Afghanistan. The Pakistan Army's attack on the Lal Masjid in Islamabad proved to be the proverbial straw that finally destroyed the charade embodied by the peace accords in the FATA, but the failure of these agreements has left Musharraf in an unenviable limbo where neither peace nor war seems able to deliver the counterterrorism goals pursued by the Pakistani state.

Third, the operational context surrounding the counterterrorism effort in the tribal areas and in Afghanistan has changed considerably— to the disadvantage of the Western coalition— since Operation Enduring Freedom began in 2001. To begin with, the Taliban movement, which was never a tight and cohesive political entity in any case, has become an even looser network of affiliated individuals and groups since it was forced from power in Kabul.

Today, the Taliban "alliance" can be characterized as a disparate congeries of several elements united only by a common religious ideology, a desire to regain power in either Afghanistan or their local areas of operation, and a deep antagonism toward the United States and its regional allies. Several distinct elements can be identified in the current Taliban coalition:

- The leadership shura centered around Mullah Omar and his cohort in Quetta and the subsidiary war councils in Quetta, Miran Shah, Peshawar, and Karachi;
- The Taliban cadres who survived the defeat in Afghanistan, which are loosely controlled by the regional shuras and continue to draw on the madaris in the FATA and the refugee camps in Pakistan for their continuing recruitment;
- The tribal networks of former mujahideen commanders like Jalaluddin Haqqani who operates in Paktika, Paktia, and Khowst provinces and provides a key bridge between al-Qaeda and the Taliban; Gulbuddin Hekmatyar who leads the Hezb-i-Islami and operates in Nangarhar, Konar, and Nuristan provinces; Anwar- ul- Haq who leads the Hezb-i-Islami (Khalis) also operates in the Nangarhar area and is believed to lead the Tora Bora Military Front; and Saifullah Mansoor, a veteran field commander who is known to be active in the eastern areas;
- The Pakistani Taliban commanders like Baitullah Mahsud, the chieftain of the Mahsud tribe in South Waziristan; Maulana Faqir Muhammad who is associated with the Tehrike- Nafaz- e- Shariat- e- Muhammad and who operates in the Bajaur Agency; Maulana Qazi Fazlullah, also affiliated with the same group but operating out of Swat; Mangal Bagh Afridi, who leads the Lashkar- e- Islami in the Khyber Agency and is believed to be part of a larger local opposition network led by Mufti Munir Shakir; and Sharif Khan and

Nur Islam, tribal leaders who have demonstrated considerable operational effectiveness in South Waziristan;

- The drug lords in eastern and southern Afghanistan, especially in Helmand and Kandahar provinces, who are either taxed or willingly contribute revenues that are indispensable for the Taliban war against Kabul;
- The sundry former anti- Soviet commanders who control small groups of fighters and are engaged primarily in criminal activities such as bank robberies, kidnappings for ransom, and assassination of local officials while they simultaneously offer their services as guns for hire;
- The disaffected Afghan Pashtun tribes, most conspicuously the rural Ghilzai, who, feeling disenfranchised in the current governing arrangements, continue to support the Taliban with manpower and sanctuary within Afghanistan; and, finally,
- Al- Qaeda, which, while distinct from all the foregoing groups in that its focus of operations remains the global jihad, nonetheless collaborates with the Taliban in order to assist the Taliban in recovering control of Kabul while it continues to preserve its sanctuary in the FATA in the interim.

The implication of such a diverse target set is that destroying the Taliban today has become much more difficult because its previously weak hierarchical structure has become even more diffuse, with truly diverse entities coordinating as necessary but with each also carrying out its own local agenda.

This reality, in turn, implies that while some specific nodes in this network will have to be defeated "kinetically" if the Taliban threat is to be erased, these tactical successes will have to be procured despite the political hesitation in parts of the Pakistani state and the real operational limitations of the Pakistani military. The complexity of Islamabad's relations with many of the constituent elements in the Taliban coalition does not help either: although Islamabad may readily cooperate in targeting some of the Pakistani Taliban commanders, drug lords, petty former anti-

Soviet captains, and al- Qaeda elements, the ties nurtured by Pakistan's military and intelligence services with the Taliban leadership and the tribal networks of key former mujahideen commanders make these targets relatively inviolate, at least in the near term. For understandable sociopolitical reasons, Pakistani leaders are also likely to find it very difficult to conduct any large-scale interdiction operations aimed at the Taliban foot soldiers and the disaffected tribes— even if only in the FATA— partly because of the unmanageable chaos that would ensue in a very sensitive area of great importance to the Pakistani state and partly because of the fact that the insurgents drawn from these groups today are truly protean, capable of participating in military operations when required but at other times fluidly mutating into ordinary tribals.

There is no doubt, therefore, that winning the war on terror in Afghanistan will require dealing with the sanctuary enjoyed by various militant groups inside Pakistan. But it is probably an exaggeration to conclude "that the solution lies not in Afghanistan, but across the Khyber Pass in Pakistan."80 What happens in Afghanistan itself is critically important—not only in regard to ongoing military operations but, more fundamentally, in respect to reconstruction, economic development, nation building, and political reconstitution—because the counterterrorism campaign will not be won until the political environment in Afghanistan improves to the point where these insurgent forces are denied the conditions that allow them to survive and flourish. As General James L. Jones succinctly stated in his testimony before the Senate Foreign Relations Committee, "I am convinced that the solution in Afghanistan is not a military one."

It is in this context that Afghanistan's— and not just Pakistan's— political failures are particularly galling. Despite the advances in developing a constitutional government in Kabul with strong international support, the Karzai regime has turned out to be conspicuously ineffective. The inability of the government to deliver basic services, education, justice, and economic development, even in those areas not directly threatened by the insurgency, has fueled great frustration with President Karzai throughout the country. The growing corruption witnessed at all levels of government only exacerbates this resentment. And the runaway upsurge in poppy cultivation, which in 2006 yielded an all- time- high output of 6,100 metric tons, has resulted in a situation where "militia commanders, criminal organizations, and corrupt officials have exploited narcotics as a reliable source of revenue and patronage, which has perpetuated the threat these groups pose to the country's fragile internal security and the legitimacy of its embryonic democratic government." The complexities of intra- Afghan politics only compound the situation further: many Pashtun groups, for example, stung by the government's inability or unwillingness to address their specific grievances, often view the local insurgents as more effective instruments for achieving their immediate security or developmental goals. Any efforts made by the government to assuage Pashtun bitterness directly, however, complicates its relations with the non- Pashtun groups, who are apt to see most initiatives aimed at bolstering central authority, reinvigorating the traditional Pashtun tribal structures, and negotiating with Pakistan as evidence of a surreptitious attempt to reassert Pashtun hegemony over the rest of Afghanistan.

The Karzai government has thus far not succeeded in steering clear of these competing pressures, and its sharply alternating policies have not helped its standing either. Its most recent stab at neutralizing the growing insurgency by implementing a reconciliation program involving the "moderate Taliban" is a good example. After resisting such an idea for a long time, in part because of opposition from former Northern Alliance figures supportive of the government, President Karzai changed course and embarked on an effort to reintegrate the less extreme Taliban members into the national mainstream.

The idea is indeed sensible in principle but difficult to implement successfully in practice. That President Musharraf is its most ardent advocate has not raised the credibility of the program particularly, because it is often viewed in Afghanistan as a Pakistani stratagem to evade fulfilling its obligations to erase the insurgent sanctuaries in the tribal areas. In any event, the notion of reconciling moderate Taliban into Afghan society, while certainly commendable if it is understood to mean coopting the poor and disenfranchised confederations such as the Ghilzai, is invariably tricky and possibly even counterproductive because of the difficulties of distinguishing genuinely alienated individuals, who might be desirous of integration, from their more diehard and utterly intractable counterparts. One very thoughtful analysis concluded:

While more efforts should have gone into reconciliation in the early days, seeking to quell the insurgency now by rewarding criminal behavior would only perpetuate a culture of impunity and betray the trust of those who have backed the new, democratic, participatory institutions. It appears that the concept of reconciliation is being used interchangeably with amnesty. While such compromise may bring some measure of short- term relief, it would ultimately do nothing to break the cycle of violence.

Not surprisingly then, this Program Takhim- e Solh, which translates roughly into the Strengthening Peace program, has not been a noteworthy success. It does not appear to have made any significant dent in the manpower available to the insurgency, even as it has increased the fissures between Karzai and his non- Pashtun allies, has created new political threats to his 2009 presidential ambitions, and has failed to undermine the Taliban's social base of support in the interim.

One news report summarized the current crisis within Afghanistan laconically by declaring: "Government corruption and poppy cultivation are rampant and public services remain a wreck; food prices are soaring, unemployment remains high and resurgent Taliban forces in the south are pressing toward th[e] capital."86 Defeating this last threat obviously represents a classic chicken- and- egg dilemma: Taliban resurgence prevents the Karzai regime from effectively extending central control in the east, south, and southeast of the country, while the lack of effective state presence in these areas is precisely what makes the Taliban's return possible in the first place. Unfortunately, the three critical elements that could help Afghanistan break out of this cruel trap are constrained for different reasons.

To begin with, and as the foregoing discussion has elaborated, Pakistan is hobbled by political hesitancy and myriad operational limitations. To make things worse, NATO forces in Afghanistan are constrained by various "national caveats," that is, operational restrictions that prevent the alliance's International Security Assistance Force (ISAF) from undertaking the necessary combat operations required to prevent the Taliban from consolidating their foothold in southern and southeastern Afghanistan. Although ISAF is formally charged with the provision of security throughout Afghanistan, the main thrust of its effort revolves around supporting the approximately thirty- four provincial reconstruction teams (PRTs) operating throughout the country.

The PRTs are joint military- civilian units of between sixty and one thousand personnel engaged in reconstruction activities aimed at enhancing local security in order to permit the larger nation-building exercise to succeed. This essentially humanitarian mission, however, presumes the consent of local residents for its success and requires the PRT to be neutral and impartial with respect to any overarching political rivalries that may otherwise characterize its operating environment. The PRT is supposed to be robust enough to defend itself against attack, but it is emphatically not intended to be the spear point of change through offensive military action. Although the vision underlying the PRT is defensible, the fact that the social change it engenders has consequences for the local balance of power within Afghanistan implies that its activities are entirely unwelcome to those who oppose the larger nation-building project. Consequently, the PRTs specifically and the international community's reconstruction activities more generally have become the target of concerted attacks by Taliban and al-Qaeda forces, especially in southern and eastern Afghanistan. It is in this context that the national caveats handicapping ISAF— some seventy- one at last count— become relevant because they prevent the various contingents that compose the 38,000-strong force from effectively engaging the adversary as required in accordance with tactical necessity.

Thus, although ISAF's area of operations has now extended to all of Afghanistan thanks to its stage 3 expansion to the South and its stage 4 expansion to the East, the differential rules of engagement under which each national contingent now operates ensures that its full combat power cannot be brought to bear uniformly over the entire battlefield— to the obvious advantage of its Taliban and al- Qaeda adversaries.

To make things worse, although ISAF is declared to be NATO's highest- priority mission, the alliance has had enormous difficulty convincing its member states to make the requisite contributions of manpower, equipment, and finance to secure victory in the combat operations in Afghanistan.

As things stand today, NATO fields some 1.2 soldiers per thousand Afghan inhabitants. Even if the 85,000 Afghan security personnel and the 12,000-odd U.S. forces dedicated to Operation Enduring Freedom are added to the number, the ratio of security forces to population hovers at about 4 soldiers per thousand inhabitants. This level of force presence is abysmal, given that a considerable body of research suggests that successful nation-building operations require at least 10 soldiers per thousand inhabitants, and preferably 20 soldiers per thousand inhabitants if there is an active conflict.

NATO thus far has simply not been able to contemplate, let alone provide, combat forces at anything approximating these levels required for success in Afghanistan. The British, the Canadians, and the Dutch have supplied the largest contingents actually involved in combat operations; although the Germans and the Italians have a significant presence, they are not involved in active combat. The French, too, while politically supportive of the ISAF mission in Afghanistan have declined to support the effort through either enhanced contributions or a restructuring of their current force posture. Although French forces remain among the most capable units within ISAF, the thousand- odd troops currently present in Afghanistan are deployed in the relatively secure areas in and around Kabul, with Paris continuing to resist NATO entreaties to dispatch these forces to the eastern and southern areas of Afghanistan where the Taliban opposition is most active.

The NATO presence in Afghanistan is thus characterized by a curious paradox: the most capable European states, largely those in western Europe, have simply declined to make the robust contributions required to win what is universally acknowledged as the "good war," while the alliance's newest entrants from eastern Europe appear far more willing to contribute to the ISAF effort even though they lack the depth of national and military resources possessed by their western European counterparts. Although the early U.S. disinclination to involve NATO in Afghan peace operations played some role in sustaining this paradox, the later European disenchantment with the U.S. war in Iraq, Washington's treatment of terrorist detainees, and the U.S. emphasis on attacking the adversary as opposed to protecting the population all appear to have contributed toward the western European inclination to stay aloof from any war- fighting entanglements.

This reluctance to contribute on the part of the stronger European allies is also reinforced partly by the presence of competing security priorities and the remarkably weak domestic support for any foreign military operations.

Above all else, however, it is owed to the alliance's failure to create a consensus on the implications of a failure in Afghanistan for European security; the lack of a clarifying continental debate on the goals, strategy, and tactics associated with winning the war against al- Qaeda and the Taliban; and the stunning unwillingness on the part of the wealthier "post- heroic" European states to actually fight a war that would require them to expend blood and treasure by remaining ensconced, deployed, and operating with their full panoply of military capabilities in southern and eastern Afghanistan until the adversary is eventually routed.

Finally, the principal combatant elements conducting Operation Enduring Freedom, through war- fighting actions against the al-Qaeda and Taliban forces in Afghanistan, are also handicapped by several limitations.

Among the most important of these is the availability of deployable troops. The 10,000-odd soldiers that the United States contributes to this combat operation, supplemented by token forces provided by the United Kingdom, Canada, and a few others, are increasingly insufficient given the growing scale and intensity of the Afghan insurgency.

Although coalition forces are superbly trained and equipped and have proved themselves devastatingly effective in combat with their Taliban adversaries, they are simply insufficient to maintain the large- scale presence that is now required to win the war in southern and eastern Afghanistan, given the virulence of the challenge.

In the initial phase of Operation Enduring Freedom, when military operations essentially consisted of search- and- destroy operations that targeted roving bands of terrorists, the current force size was probably appropriate because the superior mobility, firepower, and training of U.S. forces permitted them to sanitize large areas of territory despite their relatively small numbers. With the Taliban insurgency now nourished by local roots particularly in the Nimruz, Helmand, Kandahar, Oruzgan, and Zabol provinces, simply defeating the insurgents in battle is insufficient because they appear able to replenish their numbers relatively easily using both local recruits and imports from across the border, and, more important, they are able to return covertly to the contested districts after their tactically victorious U.S. adversaries withdraw to their rear bases.

Defeating this strategy requires a long- term presence of military forces in situ, which the division- sized U.S. combatant elements simply cannot provide. NATO's inability— and reluctance— to fulfill this role and to include combat operations whenever required merely compounds the problem with the result that the local inhabitants, especially those opposed to the Taliban, are compelled to make their peace with the insurgents merely as a means of preserving their security.

The surreptitious return of the Taliban in this fashion to any given district invariably results then in the ejection of the nongovernmental organizations working therein, the interruption of state- organized developmental assistance, and a crisis in local governance— all of which exacerbate the vicious circle that further undermines security. Given this dynamic, there is good reason to fear that, just as in Vietnam several decades earlier, U.S. and allied military forces could win every tactical engagement with the Taliban and yet lose the general war for Afghanistan.

Attempting to defeat this problem with the small number of combatant forces available only ends up overusing them. The Fort Drum, New York–based U.S. 10th Mountain Division, for example, has already deployed to Afghanistan thrice in five years, and when deployed in the field it is invariably overextended operationally because of the need to cover those alliance contingents that are unable to engage in combat operations when required because of their nationally constrained rules of engagement.

The only solution to this problem will be to beef up the U.S. military presence in southern Afghanistan: this may necessitate deploying more troops and equipment but, more importantly, entails creating a dedicated U.S. command operating under NATO aegis with full and exclusive authority to conduct the war as required without being hampered by the need to support the less able allied contingents.

The slow progress in raising the indigenous Afghan security forces has not helped either in the interim.

Most NATO officials interviewed on this subject declared flatly that the Afghan National Police is currently incapable of satisfactorily performing even basic law enforcement functions and, further, that it would be a long time before the Afghan National Army would be capable of operating as a tactical partner with allied units in counterinsurgency operations and even longer before it could do so independently.

Last, and despite many recent improvements, the coordination among the multiple national militaries engaged in reconstruction, counternarcotics, and counterterrorism in Afghanistan has simply not been as effective as it could be. In fact, problems of command and control among various coalition elements remain a serious and continuing impediment to the success of the Afghan stabilization effort. The vicious interaction of these many problems implies that the chicken- and- egg dilemmas confronting Afghanistan in regard to security and state presence are unlikely to be resolved any time soon.

On balance, therefore, the failure to eliminate the al- Qaeda and Taliban cadres in Afghanistan is owed to a complex cluster of causes. Pakistan's initial reluctance to interdict the Taliban stragglers who settled in the FATA and the leadership shuras that found homes in Quetta and elsewhere in Pakistan played an important role in permitting this organization to regenerate.

This process has been aided, however, by Afghanistan's own missteps in governance, including the failure to deliver security and economic and social development as well as to limit the runaway expansion in the cultivation of poppy in southern Afghanistan. The Pakistani effort to systematically interdict al-Qaeda while simultaneously going easy on the Taliban is riddled with inescapable contradictions. Although this strategy provided some early and important fruit, its tensions are now exploited by both the Taliban and al- Qaeda as well as by the vitally important tribal constituencies that are increasingly less bystanders than full participants on the wrong side in the ongoing war on terror in the FATA.

The operational, technical, and organizational limitations of the Pakistani counterterrorism forces deployed in some of the most inhospitable terrain in the world provides the final component of the explanation for why Islamabad has not done better. There is thus no doubt that Pakistan's reluctance to prosecute counterterrorism operations indivisibly has played an essential role in the failures along the Afghanistan- Pakistan border, but it is by no means the whole story, and any political posturing that suggests otherwise contributes neither to our understanding of the problem nor to its resolution.

2

Pakistan's Long Dalliance with Militancy

Many discussions of Pakistan's use of jihadi organizations begin with the 1980s. During this period, General Muhammad Zia-ul-Haq utilized mujahideen forces to undermine the Soviet occupation of Afghanistan. Pakistan, however, has been using proxy forces since attaining independence from the United Kingdom. In October 1947, Pakistan employed Pathan tribesmen to attack the princely state of Kashmir as its monarch vacillated on the question of whether to accede to India or to Pakistan. The rebels quickly advanced on the Kashmiri capital of Srinagar, raping and pillaging along the way. As attacking forces approached Srinagar, a panicked Maharaja Hari Singh appealed to New Delhi for military assistance. The government of India agreed to defend Kashmir if Singh would commit to join the territory to India. He complied, signing an Instrument of Accession on October 28, 1947. Shortly thereafter, a full-scale war erupted, pitting Pakistan-supported and Pakistani regular forces against the Indian military. The conflict ended in stalemate on December 31, 1948, with India controlling approximately two-thirds of Kashmir and Pakistan the remaining third. This division of territory largely set the foundation for decades of Indo—Pak conflict.

Pakistan resorted to irregular forces again in August 1965 by employing militants in an effort to seize the Indian-controlled portion of Kashmir. The militants infiltrated Indian Kashmir to precipitate an uprising, which was to be followed by a Pakistani conventional military operation to seize the territory. The plan presumed widespread Kashmiri support for Pakistan and disaffection with India. This assumption proved to be wrong; locals promptly alerted the authorities to the presence of the infiltrators, enabling Indian forces to move against them. Despite this failure, Pakistani leaders launched the follow-on, conventional military phase, thereby provoking the second Indo—Pak war. Like the first war, this conflict ended essentially in stalemate. The two parties subsequently agreed to return to the status quo as per the Soviet-brokered Tashkent Agreement of 1966.

In spite of these setbacks in 1947—1948 and 1965, Pakistan's leaders did not lose interest in using militants to help seize control of Indian—administered Kashmir. Indeed, almost immediately after the 1965 war, elements within the Pakistani military started to recruit religious zealots in the Kashmir Valley in hopes of sowing discord and promoting political upheaval within the state. To that end, the Pakistanis started to work with a newly created organization called the Plebiscite Front. While some elements of the Front were willing to limit themselves to the realm of political struggle, others wanted to resort to violence to achieve their goal of merging Kashmir with Pakistan.

These efforts suffered an important setback in the early 1970s, as India cracked down against various jihadi groups. Following Ziaul-Haq's coup in Pakistan and the Soviet invasion of Afghanistan, Islamabad renewed its use of the jihadi option. Zia-ul-Haq presided over the mujahideen campaign in Afghanistan, which played an indispensible role in defeating the Soviet Union. His death during the summer of 1988 in a plane crash prevented him from applying this strategy to Kashmir. When an indigenous uprising erupted in Indian Kashmir in December 1989, however, his successors lost little time in doing so. The Pakistanis initially backed the Jammu and Kashmir Liberation Front (JKLF), a homegrown, notionally secular separatist organization, but such support proved to be shortlived. The JKLF did not wish to join Kashmir to Pakistan. Instead, it sought the creation of an independent Kashmir encompassing both Indian and Pakistani controlled portions of the state. Consequently, the Pakistani military and Inter-Services

Intelligence agency (ISI) marginalized the JKLF, redirecting their resources toward more Islamistoriented organizations dedicated to establishing Pakistani control over Indiaadministered Kashmir. These organizations ranged from the predominantly Kashmiri Hizb-ul-Mujahideen (HuM), to the mostly externally recruited, battlehardened Lashkar-e-Taiba (LeT), whose main goal is to establish an Islamic state in South Asia, and the Jaish-e-Mohammed (JeM), whose main focus is to separate Kashmir from India and join it with Pakistan. Pakistani support for these groups fundamentally transformed the character of the Kashmir insurgency, metamorphosizing it from an indigenous independence struggle, triggered by the malfeasances of Indian rule, to an externally orchestrated effort to attrite Indian resources and seize Jammu and Kashmir for Pakistan.

Over time, Pakistan-backed militants launched increasingly provocative terror operations. On December 13, 2001, for example, LeT and JeM attacked the Indian Parliament while it was in session. Although the terrorists were defeated and no members were harmed, the assault could have resulted in a massacre of India's national legislators. In the wake of this attack, under considerable U.S. pressure, Pakistan undertook cosmetic efforts against organizations such as the LeT and the JeM, briefly incarcerating members of their rank and file. Also, on January 12, 2002, in a nationally televised speech, Musharraf stated that he would not allow Pakistani soil to be used as a launching pad for terror against India or any other country, though he did not rule out the possibility that militant groups might operate from Pakistan-administered Kashmir, which enjoys nominal independence. Despite Musharraf's apparent interest in preventing further terrorism, little changed in practice. Soon thereafter, in May 2002, the LeT were implicated in an attack on the families of soldiers stationed at an Indian military base at Kaluchak in Jammu and Kashmir. The December 2001 parliament assault had led India to undertake a massive military mobilization to coerce Pakistan into ending its support for terrorism. The May 2002 Kaluchak attack brought the two states to the brink of war. For reasons that are the subject of a vigorous debate, they managed to avoid outright conflict during these 2001—2002 crises. Nonetheless, Indo—Pak relations remained fraught as Pakistan failed to completely rein in the jihadi organizations operating on its soil.

In the wake of the 2001—2002 crises, a series of bombings rocked major urban centres across India from Bangalore to New Delhi. Indian authorities attributed several of the attacks to the LeT. Pakistani authorities in some cases ignored the charges, and in others denied any connection with the bombings. Doubts about continued links between Pakistan and anti-Indian terrorism, however, were effectively dispelled with the November 2008 assault on Mumbai. A group of 10 terrorists launched a series of carefully planned attacks against the Taj Mahal and Oberoi hotels, the Bhikaji Cama Children's Hospital, the Chattrapati Shivaji Railway Terminus, the Leopold Cafe', and the Chabad House, a Jewish cultural center. Well over one hundred civilians, several security personnel and all but one terrorist were killed in the three-day shooting spree.

Pakistani authorities initially denied any link between the Mumbai attackers and Pakistan. Overwhelming evidence that the terrorists were members of LeT and that their operation had been planned in, launched from, and directed in real time by operatives in Pakistan, however, pointed toward the contrary. No longer able to deny the Pakistan—Mumbai connection, Pakistani officials placed Hafiz Mohammed Saeed, the head of the LeT's charitable front organization, Jamaat-ud-Dawa, under house arrest in Lahore. Before long though, Saeed was free once again after a Pakistani court released the LeTchief in June 2009, citing a paucity of evidence against him. The provincial government of the Punjab subsequently withdrew terror charges against Saeed for a similar want of evidence.

The Sorcerer's Apprentice

Analysts have often cited Pakistan's support for Islamist militancy as strategically shortsighted. Islamabad has adhered to essentially the same strategy in pursuit of the same ends for most of its history, using non-state actors in an effort to alter territorial boundaries in South Asia without triggering a full-scale conventional conflict in the region. Despite its repeated efforts, Pakistan has rarely succeeded in attaining its goals. The 1947 and 1965 Kashmir wars ended in stalemate. The Pakistan-backed insurgency in Kashmir, despite its violence, has not convinced the Indians to leave the territory. To the contrary, the Indians have become more intransigent as the carnage has increased. Meanwhile, Pakistan's provocative behavior has created serious regional tensions that could trigger a major conflict, and diverted resources away from other urgent domestic priorities such as economic development, educational reforms, and infrastructure renewal. Thus, critics argue, Pakistan's asymmetric warfare strategy has largely failed. This criticism, however, is not wholly warranted. Pakistan's asymmetric warfare strategy has in fact achieved notable successes. Its support of mujahideen forces in Afghanistan played a crucial role in the Soviets' defeat. In Kashmir, the Pakistanis have inflicted serious economic, military, and diplomatic costs on India. They have also led New Delhi to adopt draconian antiterrorism policies that have badly tarnished its international image. In neither case was Pakistan forced to engage in direct combat against a stronger adversary. Rather, the use of non-state actors enabled the Pakistanis to damage the Soviets and the Indians while avoiding direct conflict and the concomitant risk of catastrophic defeat. Whatever its shortcomings, Pakistan's strategy has achieved important goals, and should not be dismissed as an abject failure.

Despite its past successes, however, Pakistan's asymmetric warfare strategy now faces the serious problem that those militant organizations, which the Pakistanis created and nurtured to execute their policy, no longer wholly share their aims or serve their interests. The militants' goals have become increasingly maximalist. Many seek not just to liberate Kashmir or to join it to Pakistan but see eventual control of territory within India proper as the true prize in their struggle. And they will not allow the Pakistani state to prevent them from attaining it. Nasr Javed, a LeTofficial, delivering a speech at the Quba Mosque in Islamabad on February 5, 2008, declared: "India is also afraid of Jihad. India fears that if the Mujahideen liberated Kashmir through Jihad, then it will be very difficult to keep rest of the India under control. Jihad will spread from Kashmir to other parts of India. The Muslims will be ruling India again." He went on to say, "The government of Pakistan might have abandoned Jihad but we have not. Our agenda is clear. We will continue to wage Jihad and propagate it till eternity. No government can intimidate us. Nobody can stop it_be it the U.S. or Musharraf."

The jihadi organizations also oppose Pakistani efforts to cooperate with U.S. antiterrorism efforts. In the wake of the 9/11 attacks, the U.S. government realized that Islamist terrorism was not an issue isolated to the Middle East or South Asia. Rather, it was a global problem that directly impacted the United States' own security. U.S. leaders also decided that they needed Pakistan to serve as a leading partner in their new "global war on terror." Thus, Washington dramatically shifted its policy. It would no longer ignore Pakistani support for militancy in South Asia, and it would offer Pakistan substantial military and economic benefits for cooperating in its antiterror efforts. In order to reap these rewards, Pakistan agreed to serve as an ally in the U.S. antiterrorism campaign. As a result, the Pakistanis were forced to limit support for Islamist insurgents in Kashmir, occasionally even outlawing militant groups. This Pakistani cooperation with the United States alienated the militant organizations. These groups, which owed their existence to Islamabad, branded Musharraf a traitor and turned against the Pakistani government.

Meanwhile, the Taliban, whose control of Afghanistan had been strongly supported by the Pakistani government, now seeks not just to retake Afghanistan, but to seize Pakistani territory as well. Factions such as the Tehrik-e-Taliban, the main Taliban group in Pakistan, have asserted control over swaths of territory to resist the central government, enforce a strict interpretation of Sharia law, and unite with the Afghan Taliban against NATO forces in Afghanistan. Pakistan would benefit from Taliban resurgence in Afghanistan: it would mean a friendly government in Kabul, afford Pakistan badly needed strategic depth, allow it more direct access to the energy-rich states of Central Asia, and reduce Indian regional influence. Islamabad, however, does not wish to cede control of its own territory to Taliban elements. These differences between the goals of the Pakistani state and the Islamist groups it helped to create and nurture have severely undermined Pakistani security in a number of ways. First, they have led to outright violence between the militants and Pakistani forces (for example, the Pakistan army has been battling Taliban elements in South Waziristan). Such conflict is costly, both in military terms and in terms of harm to Pakistan's civilian population. Second, differences with the militants have put Pakistani leaders at risk. Musharraf survived multiple assassination attempts after siding with the United States in the war on terror. And militants associated with the Pakistani Taliban succeeded in killing former prime minister Benazir Bhutto as she sought to return to office. Third, jihadi attacks on Indian targets, such as Mumbai, do not merely threaten to undo the Indo—Pak peace process but risk plunging the subcontinent into a large-scale war. In the event of another major terrorist incident in India, Pakistan could be held responsible even if Islamabad was not involved in planning or executing the attack as it evidently was not in the Mumbai case. Even an Indian government that did not wish to respond militarily could find domestic political pressure to do so overwhelming.

Significantly, this is occurring at a time when the Pakistanis can ill afford it. Islamabad would like to deescalate tensions with New Delhi and reduce the likelihood of an Indo—Pakistani confrontation so that it can concentrate on stabilizing its internal security situation in the northwest. Instead, the danger of conflict with India forces Pakistan to divide its attention between the northwest and the East, making its task of internal stabilization significantly more difficult. Thus, the Pakistani state and the jihadis whom it no longer fully controls are, to a significant extent, working at cross purposes.

Who's Your Sorcerer Now?

Following the November 2008 attacks on Mumbai, a single question echoed from New Delhi to Washington: were the Mumbai attacks simply the work of Pakistan-based militants or were they actually orchestrated by the government of Pakistan? Given the militants' increasing autonomy, however, and Pakistan's inability to reassert control over them, this was the wrong question to ask. The relevant question is: who will now play the role of South Asian sorcerer and rein in the jihadis? The natural candidates for the sorcerer's role would be the governments of either Pakistan or India. Recent events, such as the Mumbai attacks, have shown that neither is presently up to the challenge. The government of Pakistan has publicly promised to prevent its soil from being used to launch anti-Indian terrorism, but the Mumbai attacks demonstrate that Islamabad is unable to honour this pledge. India, for its part, cannot defend itself against such attacks. Despite the fact that the Indian authorities had received credible warnings of a seaborne terrorist operation, a mere handful of terrorists were able to keep Indian security personnel at bay for nearly three days, showing that the Indian authorities were caught completely off guard. India does enjoy conventional military superiority over Pakistan. This advantage does not, however, afford the Indians many good options for dealing with the jihadis. The Indians could strike across the Line of Control against terrorist camps in Pakistan-administered Kashmir, which is the most plausible option. But even if such attacks were successful, they would yield only limited benefits because Kashmiri militant camps are transitory and lack high-value human targets or physical infrastructure.

Because strikes on militant camps are not likely to be profitable, the Indians could threaten to launch large-scale attacks deep into Pakistan proper in the event of further terrorism. Although India would eventually prevail in such a conflict, victory would be costly. Nonetheless, such a large-scale confrontation might make continued tolerance for anti-Indian militancy prohibitively expensive for Pakistan, thus finally convincing Pakistan to fully renounce the jihadi option. But even if Indian leaders decided that the possible benefits of such a policy were worth its likely costs, Pakistan's nuclear capacity makes it infeasible. Given the danger of triggering a nuclear response, it would be too risky for the Indians to launch large-scale attacks deep into Pakistan's territory. In the past, India has been willing to contemplate limited conflict with Pakistan, despite Pakistani nuclear weapons (for example, the 1999 Kargil conflict). Pakistan's nuclear capacity, however, has led the Indians to explicitly rule out the possibility of launching a full-scale conventional attack on the Pakistanis. India is unlikely to change its position in the near future. A series of rapid, more limited attacks into Pakistani territory could inflict significant costs on Pakistan without triggering a nuclear exchange. The possibility of such action might stand a better chance of convincing Pakistan to abandon its support for anti-Indian militancy than the threat of all-out conventional war. India is acquiring increasingly sophisticated conventional assets and formulating a "Cold Start" military doctrine that may afford it such a capacity. Given the jihadis' growing autonomy, however, greater Indian coercive capabilities could prove irrelevant. Pakistan may be unable to control the militants' behavior even if it wants to. Thus, Indian military threats could convince Pakistan that it must rein in the jihadis, and still fail to prevent further terrorism. The jihadi networks in Pakistan are so pervasive and their strength so significant that only a firm, unequivocal decision on the part of the country's military and intelligence services to sever all links, albeit not without costs, could bring about their eventual demise. Short of such a drastic volte-face on the part of the Pakistani security and intelligence services, the hydra-headed monster cannot be slayed. In addition, a more coercive Indian approach runs a serious risk of backfiring. Pakistan's asymmetric warfare strategy has been largely motivated by its insecurity vis-a'-vis India. Thus, by augmenting its punitive capabilities, India could render Pakistan even less secure and increase its incentives to promote militancy even further.

Neither India's nor Pakistan's domestic security nor their conventional military capabilities, therefore, are currently able to solve South Asia's sorcerer's apprentice problem. Unfortunately, their nuclear arsenals are largely useless as well. Nuclear weapons facilitated Pakistan's initial adoption of a low-intensity conflict strategy against India during the 1980s and 1990s, preventing large-scale Indian conventional retaliation while militants launched attacks in Indian Kashmir. Nuclear weapons cannot now be used to eradicate the terrorists who flourished under this strategy and today wreak havoc in both India and Pakistan. And nuclear weapons limit India's future military options in dealing with terrorism_ they prevent New Delhi from taking action that, though costly, could potentially convince Pakistan to revisit their tolerance for anti-Indian militancy.

Finally, nuclear weapons pose a danger because of Pakistan's unstable political and security environment. The army, Pakistan's most powerful institution, tightly controls the nuclear arsenal. The army has enormous incentives to ensure the weapons' security, and they do not appear to be under any immediate threat. Still, Pakistan could face situations in which its arsenal might be vulnerable.

For example, if Pakistan attempted to move weapons during a crisis with India, militants could capture them as they are being transported, particularly if the jihadis had access to inside information, such as the weapons' transport schedule. Of course, even if they managed to steal a weapon, the militants would still face a number of difficult tasks, such as determining how to use it. Nonetheless, the security of Pakistan's nuclear arsenal is a genuine concern. Nuclear weapons, therefore, are not only unable to help India or Pakistan play the role of a South Asian sorcerer, they could even potentially pose dangers of their own.

TAMING THE APPRENTICE

What is the solution to South Asia's sorcerer's apprentice problem? The situation will require a radical rethinking of the region's security framework, with both India and Pakistan adopting policies that transcend their traditional comfort zones. Pakistan must truly forswear militancy, ending support for the jihadis and accepting international military and financial assistance in crushing them.

The Pakistanis need to recognize that, despite past successes, the costs of supporting militancy now outweigh its benefits. Recent events, such as the Mumbai attacks, may present Islamabad with a final opportunity to get control of the situation. If the government of Pakistan does not take decisive action against the militants soon, it may lose control of the state or find itself drawn into a catastrophic conflict with India in the wake of another terrorist attack. Pakistan has moved against terrorist organizations in the past. These measures, however, have been mostly cosmetic and of short duration. Following government crackdowns, terrorist groups have traditionally changed their names and quickly resumed their activities. Even in the wake of Mumbai, Pakistan's action against the militants was half-hearted. As noted above, Pakistani officials initially denied any connection between the Mumbai terrorists and Pakistan, arresting Saeed only when faced with overwhelming evidence of LeT's role in the attacks and releasing him soon thereafter. Given this track record, it is doubtful that Pakistan will move seriously against Islamist militancy in the near future. Only time will tell for certain.

The Indians, for their part, must take their own security far more seriously. In 1991, following a major financial crisis, the Indian government acknowledged its socialist development model's failures and adopted a new, free-market strategy for economic growth. Similarly, India must use the Mumbai attacks to wholly revamp its security infrastructure. They appear to have begun to do so.

In the wake of the attacks, the government announced that it was enhancing its maritime security capabilities, creating a U.S. Federal Bureau of Investigationlike National Investigative Agency, increasing intelligence sharing, improving the training and equipment of police and domestic security forces, and strengthening antiterrorism laws. The Indians must follow through on these initiatives.

In addition, they must address their own Muslim community's legitimate concerns, both in Kashmir and in India proper. This will reduce the incentives for continued Kashmiri insurgency, and lower the likelihood that overseas terrorists will find willing accomplices within India. If they fail to implement these measures, India's impressive economic and military gains of recent years will be for naught. Skyrocketing gross domestic product, sophisticated conventional military capabilities, and even nuclear weapons mean little when ordinary citizens are not safe in railway stations, streets, hospitals, and hotels of their own cities. And if India remains vulnerable to Mumbai-like attacks, international corporations will lose interest in the country, refusing to do business in what they view as an excessively dangerous environment. None of the steps outlined above will provide an overnight solution to the problems of Islamist militancy within South Asia. These can, however, help South Asia create its own modern-day sorcerer, dealing with the forces that Pakistan's asymmetric warfare strategy have unleashed over recent decades without triggering a large-scale conflict or nuclear conflagration. If the region fails to meet this challenge, its most pressing security problem will go unaddressed and the implications will reverberate far beyond South Asia.

3

Pakistani Islamic Militant and Madrassa

Madrassas in Pakistan are generally financed by voluntary charity provided by the bazaar businessmen and others who believe that they are earning great merit by contributing to them. Some of them are also given financial assistance by foreign governments—the Saudi government is said to help the Ahl-i-Hadith seminaries and the Iranian government the Shia ones—but there is no proof of this assistance.

And even if it does exist, it goes only to a few *madrassas* whereas the vast majority of them are run on charity (*zakat* = alms, *khairat* = charity, *atiat* = gifts etc). The Zia ul Haq government (1977-1988) tried to gain influence on the *madrassas* by distributing the alms (*Zakat*) funds to them in the 1980s. The only scholarly study of this is by Jamal Malik who points out that most of the *madrassas* who received these funds were Deobandi. However, as the *madrassas* had to be registered, this increased the government's influence over them (Malik 1996: 150-153).

The government of Pakistan gives financial assistance to the *madrassas* even now for modernizing textbooks, including secular subjects in the curricula and introducing computers. In 2001-02 a total of 1,654,000 was given to all *madrassas* which accepted this help. As the number of students is 1,065,277 this comes to Rs. 1.55 per student per year. An additional aid of Rs. 30.45 million is promised for providing computers and changing the syllabi in 2003-04 and this will come to Rs. 28.60 per student per year.

However, as all *madrassas* do not accept financial help from the government the money is not distributed evenly as the above calculations might suggest. According to the Jamia Salfia of Faisalabad, the annual expenditure on the seminary, which has about 700 students, is 40,00,000 rupees. Another *madrassa*, this time a Barelvi one, gave roughly the same figure for the same number of students.

This comes to Rs 5,714 per year (or Rs 476 per month) which is an incredibly small amount of money for education, books, board and lodging. In India, where condition are similar to these in Pakistan, the *madrassa* Mazahiral Uloom in Saharanpur (UP), has 1300 students and 115 employees and its income between 2000 to 2001 was Rs. 9,720, 649 or Rs. 948 per student per year (Mehdi 2005: 93).

The expenditure from the government in 2001-2002 was Rs. 1,654,000 for all the *madrassas* in the country and about 32.60 per cent *madrassas* do not received any financial support at all, the total spending on these institutions is very little (IPS 2002: 33). However, as mentioned above, there are plans to change this in a radical manner. In my survey of December 2002 and January 2003, *madrassa* students and teachers were asked about their income. Many did not reply these questions but those who did suggest that they mostly (76.62%) belong to poor sections of society. The teachers of the *madrassas* also mostly (61.11%) belong to the same socio-economic class as their students. The *madrassas* provide sustenance for all these poor people.

In short the *madrassas* are performing the role of the welfare state in the country. This being so, their influence on rural people and the poorer sections of the urban proletariat will continue to increase as poverty increases.

Poverty and the Roots of Religious Violence

While it can only be speculated that there is a connection between poverty and religious violence, the proposition does have empirical backing. Qasim Zaman tells us, for instance, that in Jhang—the birth place of the militant Sunni organization called the Sipah-i-Sahaba—the proportion of Shias in the affluent urban middle class is higher than other areas of Pakistan. Moreover, the feudal gentry too has many Shia families.

Thus the Sipah-i-Sahaba appeals to the interests of the ordinary people who are oppressed by the rich and the influential. Indeed, Maulana Haqq Nawaz, the fiery preacher who raised much animosity against the Shias, was 'himself a man of humble origin' and 'had a reputation for being much concerned with the welfare of the poor and the helpless, and he was known to regularly spend time at government courts helping out poor illiterate litigant's (Zaman 2002: 125).

Another leader of the Sipah-i-Sahaba, Maulana Isar al-Qasimi (1964-1991), also preached in Jhang. He too denounced the Shia magnates of the area and the peasants, terrorized by the feudal magnates, responded to him as if he were a messiah. Even shopkeepers rejoiced in the aggressive Sunni identity he helped create. When the Shia feudal lords attacked and burnt some defiant Sunni shops this identity was further radicalized (Zaman 2002: 127).

In the same manner the Muslim radicals in the Philippines too attack social and economic privilege. Indeed, Islamist movements from Turkey to Indonesia talk of the poor and the oppressed and sometimes do take up their cause. This has won them votes in Turkey where they have been suppressed by the secular military. It was also a major factor for mobilization in Iran against the Shah who was seen as being rich, wasteful, corrupt and decadent. So, though difficult to demonstrate, Islamic militancy—whether by radicalized *madrassa* students or members of Islamist or Jihadi groups in Pakistan—has an element of class conflict.

It is, at least in some part, a reaction of the have-notes against the haves. This is a dangerous trend for the country because *madrassa* students are taught to be intolerant of religious minorities and are hawkish about Kashmir. As they are also from poor backgrounds they express their sense of being cheated by society in the idiom of religion. This gives them the self-righteousness to fight against the oppressive and unjust system in the name of Islam.

The Worldview of Madrassa Students

The *madrassa* students are the most intolerant of all the other student groups in Pakistan. They are also the most supportive of an aggressive foreign policy. In my survey of 2002-2003 mentioned earlier the *madrassa* students were the only group of students—out of Urdu and English-medium school ones—who supported both overt and covert conflict with India over Kashmir in large numbers. They were also against giving equal rights (equal to Muslims) to non-Muslims and women (equal to men) as citizens. These figures and the survey itself are given in Rahman.

THE CAPACITY DILEMMA

The Pakistani military's political power is a historical legacy of the country's birth. The immediate onset of conflict over Kashmir in 1947-48 with a militarily and politically stronger India made the military central to the state's survival and placed it above civilian scrutiny. Today, after four wars with India, the military filters every internal and external development through the lens of Pakistan's rivalry with India. Civilian governments, such as the current one, headed by President Asif Ali Zardari's Pakistan Peoples Party (PPP), and those headed by Nawaz Sharif's Pakistan Muslim League (PML-N), have typically operated in the military's lurking shadow.

The military has frequently co-opted Islamists to advance its domestic and regional agendas. In the late 1970s and into the 1980s, the generals, especially the U.S.-funded military dictator General Muhammad Zia-ul-Haq, used Islamism to gain political legitimacy. Zia suppressed secular political rivals, such as the PPP, by jailing and torturing opposition leaders, banning political parties, and enacting harsh Islamic laws to appease allies in Islamist parties, such as the Jamaat-e-Islami. Zia also armed Sunni sectarian groups in order to balance the country's Shiite minority, which had been emboldened by the recent Iranian Revolution. State patronage of violent extremism deepened sectarian rifts, militarized the society, and empowered radical Islamists, all of which in turn eroded the state's own writ and authority.

Flush with U.S. cash, the generals also fomented militancy in Kashmir to keep India bleeding and sponsored fundamentalism in Afghanistan to give Pakistan strategic depth against its archrival. Yet faced with U.S. President George W. Bush's famous ultimatum after 9/11 to either cut the military's ties to Afghan militants or prepare for war, Pakistani President Musharraf ostensibly jettisoned the generals' black-turbaned allies.

He granted the United States access to Pakistani air bases, expanded Pakistan's intelligence cooperation, provided logistical support for the U.S. invasion of Afghanistan, and helped the United States with its primary objective — killing or capturing members of al Qaeda. The United States was content with this level of cooperation and did not press Pakistan to help stabilize Afghanistan or target the Afghan Taliban, who had fled to Pakistan in the wake of the U.S. invasion.

Yet by 2004, the Taliban threatened to undermine the Afghan regime from their stronghold in Pakistan, and the Bush administration demanded that Pakistan address the problem, "the sooner, the better" in the words of Zalmay Khalilzad, then U.S. ambassador to Kabul. Since then, the Pakistani military has targeted militant groups in several parts of FATA and in the Malakand region of Khyber Pakhtunkhwa (formerly the North-West Frontier Province).

But the military has a pick-and-choose approach to counterterrorism, even though terrorism poses a grave threat to Pakistan's internal security and stability. It has targeted members of the Pakistani Taliban in South Waziristan and other administrative agencies in FATA, for example, but has persistently refused to take action in North Waziristan, which is the headquarters of the Haqqani network, an al Qaeda-affiliated Afghan militant group that leads the cross-border insurgency in eastern Afghanistan. It also continues to allow top members of the former Afghan Taliban regime to operate from Pakistan's major cities, especially Quetta and Karachi. Although Lashkar-e-Taiba, a militant group that carries out attacks in India and Indian Kashmir, is formally banned in Pakistan, it continues to operate through proxies and aliases, recruiting operatives, organizing rallies, collecting funds for its "charitable" activities, and publishing proselytizing jihadist materials in plain sight of Pakistani intelligence authorities.

Although ending the insurgency in Afghanistan will require more than just eliminating militant sanctuaries in Pakistan, the Pakistani military's reluctance to target Afghan militants in North Waziristan has been a particularly sore point in its relationship with the United States. U.S. officials believe that the lawlessness of North Waziristan hampers the U.S. military effort in Afghanistan, since insurgents can easily escape to safety on the Pakistani side of the border. For its part, the Pakistani military denies sheltering the Afghan Taliban anywhere in the country and claims that it cannot expand its operations into North Waziristan because it is stretched thin by its existing deployments and is short of critical military hardware, such as attack and transport helicopters.

Several U.S. and Pakistani observers agree with this assessment. Writing on March 23, 2010, in *The New York Times*, the Brookings fellow Michael O'Hanlon argued that Pakistan "simply does not have the military capacity to make major moves against the Afghan fundamentalists." Former U.S. Secretary of State Colin Powell reportedly believes that Pakistan needs more armaments to successfully fight insurgents on its border with Afghanistan. And Maleeha Lodhi, former editor of *The News International* and former Pakistani ambassador to the United States, similarly contends that pushing the military to fight on multiple fronts is likely to strain its capacity and undermine its existing missions.

By treating the Pakistani military as a state above the state, the United States only reinforces the military's exaggerated sense of indispensability.

Yet even if capacity is a genuine issue, it is not the reason that counterrorism in Pakistan has failed. It is a pretext for inaction, rhetorically implying that the military has undergone a strategic paradigm shift, seeing militancy as a threat to national security rather than as a useful tool of foreign policy. Yet there are reasons to be skeptical. First, the Pakistani military has shown that it does indeed have the tools it needs to fight terrorism in several tribal areas simultaneously when it wants to. Besides, it already receives enough U.S. security assistance — roughly $300 million since 2002 in foreign military financing and around $1.1 billion since 2008 for increasing its counterinsurgency capabilities, to be followed by $1.2 billion more next year — to acquire the capacity it claims to so desperately need. In contrast, in 2010, U.S. aid for Pakistan's poorly paid, undertrained, and underresourced police forces, which are crucial to fighting insurgencies, totaled a paltry $66 million.

Second, it is unlikely that the Pakistani military has truly changed its calculation of the strategic value of militant groups. Before it moved into South Waziristan in October of 2009, the military cited similar shortages in resources yet was able to conduct a full and relatively successful mission there, clearing the area, capturing or killing many militants, and dismantling their bases and training camps. Indeed, the military seems to confront only those militants who threaten and attack the army itself. When the Pakistani government requested that the military go into South Waziristan, for example, it dragged its feet for months and was spurred into action only after militants carried out a deadly attack on its heavily guarded headquarters in the northern city of Rawalpindi. At the same time, it holds those groups that do not threaten it, including the Haqqani network, as reserve assets for the endgame in Afghanistan, when U.S. troops start pulling out this July and eventually leave by 2014. In fact, Pakistan's intelligence service has reportedly permitted Haqqani fighters to flee U.S. drone attacks in North Waziristan and relocate to bases in the nearby Kurram region.

Troublingly, the military's capacity alibi shifts the blame for the strength of Pakistan's violent extremists from the military — which has nurtured and legitimized the influence of radical Islamists — to civilian leaders and foreign patrons, who have supposedly neglected to provide the army with enough resources. Yet the extremists' growth and power in Pakistani society are a direct result of the military's pursuit of strategic depth against India. In fact, the military's permissive attitude toward radical Islamists has allowed them to infiltrate the lower echelons of Pakistan's security services. This worrying development was vividly demonstrated by the brutal murder of Salman Taseer, the governor of Punjab, Pakistan's largest province, by his own police guard on

January 4 for opposing the blasphemy laws. Brazen terrorist attacks have battered the military itself, and suicide bombings in major Pakistani cities, including a spate of them in 2009 that claimed over 3,000 lives, have undermined citizens' confidence in the government's ability to provide them with security. Surprisingly, such attacks have not seemed to erode confidence in the military, especially after it provided quicker and more effective relief than the government after last year's devastating floods — although trust in the military should not be confused with public support for military rule.

CAN MIGHT MAKE RIGHT?

With all the resources in the world, the Pakistani military alone would be insufficient to conquer terrorism. So far, wherever it has tried to deal with militants, it has alternated between attempting to subdue them with brute force and, when that does not work, cutting its losses by appeasing them with peace deals. Both approaches have further fuelled militancy.

For instance, the military's use of artillery and aerial strikes to "soften targets" (sometimes without sufficient warning to civilian populations) and its collective punishment of tribes (under the Frontier Crimes Regulation, the colonial-era law under which FATA is still governed) have angered and alienated locals, reportedly facilitating militant recruitment. In exchange for a cease-fire, the peace agreements have ceded territory to the militants and given them the space to openly recruit, train, and arm themselves.

The terms of the military's 2005 deal with Baitullah Mehsud, who was the leader of the Pakistani Taliban until his death in 2009, for example, stipulated that the military would release captured militants and vacate Mehsud's territory in return for a pledge that he would not harbor foreign fighters or attack Pakistani security forces. The military claims to have learned its lesson and has adopted a new strategy of counterinsurgency based on winning hearts and minds. But even in its recent campaigns, such as the 2009 offensives in the Swat Valley and South Waziristan, which were relatively more successful in terms of clearing militants and taking back territory, the military favored a heavy use of force and displaced millions of citizens. Moreover, it failed to capture or kill any significant number of senior Taliban leaders.

Militant extremism can be fought effectively only through serious governance reforms that ensure the rule of law and accountability. This will require a strong democracy, a viable economy, and well-balanced civil-military relations. In FATA, it will require abolishing the Frontier Crimes Regulation and integrating the region into the adjoining Khyber Pakhtunkhwa Province to end the Pakistani federal government's direct and oppressive rule, which the Pakistani Taliban have exploited to expand their influence, displace the already weakened tribal authority in the region, and establish parallel courts and policing systems in several FATA agencies, including North and South Waziristan. All of this seems daunting, but there is really no other long-term alternative. And despite its many failings and weaknesses, there are reasons to be optimistic about democracy in Pakistan.

If the "third wave" of democratization in the 1970s and 1980s had any lesson, it is that democracy does not necessarily require natural-born democrats or a mythically selfless political leadership. In fact, a strong democratic system can mitigate the baser instincts of politicians. If anything, the experience of countries such as Chile, the Philippines, South Korea, and Thailand in the last few decades shows that the strength and quality of democracy may be linked to the stability of the party system. This is good news for Pakistan. It is true that Pakistan's civilian politics is dominated by a few families, namely the Bhuttos, who control the PPP, and the Sharifs, who control the PML-N. In a perverse way, however, the hold of the Bhuttos and the Sharifs on their parties may be one of the main reasons that these parties have survived the military's divide-and-rule repression and may consolidate democracy in the future.

Already, the demands of governing seem to be putting some positive pressure on Pakistan's politicians. The most recent civilian government is only three years old, yet the much-derided political elite seems to have developed a consensus that democracy is the only game in town and has enacted constitutional reforms to curb outsized presidential powers — an artifact of previous military regimes — especially the power to dismiss democratically elected parliaments and prime ministers, which past military or military-backed presidents used to neuter parliament. The government has also created new parliamentary committees to appoint Supreme Court and provincial High Court judges and the country's top election officials, delegated some administrative and financial authority to the provinces, and raised the share of the federal revenue pool that the provinces receive.

The best way to further boost Pakistan's democracy will be to habituate the military to democratic norms and raise the costs of undermining democratic governance. The current parliament has already removed some constitutional loopholes that military leaders used in the past to avoid prosecution for coups. It has also proscribed the judiciary's frequent practice of legalizing military rule. But more direct attempts at exerting civilian control have backfired, including the government's short-lived July 2008 decision to bring Pakistan's secretive Inter-Services Intelligence (ISI) — which technically answers to the prime minister but in practice operates as the military's intelligence wing — under the control of the Interior Ministry. The move was reversed during a midnight phone call between an angry Army Chief Kayani and the prime minister. And now, the ongoing ethnic violence in the southern port city of Karachi and the politically charged turf battles between the PPP government and the Supreme Court over the judiciary's encroachments on executive authority — such as its sacking of top federal officials, its creation of judicial cells to monitor specific corruption cases, and its fixing of basic commodity prices — could invite renewed military intervention.

But such setbacks are not uncommon in transitional democracies and should not prevent civilian politicians from continuing to take measured steps to establish civilian supremacy. For instance, instead of staying out of defense policy completely, the civilian government should call regular meetings of the cabinet's Defense Committee to discuss and make key national security decisions. Civilians should also try to exert more control over the

Ministry of Defense, subject military expenditures to vigorous parliamentary debate, create a bipartisan parliamentary subcommittee for intelligence oversight, enact legislation to bring the ISI under civilian control, and appoint a special cabinet committee to approve top military promotions and appointments.

OUT-OF-BALANCE BUDGETS

The other critical obstacle to democratization and stability in Pakistan is the country's weak economic performance. The civilian government inherited a cash-strapped, highly indebted economy from the Musharraf regime and had to ask the International Monetary Fund for a $7.6 billion bailout in 2008 to avoid default. Last summer's heavy floods, which displaced some 20 million people and caused considerable damage to Pakistan's civilian infrastructure, dealt a devastating blow to the prospects of economic resurgence. Perceptions of widespread government corruption and civilian authorities' apparent unwillingness to cut spending have not helped. Moreover, Pakistan has one of the lowest tax-to-GDP ratios in the world — only two percent of the population pays any taxes at all — yet the government has not been able to agree on critical tax reforms.

Pakistan must also reckon with the need to alleviate the economic hardships faced by its poor. Skyrocketing inflation of basic commodity prices, chronic power cuts, persistently high levels of unemployment, and general lawlessness are fueling public resentment of the current government. Some observers fear that the downward economic spiral could play into the hands of Islamists, but there is no automatic link between economic woes and the influence of Islamists in public life. In Pakistan, Islamist influence has been closely tied to state patronage, not popular support. Islamist parties continue to perform poorly at the polls, never garnering more than 10-12 percent of the vote, whereas the two main moderate parties — the PPP and the PML-N — typically claim about 60 percent of the vote and 70 percent of the seats in the national parliament.

Still, Pakistan's civilian government must stabilize the economy to bolster public confidence in democratic institutions. It must invest in Pakistan's long-term economic development and create opportunities for the country's rapidly growing population. It may even need a long-term, multibillion-dollar Marshall Plan to help build civilian institutional capacity, rebuild areas hit by last year's floods, invest in public-sector and infrastructure projects, and plug the energy shortages that have all but crippled the manufacturing sector, especially its top-exporting textile industry. Of course, such a plan should come with proper controls to fight corruption and waste.

It is worth noting that Pakistan's economic difficulties are the result not just of bad luck and poor management, and therefore they cannot be fixed with development aid alone. They are rooted in fundamental structural problems as well: military expenditures dwarf spending on development. Pakistan has one of the world's largest out-of-school populations, yet it spends seven times as much on the military every year as on education, an investment with a higher national security payoff in the long run. Thus, the country must find a way to rationalize its military expenditures.

Some progress toward a resolution of the Kashmir conflict could induce Pakistan to scale back its military behemoth. It could also potentially reduce the attractiveness of using militancy as an instrument of foreign policy. As Steve Coll chronicled in *The New Yorker* in 2009, Musharraf and Indian Prime Minister Manmohan Singh were quite close to reaching a breakthrough accord on Kashmir in 2008, but it was aborted by the rapid erosion of Musharraf's authority in the face of domestic opposition to his dictatorial rule. The point is that only a strong, stable, and legitimate elected government will be able to mobilize the public opinion necessary to clinch a lasting peace with India. Both the PPP and the PML-N favour cooperation over confrontation in the region, and each has tried to mend fences with India, through high-level diplomacy as well as backdoor talks, only to be upbraided by the generals for compromising on national security. These parties need more room to pursue peace with India while holding the military at bay. This is something the United States can help provide, by firmly supporting democratic institutions in Pakistan even as it works with the military to fight al Qaeda.

No Means No

The Obama administration came into office in 2009 with a solid commitment to supporting Pakistan's then year-old civilian democratic government as a hedge against militancy and terrorism. The Kerry-Lugar-Berman bill, which was passed into law as the Enhanced Partnership With Pakistan Act of 2009, authorized the U.S. Congress to triple civilian development assistance to Pakistan, raising it to $7.5 billion between 2010 and 2014. The aid package was designed to signal a new era in the United States' relationship with Pakistan, shifting the focus of U.S. aid from the military to civilian democratic governance and social development. Continued military aid was also tied to a yearly certification by the U.S. secretary of state that the Pakistani military has refrained from interfering in politics and is subject to civilian control over budgetary allocations, officer promotions, and strategic planning.

Not surprisingly, the Pakistani military balked at this affront even as the civilian government welcomed the aid. Joining with opposition parties, the military publicly decried the bill as a threat to Pakistani national security and mobilized right-wing sections of the media against U.S. meddling. In response, the bill's sponsors buckled and effectively defanged the conditionality measures. Even though the text of the law is intact, the United States meekly assured the Pakistani military that the intent of the conditions was misinterpreted and that the United States would keep its nose out of the generals' business. Indeed, most contact between the two countries still occurs behind closed doors between the two militaries or between the CIA and the ISI. The CIA's use of unmanned drones against militants in FATA, which are reportedly flown out of Pakistani bases, exemplifies this lack of transparency. The secrecy of the program allows both the United States and Pakistan to escape responsibility for civilian casualties.

The climb-down on the Enhanced Partnership Act indicated that even though the U.S. Congress recognizes the folly of building exclusive alliances with the Pakistani military, it still prefers engaging with Pakistan's military over its civilian leaders. This is partly pragmatism: the military is still the most powerful institution in Pakistan. But by continuing to treat the Pakistani military as a state above the state, the United States only reinforces the military's exaggerated sense of indispensability and further weakens civilian rule.

If the United States had stood its ground, the Pakistani military would have eventually backed down. It is dependent on the United States for military aid and high-tech armaments, including upgrading its aging fleet of F-16 fighters. And although the military has leverage over Washington since it controls U.S. supply routes into landlocked Afghanistan, its bargaining position has weakened over time.

Although Washington generally remains reluctant to pressure the Pakistani military, appropriately using sticks has not necessarily meant losing the generals' cooperation in fighting terrorism. For example, the U.S. Congress warned that it would cut off U.S. aid in response to Pakistan's detention of a CIA contractor, Raymond Davis, who was arrested in January for fatally shooting two Pakistanis in the eastern city of Lahore. In the end, Davis was released from jail in March — the families of the victims agreed to pardon him after receiving compensation. His release would not have been possible without military complicity.

Such political and diplomatic pressure should be used to censure the military for political incursions. In this spirit, the United States should signal to the military that cracking down on terrorism is not a license for it to destabilize or overrun the government. The U.S. military should remind its Pakistani counterpart that interference in politics will not be tolerated and could have serious repercussions, including a downgrading of military ties, the suspension of nondevelopment aid, and broader diplomatic isolation.

Although the United States is confronted with an economic recession of its own, more civilian aid for (and trade with) Pakistan would cost relatively little compared to the money that the United States spends fighting Afghan and Pakistani extremists. And the potential dividends could be enormous: U.S. civilian aid could help secure civilian rule in Pakistan for the long haul and diminish anti-Americanism as well. To reduce the danger of moral hazard, this aid should be tightly linked to Pakistan's economic performance, progress in combating corruption, and transparency and responsiveness in government.

One relatively easy way for the United States to boost economic productivity in Pakistan would be to grant Pakistan emergency duty-free access to the U.S. market for textiles. This concession would face opposition from politically powerful U.S. textile interests, but the Obama administration should pursue this legislation on at least a temporary basis because it could crucially improve the economic stability of a vital ally by increasing the revenue it gets from this important industry.

Although a settlement of the Kashmir conflict is unlikely in the short term, Washington should continue to push both sides to achieve that goal. Of course, there are no guarantees that peace would be sufficient to reduce Pakistan's military expenditures or restrict the military to its proper constitutional sphere. But it is worth the effort because the international community has a stake in ending the nuclearized Indian-Pakistani rivalry, which not only endangers global security but also has spilled into Afghanistan.

With over a hundred nuclear weapons, a war-prone rivalry with India, and the presence of some of the world's most dangerous terrorists on its soil, Pakistan is too important to be left to the devices of its generals. For too long, the United States has sacrificed democracy for order. The results have been less than ideal, especially for the people of Pakistan. Pakistan urgently needs support from the international community to help stabilize its civilian democratic institutions and bolster its economy. Only such support will ensure its stability and reliability as a U.S. partner in the region.

MILITARY INTERVENTIONS TO MILITARY WITHDRAWALS

Military intervention in politics and military disengagement from politics are two sides of the same theoretical problem. These dependent variables are similarly rooted in the basic civil-military problématique: societies create militaries for protection but in doing so endow their militaries with the power to threaten their societies. The crux of the issue revolves around how civilian governments can exercise control over militaries that have the strength to usurp their authority, or conversely, how civilians can regain control after being kicked to the curb by their militaries. The majority of civil-military scholarship has focused on developing and refining one side of this problem: the causes of military intervention. The effort to locate the source of military interventions has produced a large and contentious literature which first emerged from the debate over the relationship between military professionalism and civilian control.

The *coup d'état* is the apex of military intervention and therefore its study became an early central tenet in civil-military relations theory. Many scholars including Huntington (1957, 1968), Finer (1962), Nordlinger (1977), Thompson (1975), Welch (1976), and Luttwak (1979)—to name only a few—have addressed the causes, typologies, and frequency of military coups. They have identified numerous and complex webs of casual factors behind military coups, which are commonly separated into opportunities and motives. Coup opportunities arise from a weakening of the civilian regime, whether it has lost legitimacy through acts of corruption, electoral fraud, or other forms of political mischiefs, or perhaps a general ineptitude at governing.

Opportunities can also be fashioned from broader conditions in the country such as a floundering political process, internal unrest, external security threats, or economic crises. In terms of motivations, coups are nearly always justified by their perpetrators to have been committed on behalf of the national interest.

Such claims, however, are commonly dismissed as camouflage to hide the military's pursuit of narrower sets of interests. Some scholars contend that the military may be motivated to stage a coup to defend or advance a particular socioeconomic class or sectional group in society. Another possible motivation is the personal interests of the military leadership who seek greater political power, glory, or riches for themselves after seizing power. Many authors have recognized one of the strongest motivations for coups is to preserve the military's corporate self-interest, which includes the preservation of the military's autonomy, hierarchical discipline, internal unity, organizational prestige, access to resources, privileges, and other aspects. Despite the abundance of coup studies, deciphering the precise causes behind a coup is extremely difficult. Apart from the sheer array of possible causal factors, none of these explanations are mutually exclusive. Nevertheless, the traditional theoretical focus on coups has fallen by the wayside in contemporary civil-military relations due to the decline of coups in many parts of the world after the 1980s as many countries stabilized along either democratic-paths, as did much of Latin America, or along military-authoritarian paths, as did much of the Middle East.

Compared to the abundant attention theorists have given to studying interventions, the other side of the coin dealing with military withdrawals is astonishingly underdeveloped. As David Pion-Berlin observes, "Although for almost every military intervention one can find a military withdrawal, the former has been the subject of literally hundreds of major studies while the later has not." Rather than looking at what causes a military to rush from the barracks and storm the palace, this perspective is concerned with what causes a ruling military to hand the palace back to the civilians and return to the barracks. Withdrawals, unlike coups, almost never transpire by sheer force of arms. Militaries have the ability to intervene in politics and seize power because they possess a monopoly on force in their society. Civilians do not have reciprocity to forcibly remove the military from power. In this regard, their relationship is decisively one-sided. Despite the military's ability to seize and hold onto power, scholars have noted that military regimes are unusually short-lived forms of authoritarian government. Ruling militaries nearly always withdraw and do so with a degree of acquiescence—but usually not with much enthusiasm. Lastly, it is important to draw a distinction between what is meant in this paper by military withdrawal, disengagement, and "returns to the barracks." These terms relate to the military's abdication from *overt* rule—the self-dismantlement of the military regime—it does not necessitate the military's full retreat from politics nor an acceptance of civilian supremacy.

There are few studies directly concerned with military withdrawal. Most of the literature has developed as secondary findings within the traditional focus on interventions and remains scattered and under-theorized. Perhaps the earliest and most important work to touch on military disengagement is S.E. Finer's *The Man on Horseback*. In the course of his inquiry, Finer observed that militaries sometimes terminate their rule, restore civilians to power, and subsequently "return to the barracks." According to Finer, a return to barracks occurs due to the combination of three conditions: "The disintegration of the original conspiratorial group, the growing divergence of interests between the junta of rulers and those military who remain as active heads of the fighting services, and the political difficulties of the regime."

Alfred Stepan offers a useful framework for understanding the complex division of responsibilities and interests that arise in military regimes. He unpacks "military regimes" into several parts. The first component is the military-as-government, which refers to the top military leaders who directly wield the political power of the state which typically comprises the ruling general or junta and a small clique of key officers and civilians. The second component is the military-as-institution, which denotes the majority of the officer corps who for the most part remain responsible for "normal" military duties. Stepan contends that if the military-as-government precipitates a crisis or otherwise endangers the corporate interests of the military-as-institution; the latter might be willing to overthrow the former to redress the problem. Even then, the military must feel it is in its best interest to transition power to civilians rather than just reconstitute another military-as-government.

Eric Nordlinger's study on praetorianism focuses on interventions and the political sociology of the officer corps. He briefly touches on the motivations behind disengagement, suggesting that sometimes militaries prefer the "relative political purity" of the barracks to the unpleasant governing process. Noting the military regimes are characteristically short-lived, he identifies three paths by which military regimes are supplanted by civilian governments: civilian pressure which forces the military from power (extremely rare), military countercoups which return power back to civilians (somewhat rare), and voluntary disengagements (the most common). Nordlinger identifies the military's corporate interests as among the most important reasons behind a voluntary withdrawal.

In terms of literature primarily concerned with military withdrawals, Christopher Clapham and George Philip diagnose factionalism as a major problem for military regimes. In the long-term, political intervention is corrosive to military unity. They posit that all military regimes face a common political problem in preserving their ruling interests with their limited capacity for political organization and management. Claude Welch, exploring the conditions for successful "long-term" military disengagement from politics, contends that withdrawals are based on the military's corporate interests and broader dynamics such as domestic conflict and the economy. Many of the works on military withdrawal dovetail nicely with the comparative politics literature on transitions from authoritarianism. Most of these approach the matter of military withdrawal from the normative standpoint of how civilians can best muzzle a politicized military and return it to the barracks. Yet as Welch points out, "No single, coherent school of thought exists regarding the causes and consequences of returns to the barracks and the pathways of liberalization and democratization." Some scholars have poked and prodded at the issue of diverging interests in military regimes within the context of disengagement but there have been few direct inquiries and even fewer substantive case studies into its potential theoretical applications for civil-military relations.

4

Pakistan's Military, Religion, Politics and Terrorism

During the 1950s, if one were to attempt to predict which of the new Muslim states that emerged during the 20th century would pose a major threat to global peace and security, Pakistan would be very much at the bottom of the list. Pakistan was then widely regarded as a beacon of moderation: a highly tolerant secular state and a strong ally of the West in its conflict with the Soviet Union. Since the attacks on the United States on 11 September 2001, however, Pakistan has come to be regarded as the world's epicentre of terrorist activity committed in the name of Islam. Currently, the Pakistan state is waging a bitter war with terrorist groups many of whom are also actively supporting the Taliban in fighting the US and its allies in neighbouring Afghanistan. Pakistani nationals have been involved in terrorist attacks on India, Britain and the United States. In Pakistan itself, sectarian violence between extremists from the majority Sunnis perpetrated against the minority Shia sect has involved assassinations, attacks on religious processions and places of worship, and, most deadly of all, suicide bombings.

The major precondition for the emergence of terrorism during the 1980s has been the ongoing structural weaknesses of Pakistan. Ever since its formation in 1947, Pakistan has been ruled either by weak ineffectual civilian governments or military dictators both of whom have failed to address Pakistan's problems particularly relating to good governance and the maintenance of law and order. Weak governments, both civilian and military, have had a poor record in combating terrorism. Indeed, some politicians and elements within the armed forces have supported extremists for political advantage.

In addition, three specific major political developments provide an explanation for the terrorist phenomenon. The first is the long-standing bitter dispute between India and Pakistan over control of the Kashmir Valley that had been partitioned between India and Pakistan in 1947. Ever since, Pakistan has felt threatened by its much more powerful neighbor India and the countries have waged two major and one localized war over Kashmir. Pakistan governments – both civilian and military – have trained, financed and used terrorist groups to fight a proxy war in Indian–ruled Kashmir. This policy backfired after Pakistan was coerced by the United States into supporting the disastrous highly unpopular invasion of Afghanistan in October 2001 which is regarded throughout the Islamic world as an attack on Islam itself. As a consequence, many of the jihadi groups turned on the Pakistani government and security forces which previously had nurtured them.

The second major development was the military dictatorship of General Zia ul-Haq who ruthlessly governed Pakistan from 1977 to 1988. In part because of his religious zealotry but also to build his legitimacy and power, Zia attempted to Islamize Pakistan according to his own narrow interpretation of Sunni Islam. Under Zia the tolerance so long characteristic of Pakistani Islam began to break down. The most damaging consequence of Zia's Islamization policy was the outbreak of on-going sectarian violence between the majority Sunnis and the minority Shias, who had been threatened by Zia's attempts to impose Sunni law on the country. These sectarian terrorist organisations were the forerunners of many other terrorist groups that have plagued Pakistani society since the 1980s.

The final, and, in many ways, the most critical factor was the impact of the Soviet invasion of Afghanistan in 1979. The spontaneous uprising of the Afghans assumed the form of a holy war or jihad which was strongly supported by Pakistan. The

Pakistan military, particularly its intelligence service, the Inter-Services Intelligence (ISI), channeled lavish funds and weapons, supplied largely by the United States and Saudi Arabia, to the most extremist groups of the mujahedin or holy warriors who fought the Soviets. After the Soviets had left Afghanistan in 1989, the numerous well trained and well armed jihadists were recruited, with the tacit support of Pakistani governments, by the many terrorist groups active in Pakistan and in Indian-ruled Kashmir. In addition, Saudi Arabia used the Afghanistan jihad to promote its narrow Wahhabi ideology within Afghanistan and Pakistan itself. Wahhabism is implacably hostile both to Shias and to Sufism, the mystical more tolerant form of Islam that is widely practised in Pakistan. Many of the Sunni extremists engaged in anti-Shia and anti-Sufi acts of terrorism have drawn upon Wahhabi doctrines to justify violence whose roots lie in political, economic and social rivalries.

The historical analysis demonstrates clearly that Islam as a belief system played little or no role in the rise of terrorism in Pakistan. Although dubious interpretations of Islamic teachings, which have been rejected by mainstream Islamic scholars, have been used to justify terrorist actions, the history of terrorism in Pakistan refutes the belief held by many Western political leaders, the media and a great many Western academics that 'Islamic extremism' is one of the primary drivers of contemporary terrorism and that Islam is a prime security threat facing Western countries. Unfortunately, the mainstream Western media continues to report and explain acts of terrorism largely in terms of their roots in religious extremism without reference to the political and historical contexts. Researchers also need to challenge the assumption held by many Western politicians and the media that Muslims engaged in terrorist actions are irrational religious fanatics whose repression justifies the abuse of human rights through torture, extrajudicial killings and other violent forms of counter-terrorism. Finally, contrary to the popular view held in non-Muslim countries, the major victims of terrorism in Pakistan committed in the name of Islam have been other Muslims – not outsiders. The major struggle today is not between Islam and the West but rather within Islam itself between the majority of Muslims who desire to live at peace with their neighbors and the small but powerful minority who want to impose their extremist forms of Islam on their fellow Muslims and non-Muslims alike. More in-depth studies of Pakistan and other Islamic states are needed in order to understand the complex social, economic and political problems that have nurtured violence that has been committed in the name, if not the essential spirit, of Islam.

THE RISE OF RELIGIOUS FUNDAMENTALISM IN PAKISTAN

Religious fundamentalism has become a powerful and dangerous force in Pakistan, due mainly to the opportunism of successive political leadership that has pandered to it. Militant sectarian religious groups and parties, led by half-educated and bigoted mullahs, many of them armed to the teeth, are holding our civil society and the state to ransom. They threaten the very fabric of Pakistan society.

Threats of disruption from religious parties have escalated in recent decades. They have steadily grown in strength since the time of General Zia. They now claim that they are the true custodians of Pakistan and that it was they, the mullahs, who had fought successfully for Pakistan, to establish a theocratic state for Muslims. Facts contradict such claims. With the exception of Ghulam Ahmad Parvez's pro-Pakistan *Tulu-i-Islam,* group, all religious groups and parties, including the *Jamiat-i-Ulama-i-Hind,* the *Majli-i-Ahrar* and the *Jamaat-i-Islami,* had all bitterly opposed the Pakistan Movement and abused its leadership which was secular.

The Muslim League, the Party that led the Pakistan movement, was a party of modern educated Muslim professionals and government job seekers (whom, for the sake of brevity, we may call the 'salariat'). It had little to do with the outlook of bigoted mullahs. It was free of any millenarian ideological pretences about creating an Islamic state. *It was a movement of Muslims rather than a movement of Islam*. Behind it was a new class of English educated Muslim professionals and government job seekers that came into being in the 19 century. It got organised politically by the turn of the century, seeking a better deal for themselves vis-à-vis Hindus who were advancing relatively more rapidly in these fields.

When the Muslim League was founded in 1906 at a meeting convened by Nawab Salimullah at Dhaka, the new party was immediately hi-jacked by the Aligarh group led by Nawab Viqar ul-Mulk. Aligarh was at the vanguard of the new Northern Indian Muslim *salariat* class, the sons of the Muslim *Ashraf*, who were deeply conscious of the loss of their privileges with the advent of British rule and the relatively more rapid rise of Hindu educated classes. The main base of the Muslim salariat was in UP and Bihar for, at that time, its was relatively weaker in the Muslim majority provinces.

The Muslim League was focused entirely on its secular demands of western educated Muslim professionals and the salariat. Attempts to place the issue of Islamic ideology on the agenda of the Muslim League were both rare and invariably unsuccessful. Arguably, the earliest of such attempts was one by Shibli Numani to Islamise the Aligarh syllabus. Shibli was explicitly committed to theocratic values and wanted to shift the emphasis of the Aligarh syllabus away from English and modern sciences, towards Islamic learning and the Arabic language.

The response of the Muslim salariat class to that attempt is exemplified by the remarks of Sir Raza Ali, who was a close collaborator of Sir Syed's immediate successors, Muhsin ul-Mulk and Viqar ul-Mulk. With them, Raza Ali was at the centre of the Aligarh establishment.

In an article in the daily Statesman opposing Shibli's move, he remarked that the idea of reviving Arabic knowledge was, of course, beguiling for Muslims. But he warned that they should not ignore the demands of our times, for the most urgent need of Indian Muslims was to be offered education that would be beneficial in the affairs of this world; education that would help their coming generations to earn their livelihood. Sir Raza Ali spelt out the principal concern of the educated Muslim middle class at the time. Their concern was not about a hypothetical return to original Islam and the creation of an 'Islamic State', ruled over by mullahs, that Shibli had dreamt about. Shibli had to leave Aligarh, for it was not the place where his theocratic ideas could flourish.

Among the rare attempts to bring the issue of 'Islamic Ideology' on to the agenda of the Muslim League was one that was planned for the Delhi Session of the AIML in April 1943. One Abdul Hameed Kazi (backed by 'Maulana' Abdul Sattar Niazi) canvassed support for a resolution, which he intended to table. That would commit the Muslim League to an Islamic ideology and the creation of an Islamic state. But pressure from everyone around him forced Kazi to abandon the idea. The resolution was not even moved. The Pakistan movement remained firmly committed to its secular concerns. In his keynote speech before the inaugural meeting of Pakistan's new Constituent Assembly, on 11th August 1947, Mr. Jinnah spelt out the *Pakistan Ideology,* namely the secular and tolerant vision of the new state. That speech was not a sudden aberration, as some Islamic ideologists, and General Zia's hacks, were later to allege. It was consistent with what Mr. Jinnah had been saying for decades. The Muslim League had always been committed to a secular society.

Following Mr. Jinnah, his political successor, Liaquat Ali Khan, too reiterated the Muslim League's secular values. When Liaquat moved the Objectives Resolution in the Constituent Assembly in March 1949 he declared that 'As I have just said, the people are the real recipients of power. This naturally eliminates any danger of the establishment of a theocracy.' Despite that clear statement by the mover of the Objectives Resolution, later religious ideologues, notably General Zia and his hacks, have claimed that the Objectives Resolution was a charter for the imposition of the 'Sharia' (as they would interpret it) although the word Sharia does not occur anywhere in that Resolution. Their argument is based on some conventional generalities in the Resolution, which said that 'Muslims shall be enabled to order their lives, in the individual and collective spheres, in accord with the teachings and requirements of Islam as set out in the Holy Quran and the *Sunna'*. That, did not amount to a charter for the creation of a theocratic, 'Islamic' State.

Liaquat's position on the Muslim League's traditional secularism was, however, soon to be reversed. Not so very long after the Objectives Resolution was passed, Liaquat began to change his tune for his political base was threatened by of splits in the Muslim League in the Punjab, which was the power-base of Pakistan's ruling elite. That was due to factional conflict between Daulatana and Mamdot who left the Muslim League to form a rival Party. Liaquat was now in a panic. He decided to exploit Islamic rhetoric, to hold together his crumbling Party. He began to speak of 'Islam in Danger'. He also began to equate loyalty to the Muslim League with loyalty to the state. Those who opposed him or his party were denounced as traitors.

There was, however, a second and a much more important reason why Liaquat decided to abandon his secular stance. Powerful regional movements had arisen in East Bengal, Sindh, Baluchistan and the NWFP, whose people felt that they were not being given their due in a Punjabi dominated Pakistan. They demanded regional autonomy and fairer shares of resources. The Centre, which was seen as 'Punjabi', was in fact dominated by a cohesive bureaucracy, under Chaudhri Muhammad Ali as Secretary General to the Government. It was the centralised bureaucracy that ruled Pakistan whilst politicians, including Liaquat, went through the motions.

Arguably, it was the challenge to the centre from regional movements which was the more important factor in precipitating Liaquat's ideological *volte-face.* Abandoning Mr. Jinnah's (and his own) firm stand against pandering to the mullahs, Liaquat sought to negate regional demands by issuing calls for 'unity' in the name of Pakistan and Islam. We were all Pakistanis and Muslims, it was now argued, and therefore we could not be Bengalis or Sindhis or Baluch.

The bureaucracy, rather than Liaquat, was in effective control, and it was not prepared to make any significant concessions to the mullahs. The mullahs could be given a visible public role, but without any real share in power. For that purpose a *Board of Talimaat-i-Islamia,* was set up. It provided a few jobs for some senior mullahs, the *Ulama.* But the Board was to be no more than a façade for the new found religious rhetoric of politicians. It was not to have any real powers. Its function was purely advisory and that too only on matters that were referred to it. When the Board did make some suggestions they were unceremoniously ignored. Nevertheless, the *Ulama* seemed to be content with the arrangement. They remained quiescent for nearly two decades. Recalcitrant Mullahs, such as Maulana Maududi, found themselves in jail. The mullahs were under control. That basically peaceful scene was disturbed only temporarily in 1953, when Islamic militants launched Anti-Ahmadi riots in the Punjab an d Martial Law was proclaimed. Although religious zealots of the Majlis-i-Ahrar and the Jamaat-i-Islami led the riots, they were in fact being used by cynical political forces, led by Punjab Chief Minister Mumtaz Daulatana. That was done in the context of US attempts to destabilise the Nazimuddin Government at the centre and to counter the Bengal group of MPs in the matter of the proposed Pakistan-US military Alliance which they opposed. That is a long and complicated story.

A decade and a half later, religious rhetoric was indulged in by the illegitimate regime of General Yahya Khan, but without conceding any formal role to the mullahs. General Sher Ali, redefined 'Pakistan Ideology' as 'Islamic Ideology'. The Yahya government's primary concern was to de-legitimise the increasingly powerful Bengali nationalism. Yahya's Bengali adviser, Prof. G. W. Choudhury, had persuaded him and his coterie of Generals, that East Bengali nationalism was limited to only a handful of intellectuals, who were in the pay of the Indians and that the vast majority of Bengalis had no sympathy with them. That tragically false picture could account for the ferocity and reckless manner in which Yahya tried to suppress the Bengali people in 1971. Would they have embarked on that policy if Yahya had even the slightest inkling of the depth of Bengali feelings ?

The mullahs were quiescent, however, until they were stirred into action by the foolish populist rhetoric of Zulfiqar Ali Bhutto who misguidedly decided to exploit religious ideology. Thereby Bhutto sowed the seeds of his own destruction, for the re-activated mullahs became the vanguard of the campaign against him. That set the scene for Gen. Zia's *coup d'etat.*

It was under General Zia that narrow and bigoted religiosity became state policy. The General sought the political support of the mullahs for his illegal regime, for he had no other political base. He also sought financial support from the Reagan regime in the US. Both of these objectives, he thought, could be secured through an Islamic *Jihad* which he proclaimed against the Soviet presence in Afghanistan.

The CIA joined took over the task of organising armed religious groups in Afghanistan, in cooperation with Pakistani agencies. When the Russians left Afghanistan, however, the CIA was withdrawn precipitately from the scene, leaving it to Pakistan to deal with the mess that they had created. Foolish Pakistani policies since then, especially under Benazir Bhutto and her successor Nawaz Sharif, got Pakistan even more heavily involved with these once US sponsored 'terrorist groups'.

The present government has done little to turn away from these policies to extricate Pakistan from the mess that was inherited from Zia's Afghan policy. When he seized power illegally, Zia badly needed some source of legitimacy for his regime. Being politically bankrupt, he decided to exploit the credulity of Pakistani Muslims by invoking Allah.

He claimed to have experienced *ilham* (a divine revelation) in which, he declared, he was enjoined by the Almighty himself to Islamise Pakistan and to transform it into a fortress of Islam. New 'Islamic Laws' were promulgated that were crude and cruel distortions of Islamic teachings, such as his *Hudud Ordinance* which, for example, had the effect of punishing a rape victim (for fornication) while the perpetrator of the rape went scot-free because of impossible conditions of proof now needed to prove his guilt!

Zia also bequeathed to his successors undemocratic Shariat Courts, that are answerable to no one. They issue binding decisions on the state and on the people, in the name of the Sharia. That role, in the name of Islam, is rejected by the philosophy of Sir Syed Ahmad who pointed out that Islam did not decree the office of a Pope with powers to issue binding decrees in the name of the faith. Islam, he said, is a religion of the individual conscience. No person or institution has the right to issue binding *fatawa*, laying down what Islam is and what it is not. Indeed, no other Muslim country has the equivalent of our Shariat Courts. They were set up by Zia's illegitimate regime and should be dissolved.

The *Shariat Courts* are manned by persons who hold rigid religious views. Their most damaging decision so far is an order that requires the abolition of interest, 'in all its forms', by 30th June, 2001. This threatens to bring Pakistan's already very shaky economy to a complete halt. No enemy of Pakistan could have devised a more potent weapon to destroy the country. In arriving at their decision the judges of the Shariat Bench of the Supreme Court set aside the advice of a very large number of scholars who came before it as witnesses, who resisted this interpretation of the *Sharia.* Instead, the Court appears to have been misled by bogus claims of 'Islamic Banking'.

They seem to be ignorant of how a modern economy functions and do not seem to have understood at all the obvious implications of their decision in a modern day capitalist economy such as that of Pakistan. They appear to be ignorant of the difference between interest in a modern capitalist economy *(sood)* and usury (riba) in pre-capitalist economies to which Quranic strictures apply. What the Shariat Courts have produced is a time bomb which, if allowed to go off, threatens to blow up Pakistan's economy.

The present Government seems to be paralysed in the face of the die hard religious lobby which seems to be triumphant about this. It has poor advisers. As soon as the Shariat Appellate Bench of the Supreme Court announced it decision, the minister of Finance, who is an ex-banker declared, without pausing to think, that the Court's decision would be implemented in full. But, after months of deliberations by several high powered committees, the Government still has no idea whatever of what is to be done. It speaks with two voices.

At a recent meeting, the Federal Minister for Religious Affairs declared that the Government has drafted all required laws and regulations, which are ready to be promulgated and that the Government is ready to implement the Shariat Court's decision in full, and without qualifications. But at the same meeting, the Governor of the State Bank of Pakistan (the country's central Bank) declared that they do not as yet know how the Shariat Court decision can be implemented. He said that the Government needs more time to work out viable solutions and that it has asked for an extension of time.

The Government does not seem to understand the gravity of this issue. They should know that they cannot allow the economy to collapse. But they also appear to be too intimidated by religious fundamentalists to overturn the Shariat Court's decree. Meanwhile, the top nine religious parties in the country have declared that they will launch a mass anti-Riba movement, on the lines of the movement that brought down Zulfiqar Ali Bhutto, if the Government fails to abolish interest by the date laid down by the Shariat Bench of the Supreme Court, namely the end of June, 2001. They have declared, ominously, that the time has come for a decisive war between Islamic and secular forces in the country. A major factor in the present situation is a development since the time of Zia. That is the proliferation of *deeni madaris,* religious schools, that have spread throughout Pakistan. They receive generous foreign funding, not least from Middle Eastern states like Saudi Arabia. The *deeni madaris* have little difficulty in recruiting pupils (*taliban*), who are turned into fanatics, ready to die for what they are taught to believe are sacred causes. A factor that has greatly helped their recruitment is the creation of a huge number of unemployed families, people without a livelihood and without hope, as a consequence of farm mechanisation, especially in the Punjab. Every tractor displaces at least a dozen families of sharecroppers. Hundreds of thousands of them are now without a source of livelihood. In that context, the appearance of the well financed *deeni madaris,* who take over their children, give them free 'tuition', accommodation and food, cannot appear to be anything other than a great blessing. The enthusiastic young *taliban,* are taught to recite the Quran. They are also indoctrinated, their minds filled with distorted and intolerant ideas about what Islam is and what it prescribes.

The *taliban* are thus turned into fanatics. Most of the *'deeni' madaris* also give them military training for *jihad* initially ostensibly against the Soviets and now for the liberation of Kashmir. But already Pakistan itself is experiencing the inevitable heavy fall out from this. The armed groups, many of them with battle-hardened *taliban,* are in the vanguard of sectarian killings throughout Pakistan, which are on the increase; killings of members of rival sects, Sunnis against the Shi'a, Deobandi Sunnis against Barelvi Sunnis and so on.

They have also begun to issue threats against the state itself and the society in Pakistan. Instead of a viable policy designed to disarm and liquidate such groups, successive regimes in Pakistan have pandered to them. The current military government, unlike the military regime of General Zia, has not indulged much in religious rhetoric, except for the occasional utterances of its Federal Minister for Religious Affairs. Indeed, the Government's liberal interior minister, General Moinuddin Haider, has given calls, from time to time, about doing something to bring the so-called *deeni madaris* under some sort of control, reforming their syllabi to introduce some useful, career related, educational input into their activities. For that he has become the *bête noir* of the religious parties, who have warned the government, firmly, against meddling in their affairs.

The government, for its part, seems to be intimidated by the militant Islamic groups. In December last, for example, one *Maulana* Muhammad Akram, leader of the *Tanzimul Ikhwan,* threatened to march on Islamabad with 'hundreds of thousands' of his followers, to force the Government to promulgate the *Sharia.* The Government's response was to placate him. It despatched the Punjab Home Secretary and the Inspector General of Police to parley with Akram.

That was apparently not enough, for it then sent Dr. Mahmood Ghazi, the Federal Minister for Religious Affairs, as reinforcement. After long drawn out talks, Maulana Akram 'graciously agreed' to defer his plan to storm the capital. It has been suggested by the media that Maulana Akram has 'a lot of influence among middle-ranking officers of the army'. If that is so, that must surely be extremely worrying. Could it be that which explains the Government's apparent paralysis in the face of serious threats from fanatical religious groups? It must know that a do nothing policy will not solve anything. Left to itself, the situation can only get worse.

Theories of the state, democratic or otherwise, are premised on the state's monopoly of legitimate force. But here we have a situation where the state's monopoly of force is undermined by the numerous armed religious groups (who often work in concert) that have agendas of their own. The Government must realise that the more they try to accommodate religious zealots, the stronger and the more intransigent they become. What the situation demands is a firm and well thought out policy to disarm such groups and bring them under control. It is surprising that Pakistan's professional military does not yet seem to have realised the very serious threat that this situation poses to itself as well as to the State and society as a whole. In the meantime, until something is done, Pakistan will continue to stagger towards an uncertain future, with contradictory state policies.

THE GROWING RELIGIOUS FUNDAMENTALISM IN PAKISTAN

The religious fundamentalists in Pakistan are once again on the full swing. They are very much encouraged by the outcome of the general elections in Pakistan. In overall, they have got over 16% of the total votes caste in the elections. But in the national assembly, they have emerged the second largest parliamentary group leaving behind Pakistan Peoples Party. Thanks to the support of the conservative Muslim League Nawaz MLN that their nominee for the prime minister Fazal Rehman got 86 votes while PPP trailed behind with 71 votes. The pro military Muslim League Q group was able to fetch the needed 172 votes for the Prime Minister lot.

The upsurge in the fundamentalist support was witnessed on 19th November 2002 when over 70,000 turned up for the funeral of Aimal Kansi in Quetta Baluchistan. This was the largest ever funeral in the whole history of Baluchistan. Aimal, body was brought from US where was awarded the death sentence after found guilty of killing two CIA officers in 1993. Till his last breath, he was very much proud of what he has done to the American imperialism. He has become another hero of the fundamentalists after Assama Bin Laden.

Another sign of the growth in religious fundamentalism was seen on 24th November when activists of Lashkar Tayaba, the banned religious group in Pakistan took over for six hours two temples in Jammu district of Indian held Kashmir. The incident resulted killing of the two and 10 more in the struggle to re-hold the temples by the Indian forces.

There have been more incidents like this during the week in Kashmir resulting over 20 deaths mainly of Indian army men. This is no incident. The leader of Lashkar Tayaba Hafiz Saeed was released last week in Pakistan. The Pakistan authorities would not accept at Lahore High Court only a month before that he is held up with them. ? Withdraw your writ petition if you want your husband to be released? Was the message of the intelligence agencies to the wife. Later the wife of Hafiz Saeed was forced to withdraw her write petition. Hafiz Saeed as brought to his hometown after being held for over a year and was house arrested. Lahore High Court declared the move as illegal. Since his release on 18th November, he has addressed many thousands in several cities of Punjab. At Faisalabad, the third largest city of Pakistan, he spoke to over 50,000 who came to greet him after his release. Many women threw their children in the air and begged him to take them for Jihad. ? Jihad can not be stopped by any mean,? he declared at the meeting.

Lashkar Tayaba was the main religious group promoted by the military intelligence of Pakistan during the nineties to carry on jihad in the Indian held Kashmir. Many youth were provided the military training at camps set up by the group in different parts of Pakistani held Kashmir. "Suicidal missions are the only way forward to further the message of Jihad" was the main philosophy of the group training. The 11th September 2001 changed the priorities of the military intelligence. The Lashkar Tayaba was asked to wind up the camps. The leader was kidnapped. The military intelligences thought that it would be all over by these actions. That is been proved all wrong. The ghost of religious fundamentalist propped up by the military intelligence is out of control and is in a process of changing its colour. From pro military group, it is fast becoming an anti military group in Pakistan.

In the eighties, the religious fanatics were very closely linked with American imperialism. In the nineties, they left them on their own. From the beginning this century, the fanatics have taken roots among the general consciousness of the masses in Pakistan as an anti imperialist force. ?It is war between Islam and American infidels,? says Samee-ul-Haq, one of the main leaders of MMA, the religious political alliance in Pakistan. He was also the main supporter of the Talban regime.

While in the nineties, the American imperialism has left them on their own but not the major part of the establishment in Pakistan. They wanted to use them against their traditional rival Indians. They had also the illusions that a stable regime in Afghanistan would give them access to the markets of the Central Asia. So the formation and the support for Talban were the main priorities. All that changed with 11th September. The crushing of Talban in Afghanistan by bombing of US imperialism has not curbed the spread of religious fundamentalism. It has spread in a different form in Pakistan at present. Leon Trotsky, the architecture of the Soviet revolution of 1917 in Russia, once quoted ?You can not crush the will of the masses to change the society?. The will of the most of the masses to change the society has not emerged, as was the case in the past, through the left forces in the region. Rather through the religious sentiment. The general elections in Pakistan held on 10th October gives some glimpse how they have emerged as a serious political force in Pakistan. The fundamentalist united in one main group called Mutehida Majlas Ammal MMA (United Action Forum) won the most seats in two provinces. They took considerable votes in all other constituencies. But the most alarming fact was their support in the two major cities, Lahore and Karachi. At Lahore, they won three national assembly seats out of 13 and in Karachi, a neck-to-neck fight against the MQM, the immigrant mass force. MMA got 5 out of 20 seats in Karachi but it was very closely defeated in all the other 15 seats. MQM fetched 12 in the end. The MMA anti US rhetoric, which played a seminal role in wooing voters elsewhere in the country, played important part in their victory. But their campaign in Karachi was also centered on the issues like health and education. Mayer belonging to MMA already rules the local government in Karachi. MMA captured 29 out of 35 National and 52 out of 99 provincial assembly seats in North West Frontier Province (NWFP). In Baluchistan, it got 6 out of 13 National and 14 out of 51 provincial seat. In over all, MMA got nearly 3.2 millions votes. While the main bourgeoisie party MLQ got 7.3 millions. PPP fetched the most votes, nearly over 7.4 million votes. The total vote caste in Pakistan was over 28.9 millions. MMA got over 52 per cent of its seats in the low turnout areas. The fragmentation and disenchantment of the secular vote coupled with increased mobility and motivated election campaign by the MMA are definitely factors that cannot be ignored.

The conservative Muslim League, the main bourgeoisie party in Pakistan was split on the question of the support for military. A large part of it went to support the military rule while the rest under MLN supported the religious fundamentalist on the name of seat adjustment in many parts of Pakistan. MLN was taking revenge from the military as their leader Nawaz Sharif was ousted from power in October 1999. Later he was forced to leave Pakistan and now reside in Saudi Arabia. In the process, the MMA got more votes and seats than the MLN. MLN strategy made the fundamentalist stronger and is now no more close associates of the MLN. In fact MLN is fast becoming a tail end of the fanatics in Pakistan. MMA took more advantage of the lowering of the vote age from 21 to 18 than another political group. The Pakistan Talban from the Madrasas, the religious schools, over 70,000 of them in Pakistan, energetically worked for the successful campaign of the MMA. ? He who has the youth has the future,? Lenin said once. The majority of the youth is fed up with the system. "They are all corrupt", is the argument presented in most of the discussion among youth. ?Only Islamic revolution is the answer? you hear very often.

After the general election, the strategy of MMA was to give an impression to the masses of Pakistan that they are ready to shares the power but it has to be on their principal position. To attract and enlarge their support among the petty bourgeoisie, the

MMA in words at least has become champions of the democracy and defendant of the 1973 constitutions.

The constitution, unanimously passed by parliament under Bhutto government, is a combination of capitalist democratic values and religious norms. The MMA also opposed the constitutional amendments by General Pervaiz Musharaf regime to give him more dictatorial powers as president.

The Legal Framework Order (LFO) was announced on 21st August 2002, giving powers to president to sack the government anytime he likes and also powers for important postings in the establishment. This strategy has earned MMA some more respect and they are not seen as power hungry as was the impression of them in the past.

The religious fanatics have supported most of the military regimes in Pakistan history. Only this time, they opted to remain in opposition in the center. They are more likely to form the provincial government in North West Frontier Province (NWFP) which is next to Afghanistan and could be part of the government in Baluchistan. They have not gone to share the government at the center because of their perspective to become a mass force at national level. ? Had Punjab been awoke like the other province, the Islamic revolution in Pakistan would have been complete in this elections? cried Qazi Hussain Ahmed, the main leader of the most organized Jamaat-i-Islami; JI is a decisive component of MMA. It is JI successful political strategy of forming political alliance of all the religious forces that has won the mass support for the MMA. ?They are never united and can never be united? was the main arguments of the some of the Left intellectuals during the past years. MMA has at least made these intellectuals think twice before they bring this argument against them.

The unity process of the religious forces started long before the 11th September realizing the political vacuum after the failure of the successive civilian regimes to solve any of the basic problems of the masses in Pakistan. The 10 years of successive failed regimes of PPP and MLN after the fall of the last military regime in 1988, has provided the opportunity to the religious forces to exploit the opportunity.

In 1993, the JI formed a Pakistan Islamic Front with some minor Islamic groups to contest the general elections. The PIF failed badly and fetched less than 3 per cent of the total votes. In 1995, Mutehida Jakjehti Council (United Solidarity Council) was formed mainly to address the question of sectarian killings. In 2000, almost 29 religious groups formed the Islamic Mutehida Inqilabi Mehaz IMAM (Islamic United Revolutionary Front. This was mainly to deal with the Western ideas spread by the NGOs in the NWFP and Baluchistan. Jamiat Ulemai Islam under Fazal Rehman played the main role in this group. In June 2001, MMA was founded at the initiative of Jamaat-i-Islami. After 11th September, over 40 different religious groups formed Pak Afghan Defense Counsel. The MMA all eyes are on Punjab, the most populated province with over 64% of the total inhabitants living in this rather prosperous area of Pakistan. Many villages in Punjab particularly in Southern Punjab have young martyrs. Those who have been killed Kashmir or Afghanistan. These ?sacrifices? are laying a strong foundation for the possible growth of the religious political influence on those areas where MMQ is yet to become a majority. MMA activists unlike the main bourgeoisie parties are not driven by careers or greed. They are from the middle and working class background committed for a change. Most of the elected members of MMA from NWFP are from poor background and are seen by many all the time on cycles. This is contrary to elected members of rich parties who are on land cruisers and Mitsubishi Pajeros. The class question is very much in the mind of many who have gone to support the MMA in the recent elections. In the absence of the any significant left force in Pakistan MMA have echoed the class sentiments mixed with religion.

Would the American imperialism tolerate the growing influence of religious fundamentalism in Pakistan? The Americans has so for relied on the military generals to do the dirty job. Musharaf has done it very happily. But the political situations are getting out of control. The formation of the MMA government in NWFP will bring new contradictions between the new government in he center with the provincial government. The under ground Talban will feel easier in surfacing in NWFP under a religious government. Already new social tensions have emerged in the area. Women rights, human rights advocated in the province are under attack. NGO's in these fields must wind up their offices? is the hidden message by the fanatics. The Sunday regular weekly off day will be once again replaced by Friday by the new provincial government. ?Beard is a must,? the new young elected leaders of MMA are advocating for every Muslim. ?Women must obey the Islamic norms and must cover themselves?. It is Talbanisation of Pakistani society in a different form. It is not yet advocating an open Jihad like the Alqaida did. But it is in the oven.

So NWFP and Pakistan could be the next target of all the propaganda of the US imperialism after Iraq. Any attempt by the center to dissolve or suspend the provincial government at NWFP will result in more civil war like situation. In 1974, the united government of the nationalist and religious fundamentalist was dissolved by Bhutto under the pressure of Shah if Iran, a guerilla war started in Baluchistan. Many were killed and many went to Afghanistan in exile. Now nationalist have diminished to large extent for the time being in this election, as they were seen as pro imperialists force. Many of these nationalists supported the American bombing in the false hope that it will crush the religious threat at home as well.

More dark period is heading Pakistan unless new initiatives is been taken by the Left and progressive forces to stop the onslaught of the fanatics.

The handing over the recorded message of Asama Bin Laden in Islamabad to Algezeera tele network shows how things can develop in Pakistan. The possibility of the presence of Asama Bin Laden in Pakistan, the pro Talban provincial government in NWFP, the growing influence of religious fundamentalism in Punjab and Sind can force the newly elected pro Musharaf regime to take drastic actions against them. This in return will make the life of ordinary Pakistani more difficult. And it will make the ideas of religious fundamentalism more popular. Labour Party Pakistan had foreseen the recent growth of religious fundamentalism. It has declined to side with them on any issue. It has opposed the American bombing alongside with the condemnation of religious terrorism. It is adopting the policy to oppose the recently formed new civil pro Musharaf regime. The new civil regime is no change for the masses. It is the continuation of the Musharaf regime in civilian cloths. It will carry the IMF; World Bank dictated policies on the name of reform agenda. The religious fundamentalist will also oppose the reform agenda but only in words. Initially they are showing a very liberal face to the West. They have already said that privatization is a must. But under the pressure of the masses, they can make big noise against the economic exploitation of the people by the Multi nationals alongside with the social and political repressions. The hypocrisy of the fundamentalist can only be exposed with a united action of the trade unions, Left and progressive forces.

PAKISTAN'S MILITARY RULERS

On a rural road in southern Punjab I saw an official government sign sporting a curious message. "My Dear Countrymen, Army will never disappoint you like the past." It was signed: Pervez Musharraf.

Musharraf is the military dictator of Pakistan who, in Blairite-style, has rebranded himself as the country's "Chief Executive". He and his supporters are keen to present the latest army coup as something new and different, and they have proclaimed a wide-ranging agenda of social and political reform. What may be new this time around is not so much the soft sell as the fact that so many of the intelligentsia, as well as a section of the NGO leadership, is willing to buy it. Further down the social scale, scepticism is stronger – as indicated by Musharraf's roadside appeal.

The coup was staged not, initially, in defence of the interests of Pakistanis against the increasing lawlessness of the Nawaz Sharif government, but in order to stop Nawaz Sharif from replacing Musharraf as army chief – something Sharif, as the elected prime minister, had every right to do.

Apologists for army rule (not least in the British foreign office) cite the notorious corruption of Sharif and other mainstream politicians as justification for the suspension of the constitution.

But the deformations in Pakistani politics are not the result of too much but of too little democracy. Even when elected governments have been in office, the military has carefully circumscribed their field of action, and indeed pulled the plug on one after another. Many of the country's chronic problems can be traced to its door. It has funded, promoted and armed the right wing religious factions, has been complicit in the drugs trade, and has siphoned off half the national budget for decades. The culture of patronage and corruption which Musharraf now inveighs against is very much the creation of several decades of army influence.

Now the military is aiming to micro-manage the whole of Pakistani society. Military officers have been installed at the top levels of a wide variety of institutions, from district and municipal administrations to the railways, the water and power development authority, universities, PIA, not to mention the cricket board. The army also proposes to institutionalise "economic monitoring" – ostensibly to stem tax evasion – while pursuing the classic IMF 'restructuring' agenda: deregulation, privatisation, globalisation. These are the policies broadly pursued by both Benazir Bhutto and Nawaz Sharif; the only difference now is that the military can implement the programme without being inhibited by concerns about electoral unpopularity.

In the short run, this has meant increases in furnace oil (a staple commodity), the imposition of a general sales tax, a coming hike in railway fares, and substantial job losses across the public sector. A taste of things to come was seen at a recent protest against 'retrenchment' in Karachi, where the army and police baton-charged demonstrators and arrested leaders of two local political parties.

The two major political parties – the Bhutto-led Pakistan People's Party and the Sharif-led Pakistan Muslim League – are both exhausted and widely distrusted. Initially, apart from the PML, which the army had chucked out, only the Pakistan Labour Party unequivocally denounced the coup. Now that Musharraf has said explicitly that he will never hand over power to either Sharif or Bhutto, and any return to civilian rule has been postponed to the indefinite future, the PPP, the PML, and a number of regionally-based parties are calling for an end to military rule.

Imran Khan's Tahriq-I-Insaf has joined the right wing religious parties in calling for "accountability first, then elections". This is echoed by a substantial section of the intelligentsia, who argue that there is no point in a return to democracy unless the army first cleanses the country of "corrupt politicians."

Accordingly, the army has launched a high-profile "accountability" drive, and has arrested several hundred politicians from the major parties. A determined, impartial and transparent accountability drive is certainly needed in Pakistan – but that is not on offer from the military. Indeed, the military and the judiciary have been explicitly excluded from investigation. Meanwhile, accused politicians are being detained for long periods without charge and when they finally get to court they are assumed guilty until they prove themselves innocent.

These are show trials (the biggest and best publicised being the trial of deposed PM Nawaz Sharif). Although the victims are themselves some of the most rotten exploiters in Pakistani society, trials of this nature will only further brutalise the administration of 'justice' in Pakistan. In the course of the trial, Sharif's lawyer was assassinated and his wife was threatened with a charge of high treason. Now that he has been found guilt of kidnapping and other serious offences, Sharif himself has been handed a life sentence.

Meanwhile, the Pakistan Labour Party, one of the only political organisations to oppose the coup, is subject to increasing harassment. Its offices have been raided and its leaders imprisoned. The iron fist inside the military's velvet glove is becoming ever more apparent.

Musharraf is being promoted, at least in the west, as a liberal secularist, but that counts for little compared to the climate among the top army leadership as a whole. Here the wind is to the right, with hard-line Islamicists rising in the army leadership. Musharraf himself has called for the uniting of all the 'jehadi' groups – armed right wing religious fundamentalists – under one command to prosecute the war against India in Kashmir.

Over the years of the Cold War and the conflict in Afghanistan, the army and the jehadi groups became symbiotically intertwined.

In contrast, ordinary Pakistanis, when given the chance, have voted overwhelmingly against fundamentalism (the right wing religious parties have never captured more than 7% in an election). In Pakistan, popular Islamic tradition is secular and tolerant – and acerbically sceptical about the pretensions of the mullahs. That's why the fundamentalist groups and their sponsors in the army focus so heavily on the Kashmir question, which A.R. Rehman, director of the Human Rights Commission of Pakistan, aptly calls "the last refuge of the scoundrel" – in both India and Pakistan.

Since the coup, the base of Pakistani society has been largely quiescent. People are worn down by the cycle of dictatorships and the failures of civilian politicians, not too mention the burdens of nearly a decade of economic recession. The civil society movements are disorientated by the collapse of their leadership, and the trades unions have issued only the most guarded criticisms of military rule. Nonetheless, Pakistani people have a long tradition of resistance to tyrants (they've already overthrown several of them), and it is only a matter of time before that tradition surfaces once again. All the locally-based social activists I spoke to made clear that they regarded the military's designs on Pakistani society as malign. They are now preparing themselves for a long period of struggle.

Frighteningly, time is not on their side. Apart, possibly, from the Cuban missile crisis, it's unlikely that the human race has ever been closer to experiencing a nuclear war than we are at the moment. Before the Kargil conflict in the summer of 1999, there had never been a serious conventional military war fought directly between two nuclear weapons states. And before the Pakistani coup, there had been a civilian check on the military deployment of nuclear weapons in all the countries which possessed them. In India, the right wing Hindu communalist BJP government is whipping up violent anti-Pakistani sentiment and levelling near daily threats of extermination against its neighbour. This strengthens the Islamic right within the Pakistani army (and the jihadi groups in the streets), which in turns provides a handy justification for the BJP's drive to transform India into a militantly 'Hindu' society. The two regimes are now inter-locked in a grisly dance of death. However, in both India and Pakistan, the elites tend to read their own brand of strident but insecure national chauvinism into the public at large.

ROLE OF THE MILITARY IN POLITICS IN PAKISTAN

August 14, 1997 will mark the 50th anniversary of Pakistan's creation [now this should be read as ' has marked' - authors]. Sixteen of these fifty years were spent under direct martial law regimes and democracy could not flourish. India, which gained independence from the British at the same time, has always been recognised as the world's largest democracy; with military coups unthinkable, it can boast of a strong parliament, free press and an independent judiciary. In Pakistan these institutions did not, or were not allowed to strengthen and this remains one of the biggest reasons why the military intervened, directly or indirectly, in politics and state affairs throughout Pakistan's half century of history.

This paper looks into the history of Pakistan in relation to the role played by the military in it. It discusses the ambitious generals' psyche, their arrogance and a smug belief in their ability to do things better than civilians. They took it upon themselves to 'sort out' the mess created by politicians and become the nation's 'saviours'. It is divided into sections roughly corresponding to military eras in chronological order - how an image-building process took place and from the small but fully-disciplined elite of the colonial era, the military emerged as a 'sacred cow' answerable to none. It also looks into the various institutions that helped entrench military rule and concludes with a review of the present situation in light of the 13 amendment in the Constitution and its implications.

MILITARY DISENGAGEMENT FROM POLITICS

It is not surprising that the recent spate of political clashes between the Pakistani civilian government and the military has generated widespread speculation among policymakers that a military coup could transpire in Islamabad. Pakistan has experienced four military coups and thirty years of military rule since the nation achieved independence in 1947. The Pakistani military is indisputably the most powerful political actor in one of the world's most dangerous countries due to the nation's political instability, violent internal strife, and its enduring rivalry with a more powerful India. In the civil-military literature on Pakistan, there are an abundance of explanations for the military's political hegemony, the causes of military takeovers, and the consequences of its dysfunctional civil-military relations for democracy. Rather than examining why and how the military intervenes in politics, this paper will look at the other side of the coin: why and how the military chooses to disengage from politics.

Given the scholarly focus on military interventions in Pakistan, there has been little rigorous inquiry into why and how its four military regimes have ended, and even less investigation into the pivotal role the military has served in facilitating each transition and the implications this has for the wider body of civil-military relations theory. The central research question of this paper is: Why does the Pakistani military return to the barracks? It will explore the underlying causes that have led the military to abdicate from direct rule, arguing that withdrawals are best explained by the divergence of interests between the leaders of the military regime, who seek to preserve their grip on political power, and the active leaders of the armed forces, who seek to protect and advance the corporate interests of the military. This breach is the key motivation for the military to return to the barracks. The opportunity for withdrawal is triggered when the regime encounters political difficulties consolidating its authority, which often backfires by rejuvenating civilian opposition and requires the regime to turn to the military to enforce its will. So long as the domestic opposition to the regime does not pose a direct threat to the military's core interests and there are viable civilian alternatives available, the military will seek to return to the barracks rather than incur the costs of repression.

This paper begins with an overview of Pakistan as a case study and a review of the civil-military relations literature related to military interventions and military withdrawals. It will then outline the civil-military scholarship related to Pakistan and provide an overview of its civil-military relations. This is followed by a short background outlining Pakistan's political history after independence. Next, it presents a detailed examination of the conditions that have led to the end of Pakistan's four military regimes in 1968, 1971, 1988, and 2008 and illustrates how the divergence of interests between the active leaders of the armed forces and the leaders of the military regime eventually caused the former to prefer a return to the barracks. The paper then analyse the commonalities and patterns of behaviour in these cases to explain how and why this divergence of interests takes place and concludes by reviewing the causes of military withdrawal in Pakistan, providing theoretical implications, and offering paths for further research.

The Case of Pakistan's Praetorian Military

Pakistan is an exceptionally rich case study for civil-military relations for several reasons. First, Pakistan has proven resilient in the face of the waves of democratization over the past few decades that contributed to widespread changes in civil-military relations in previously coup-prone corners of the world. Indeed, the basic question of civilian control in Pakistan remains a highly contentious political issue today. Second, Pakistan's political system is characterized by its strong praetorian military, which has repeatedly overthrown weak civilian governments. The country has experienced four military regimes that have ruled the country for over thirty years under Ayub Khan (1958-1969), Yahya Khan (1969-1971), Zia ul-Haq (1977-1988), and Pervez Musharraf (1999-2008). Third, Pakistan is a critically important state for U.S. policymakers. Pakistan is a strategic mid-tier regional power that possesses nuclear weapons. It has served as a frontline state during the Cold War and reemerged as such in the War on Terror as a hotbed of Islamist extremist groups including al-Qaeda. Lastly, Pakistan's turbulent relationship with its powerful nuclear-armed neighbour India has produced several major wars, countless skirmishes, and enough saber-rattling to foster a near-perpetual crisis atmosphere in the subcontinent.

While the Pakistani military is extremely politicized, it has remained a highly professional organization with a significant degree of internal discipline and cohesion. The most powerful political and military position in Pakistan belongs to the Chief of Army Staff (COAS), which is currently filled by General Raheel Sharif. The COAS heads the Army Combatant General Headquarters (GHQ) in Rawalpindi and represents the Army in the Joint Chiefs of Staff Committee (JCSC), a body charged with inter-service coordination.

At the very top of the Army's hierarchy, the COAS has a broad portfolio of military and non-military duties, the latter including managing the Army's relations with the civilians, brokering deals amongst the political parties, and supervising the military's policy fiefdom (especially in foreign affairs). The COAS always led Pakistan's military takeovers and subsequently served as the head of state or returned the military to the barracks. Besides coups, the military's principal method for interfering in the civilian political process is through the Inter-Services Intelligence (ISI) directorate. The ISI exists outside of the formal military command structure but informally serves under the COAS. The ISI has a domestic political-wing that monitors and intervenes in domestic politics on the military's behalf.

What Causes the Pakistani Military to Return to the Barracks?

In the civil-military literature on Pakistan, there are ample explanations for the military's political interventions and the causes and consequences of the country's frequent interventions. Many of the independent variables scholars have offered to explain military interventions in Pakistan fail to account for military withdrawals (and why repeated interventions transpire). The first and most prominent explanation offered is the weakness of the country's civilian political parties and democratic institutions compared to the physical and political strengths of the military. Second is that the military receives the lion's share of the national budget in addition to the enormous business empire it has amassed. The third argument focuses on the external security environment, primarily Pakistan's fierce rivalry with India and the existential threat Islamabad feels from its more powerful neighbour. Unfortunately, these arguments predict stability for military rule in Pakistan. They cannot explain the variation in military rule over time and why the military returned to the barracks in 1971, 1988 and 2008 or its bungled efforts to hand power to the civilians after staging a countercoup in 1969. Surveying the explanations for the instability in Pakistan's regimes, Paul Staniland concludes, "The unanswered puzzle is why Pakistan has not become a military ruled bureaucratic-authoritarian state despite three sustained attempts to build precisely such a regime...Scholars assume that the army simply could not maintain its rule, but comparisons make it clear that military-backed authoritarianism can be enduring."

The literature covering military withdrawal in Pakistan is quite small, paralleling the small segment the study of "returns to the barracks" occupies in the field as a whole. Mazhar Aziz uses path dependence and a historical institutionalism framework to explain how early political arrangements and military interventions compounded to shape civil-military outcomes, diagnosing that the corporate interests of the military are key. Hassan Askari Rizvi offers a comprehensive investigation into the military's role in politics, coups, and the character and policies of the military regimes. Rizvi does discuss the causes of military withdrawals in Pakistan, but unfortunately his basic framing of the phenomena is somewhat inelegant. Moreover, a host of independent variables used to explain military withdrawals in other countries do not fit Pakistan's often peculiar circumstances. For instance, a common cause of withdrawals is rampant factionalism within the military. Yet every coup and withdrawal in Pakistan has been led by the active head of the Army, supported by the top brass, and received cooperation down the command structure. As Staniland notes, "...the army enters into and withdraws from politics cohesively." There has never been a serious coup attempt in Pakistan emanating from junior officers, spontaneous unit uprisings, or a non-military party. Although the military is extremely politicized, it has remained a highly professional organization with a significant degree of internal discipline and cohesion.

Accordingly, this paper utilizes the works of Finer and Stepan to disaggregate a military regime into two echelons: the regime or military-as-government led by the political heads of the Army and the military or military-as-institution led by the active leaders of the armed forces. This paper argues that withdrawals in Pakistan are best explained by the divergence of interests between the leaders of the military regime, who seek to preserve their grip on political power, and the active leaders of the armed forces, who seek to protect and advance the corporate interests of the military. The breach between the two echelons is the key motivation for the military to stage a return to the barracks. The opportunity to withdraw is triggered when the regime encounters political difficulties consolidating its authority and faces off against a revitalized civilian opposition which requires the regime to wield to the military as an instrument of repression. So long as the domestic opposition to the regime does not pose a direct threat to the military's core interests and there are viable civilian alternatives available, the military will seek to return to the barracks rather than incur the costs of repression.

Pakistan's Historical Context

Pakistan's armed forces are a legacy from the British Indian Army that was inherited upon the nation's independence in 1947. At that time, the military was instilled with a tradition of civilian supremacy from the colonial administration. Pakistan's violent separation with India and the dispute over the Kashmir region, which led to the indecisive Indo-Pakistan War of 1947-48, served as the first test for the Pakistani Army. The early period of post-independence politics in Pakistan were dominated by the Muslim League led by Muhammad Ali Jinnah and Liaquat Ali Khan, who respectively served as Governor General and Prime Minister. The League had been a potent force within the political environment of British India because it had served as a mass platform for the Muslim minority. While committed to democracy, the League's leaders believed they were entitled to govern the country they had forged but discovered religion was no longer a salient rallying point once the nation had separated from India. Pakistan was a fragmented nation with intense political cleavages along provincial, ethnic, sectarian, tribal, and socioeconomic lines. Furthermore, West Pakistan and East Pakistan were separated by a thousand miles of hostile Indian-territory. The country was dominated principally by Muhajirs and Punjabis of West Pakistan who filled the upper-echelons of the League, the other political parties, the civilian bureaucracy, and the officer corps. A major dilemma emerged in the late 1940s which would become the central political problem in Pakistan for several decades: the Muhajir and Punjabi politicians became reluctant to initiate democratic processes because it would guarantee an enormous permanent shift in national political power to the numerically superior Bengalis of East Pakistan. With West Pakistan certain to lose out to East Pakistan in any fair electoral contest, the country's political development stalled. For over a decade after independence, the politicians could not reach a final agreement on a constitution and other electoral arrangements. The League fragmented into opposing factions. Instability amongst the political parties led to a rapid turnover in leadership, with seven prime ministers rising and falling between 1951 and 1957 before the first military coup occurred in 1958.

The Ayub Khan Regime: The Countercoup

After seizing power in 1958, COAS General Ayub Khan promoted himself to Field Marshal and Supreme Commander of the Armed Forces. General Muhammad Musa replaced Ayub as the COAS and was widely seen as a compliant apolitical officer. More than subsequent military rulers, Ayub kept the military at arm's length in the day-to-day running of the country, largely relying on the bureaucracy to administrate. Nevertheless, a number of senior officers did join Ayub in the military regime, becoming ministers, governors, and wearing other political hats.

Replacing the parliamentary government, Ayub introduced "Basic Democracy" and the 1962 Constitution. Basic Democracies were local apolitical party-less councils meant to bestow legitimacy on Ayub's rule by electing him president in 1960 and 1965. Over time, he relied less and less on his staff and corps commanders for policy advice and more on civilians, like his foreign minister Zulfikir Ali Bhutto, who became one of Ayub's closest confidants. In addition to providing the military a relatively high degree of autonomy from the military-as-government, Ayub provided the armed forces with large increases in defence expenditures and secured enormous U.S. military aid packages for modernization.

The first visible splits between Ayub and the military took shape in 1964-65. Ayub, Bhutto, and others in the military-as-government saw the window of opportunity for a favorable resolution of the Kashmir dispute was closing and began plotting a military solution, over the objections of the military-as-institution. Ayub delegated the planning for the operation to a joint civilian-military cell, which was dominated by Bhutto's men from the Foreign Office and some intelligence officers.

The influence of Bhutto and the Foreign Office on military planning undercut the military's chain of command and threatened its autonomy and unity. The regime's final plan was a half-baked scheme that would unfold in two phases. The first phase called for as many as 30,000 "guerrillas" to infiltrate across the Line of Control (LOC) into Indian-controlled Kashmir and instigate an uprising.

In the second phase, an Army division would swiftly cross the LOC and seize strategic areas before the Indians could react. COAS Musa Khan and other senior Army officers raised objections with Ayub over the plausibility of the plan's success and the risk high of escalation, which Ayub dismissed. The Army was confident that if India felt it was losing the fight in the Vale of Kashmir, it would launch a massive counterattack across the international border in the Punjab, a fight the Army knew it was unlikely to win. The COAS and the GHQ, as one general later wrote, viewed the entire ordeal as "...a bastard child, born of the liaison between the Foreign Minister [Bhutto] and General Malik [Division Commander in Pakistani Kashmir]." Accordingly, the military high command shirked in supporting planning for the war. The GHQ delegated responsibility for the Kashmir operation's planning and execution solely to Malik's divisional headquarters and made no effort to notify its combat commanders or otherwise prepare the Army and the other services for war.

The Second Kashmir War in 1965 ended with Pakistan's acrimonious defeat. After Pakistan achieved some success in Kashmir, India launched an armored counterattack into the Punjab and caught Islamabad's forces there entirely unprepared. The military-as-institution became disenchanted with Ayub and Bhutto's mishandling of the war and the ceasefire agreement that resulted in no change of territory. Senior combat commanders and mid-level officers were extremely dissatisfied with the poor generalship displayed by the GHQ. Musa Khan was replaced as COAS by General Yahya Khan, one of Ayub's protégées. The breach between Ayub's regime and the military rapidly diverged after the war and was soon exacerbated by the regime's declining political support and the rise of popular political parties. After the war, Bhutto split with Ayub and departed from the regime. He formed the Pakistani People's Party (PPP) in 1967 on a populist, socialist, and anti-Ayub platform which gained a large following among the Punjabi majority in West Pakistan. In East Pakistan, the Awami League (AL), a Bengali nationalist mass political party with a separatist agenda, was also on the rise and further threatened the military regime's legitimacy.

The shell game of Ayub's Basic Democracy soon collapsed upon the emergence of popular opposition parties demanding a return to parliamentary democracy. The heightened agitation by civilians, however, was not the decisive blow to the Ayub regime. As Stepan points out, "the loss of civilian support must somehow be transformed into a tangible cost or a direct threat to the military-as-institution." The political opposition increasingly fanned civil unrest, which led Ayub to seek to ratchet up repression by imposing martial law and calling out the Army in early 1969. For the military, violent suppression of the mass protests, especially in the Punjab where it recruited the majority of its officers and enlisted personnel, came at a high risk to its corporate interests by threatening its unity and prestige. Given the massive breach between interests of the military and those of the regime, the military no longer saw its best interests vested in the perpetuation of the Ayub regime and became willing to sacrifice the military-as-government to quell the unrest.P58F P Army Chief Yahya Khan, with the consensus of the Army brass, refused to enforce martial law on behalf of Ayub and in effect staged a bloodless countercoup. Having lost the support of the active leaders of the Army, Ayub subsequently resigned his office and handed power to Yahya.

The Yahya Khan Regime: The Generals' Revolt

General Yahya Khan assumed the presidency from Ayub in March 1969. He formed an entirely new military-as-government that included far more dual-hatted officers than under Ayub. Yahya promoted his close associate General Abdul Hamid Khan as COAS. Yahya moved quickly to address many of the underlying political issues that had plagued Pakistan's domestic political order since independence in order to extradite the military from direct power.

He abrogated Ayub's 1962 Constitution and announced free elections would be held in late 1970 for a National Assembly, which would draft a new constitution and guarantee East Pakistan proportional representation with West Pakistan for the first time. The regime and the military felt there was some risk to the military's long-term corporate interests by returning the civilians to political power, and especially enfranchising the Bengalis. Yet these fears were placated by intelligence reports throughout the campaign that showed a roughly even split among the various opposition parties in each wing of country. The regime believed it could act as an arbiter among the divided parties in a deadlocked legislature to protect the military's long-term interests.

The military regime's plan to withdraw was entirely derailed by the election results. The Awami League attained an outright majority in the legislature, sweeping all but two of the seats in East Pakistan. Bhutto's PPP won roughly two-thirds of the seats in West Pakistan. After the elections, the AL issued six hardline demands on regional autonomy including East Pakistan's right to form its own military. Bhutto refused to form a government with the AL. In March 1971, after negotiations between the parties and the regime failed, Yahya declared the National Assembly would be indefinitely delayed. East Pakistan descended into open revolt and the AL soon declared the region's independence as Bangladesh. Yahya, supported by the Army (minus the few Bengali regiments which mutinied), unleashed a brutal military crackdown in the East. The situation devolved into a full-scale civil war in which hundreds of thousands of civilians were killed by the military over the course of nine months. India invaded East Pakistan in

November 1971 to support the Bangladeshi rebels in response to the massive flow of Bengali refugees into India triggered by the fighting. Pakistan retaliated by launching an invasion from West Pakistan into India in early December. Within several weeks, India successfully routed the Pakistanis along the two fronts, captured a third of the Pakistani Army that was trapped in the East, and forced Yahya to capitulate.

Days after the dismemberment of Pakistan and the catastrophic military defeat to India, Yahya and his cadre indicated that the regime would remain in power. At that point, many of the Army formation commanders and senior headquarters officers stepped in. The Yahya regime had been a complete disaster not only for the country, but for the military as well, as morale and prestige hit rock-bottom and unity frayed. Acting on the demands of many lower commanders, Chief of General Staff (CGS) Lt. Gen. Gul Hassan, who occupied the tier directly under the COAS, sent an explicit threat to the regime: unless Yahya and the military-as-government resigned *en masse* the next day, tanks would roll into the capital and unseat them. COAS Gen. Hamid Khan, who was seen by his subordinates as a Yahya lackey, assembled the senior officer corps to see if he would be an acceptable replacement—an idea floated by several in the regime—but he was rejected. Yahya, the military-as-government, and Gen. Hamid were forced to resign in late December. Once the top echelon of the regime was removed, Gen. Hassan was appointed acting COAS and the Army quickly arranged for Bhutto and the PPP to assume the reins of power and returned the military to the barracks.

The Zia Regime: The Fortuitous Plane Crash

General Zia-ul-Haq and the Army seized power in 1977 after Bhutto rigged parliamentary elections and attempted to have the military impose martial law to quash opposition protests. Early in his regime, Zia made considerable efforts to make the military-as-institution a stakeholder in his regime. Zia had not truly established himself as the head of the Army before the coup, and in the first few years of his rule was respectful of the senior officer corps and solicited their policy views. As Rizvi claims, "The key to the invulnerability of Zia-ul-Haq was the support he enjoyed from the senior Army commanders." Furthermore, plenty of incentives were given to the military in terms of increased defence expenditures and personnel pay, as well as huge tracts of agricultural land, residences, bank loans, and other side perks.

The military favored free elections and a return to democracy in the early 1980s. Nevertheless, it was content to go along with Zia's efforts to legitimize his government so long as it did not threaten the military's self-interests. A referendum was held in 1984 that gave Zia a five-year term as president. Like Ayub, Zia oversaw general elections for a sham non-party legislature the following year and handpicked a civilian politician, Muhammad Khan Junejo, as his Prime Minister, after which martial law was finally lifted. Zia had miscalculated Junejo and the legislature, which proved to be more dynamic than anticipated and unwilling to act as the rubber stamp Zia wished. The relationship between Zia and Junejo caused rising political divisions within the military-as-government while revived opposition parties such as the PPP began clamoring for the end of military rule and a return to parliamentary democracy. The military's corporate interests became tangled in the Zia-Junejo feuding, as they quarreled over cabinet appointments, military spending and perks, promotions for the top-brass, and Zia's dual-hatted role as he clung to the ceremonial title of Chief of Army Staff (whose actual responsibilities rested with the VCOAS).

The military not only resented Junejo's forays into its autonomy, but also Zia's meddling in its internal affairs and his inability to protect the military's corporate interests from his own faux civilian government. The period of collaboration between the military-as-government and the military-as-institution was at an end. As Zia civilianized his rule, he distanced himself from the military-as-institution. Where once Zia had shrewdly dabbled in the promotions and assignments of the top brass, by the late 1980s his interference in the Army's hierarchy had evolved into blatant nepotism, a disregard for the rigid promotion system, and an undermining of the chain-of-command. Zia surrounded himself with civilians and loyal officers. He even wed his children with some of those senior officers to build kinship alliances. The officers that Zia did not trust were denied promotions to key postings or subsumed into the ever expanding number of active and retired officers running the civilian bureaucracies where they could amass fortunes for themselves but held no command. Zia rotated three VCOAS during his tenure, ending with Gen. Mirza Aslam Beg, who was appointed in 1987.

The turnover of personnel at the top and the passage of time required Zia to promote relatively junior officers to senior posts. He also stopped seeking political input from senior officers. Zia's meetings with the corps commanders and top-brass became more and more infrequent and devoid of discussion and debate. Zia undercut Beg and GHQ's command, preferring to meet with the younger corps commanders and even lower officers in private where he would dole out patronage.

The political tensions within Zia's regime, and between the regime and the military, came to a head in the summer of 1988. In April, an ISI munitions dump used to arm the Afghan mujahedeen exploded in the heavily populated military capital of Rawalpindi, killing hundreds of civilians. To stem public outrage, Junejo demanded the resignation of the head of the ISI and the directorate's former head then serving as CJCS, perhaps the two generals with whom Zia was the closest.

In May, Zia responded by dismissing Junejo and dissolving the legislature. He did so without consulting with the VCOAS or corps commanders, and then ordered the weary Army to seize key buildings and arrest the civilian leaders of Zia's own government. Despite the political setbacks and rising unrest, Zia began making plans to reconstitute his government with new elections and stay in power. In August 1988, Zia, along with most of his closest military aides and the U.S. Ambassador to Islamabad, were killed when their C-130 crashed shortly after departing from a tank demonstration where much of the Army high command was in attendance. Upon Zia's death, the leadership of the country passed to VCOAS General Beg. Within hours of Zia's death, Beg, the corps commanders, and the GHQ staff reached a unanimous decision to return to the barracks. A civilian caretaker government was appointed to oversee free elections held in November 1988 in which the PPP under Benazir Bhutto, ZA Bhutto's daughter, regained power.

The Musharraf Regime: Pulling the Plug

Pakistan's fourth military regime occurred under COAS General Pervez Musharraf, who seized power in October 1999 after the civilian government under Nawaz Sharif attempted to fire Musharraf amid rising civil-military tension over Sharif's peace overtures to India and the military's subsequent provocation and defeat in the Kargil War.

In its formative years, the Musharraf regime's relationship with the military preceded much like the early years of the Zia regime. Defence spending increased, as did side benefits for the officer corps. Musharraf was deferential to his corps commanders and mindful to safeguard the military's corporate interests from his political endeavors. Musharraf anointed himself president and held faux elections for parliament with his own political party, the PML-Q, while he crushed the PPP and the offshoot of the Pakistani Muslim League loyal to Nawaz (PML-N).

By late 2006, however, Pakistan was besieged by surging militant violence pouring out of the Afghan border area where the Army was waging a war against rural tribes aligned with al-Qaeda and the Pakistani Taliban.

Amid the backdrop of the escalating extremist violence, the regime began to unravel in 2007 in the run up to Musharraf's presidential reelection and parliamentary elections as the military withdrew its support for the government. The judges Musharraf handpicked for the Supreme Court started to challenge the legality of the military regime, mainly his unconstitutional dual-hatted role as President and COAS. In response, Musharraf suspended the highly-respected Supreme Court in March, igniting riots across the country that lasted until his successful reelection in October. As protests demanding a return to democracy gripped the major cities, Musharraf acquiesced to the domestic and U.S. pressure to allow the PPP and PML-N to contest the next parliamentary elections in early 2008.

After the Supreme Court threatened to invalidate his reelection due to his position as COAS, Musharraf declared a national emergency, abrogated the constitution, suspended the court again, and ordered the Army into the streets to quell the unrest. Divisions between Musharraf and the military rapidly grew during the two-month emergency and the subsequent run-up to the parliamentary elections. The senior officers were likely extraordinarily unhappy with Musharraf's decision to have the Army forcibly step in to protect his political fortunes. Several weeks into the emergency, Musharraf stepped down as COAS and retired from the Army—the first of Pakistan's military rulers to relinquish the title and leave the military while in office—and was succeeded by General Ashfaq Parvez Kayani. In concurrence with the corps commanders, Kayani sought to refurbish the military's unity and prestige, and he signaled that the Army would no longer jeopardize its corporate interests for Musharraf, who would have to survive politically on his own laurels. Kayani ordered the hundreds of active duty officers assigned to civilian positions back into military service. To prevent Musharraf from politicking to his commanders, Kayani placed a ban on officers taking meetings with Musharraf or partaking in any political activity. The next month, hundreds of retired senior Army officers demanded Musharraf's resignation—a clear signal he had lost the support of the military. Days before the February 2008 parliamentary elections between Musharraf's PML-Q party and the opposition parties, Kayani ordered the Army and intelligence agencies not to interfere with or otherwise rig the polls. While Musharraf was still chief executive, his regime was on political life support and the Army was pulling the plug on the besieged military-as-government and returning itself to the barracks.

Without the military's backing, Musharraf's party was trounced at the ballot box by the PPP and PML-N. Suddenly, Musharraf faced near-certain impeachment from the new hostile parliament and likely criminal charges from the Supreme Court. Musharraf considered removing Kayani and dissolving the legislature, but he lacked supporters within the Army after Kayani had the handful of commanders still believed loyal to the beleaguered president reassigned. In August, Kayani reportedly informed Musharraf it was time for him to resign rather than fight the impeachment charges. In exchange the Army would secure him immunity from prosecution. With no leg to stand on, Musharraf resigned from the presidency and was replaced by President Asif Ali Zardari, Benazir Bhutto's widower and the leader of the PPP. In this instance, the military returned itself to the barracks and was content to sit idly by and watch Musharraf's regime crumble, confident its corporate interests were best served—at least for now—under a civilian government.

Inferences: What Causes Pakistan's Returns to the Barracks?

The Pakistani military has played a crucial role in ending the nation's four military regimes, and facilitating a return to the barracks and the transition to civilian government. Many scholars, however, have accepted returns to the barracks in Pakistan as an inevitability given the immediate circumstances surrounding them: a disastrous defeat on the battlefield (1971), the sudden death of the ruling general (1988), and widespread civil discontent (1969, 2008). Although these were certainly proximate causes, none of them alone were ultimately sufficient to force the military to withdraw. Rather, these factors presented the Army with opportunities to return to the barracks, and they mattered to the extent that each pushed apart or pulled together the interests of the active leaders of the armed forces and the leaders of the military regime. These events and their political contexts altered the military's underlying preference for how best to safeguard its corporate interests from reinforcing the status quo regime to selecting an alternative regime and staging a return to the barracks. Assessing Finer's three conditions for military withdrawals, the disintegration of the original conspirator group and the political difficulties of the regime can be seen as sub-variables of the divergence of interests between the military-as-government and the military-as-institution. Furthermore, there are several commonalities and patterns in these cases to explain how and why the divergence of interests occurs.

The Vice of Origin Problem: In the aftermath of a coup, the military regime's authority to govern is *pro tempore*. There is a fusion among the military and the newly-formed regime with shared interests and common goals, which allow the two to operate in relative harmony compared to the ousted civilian government. The threat to the military's corporate interests which triggered the coup is righted by the establishment of the military regime. In due time, the military rulers recognize they cannot rely on the military as a blunt instrument to provide legitimacy by force and expect it to repress domestic opposition in the long-term. The regime begins down a rocky path to legitimize itself through sham liberalization efforts. So long as the military's corporate interests are secured, it lends support to the regime's effort to legitimize itself. The rifts between the military and the regime are still young and shallow, but the regime's political difficulties at achieving legitimacy begin to drive a wedge between the two.

Rewards and Punishment: Pakistan's military regimes, like their civilian counterparts, have all suffered from severe control problems. Military and civilian leaders' efforts to control the military have generally been all carrot and no stick. The regimes are quick to provide economic incentives to the military by increasing defence spending, securing foreign arms suppliers, increasing pay, and providing side benefits. Neither military nor civilian leaders have engaged in elaborate coup-proofing measures, doubtlessly because such efforts would draw the ire of the military which would face a threat to its unity and monopoly on force. While both military and civilian leaders have frequently tinkered with the promotion system and top-brass assignments to install loyalists, these efforts prove inadequate. Moreover, wholesale liquidations or mass purges of the officer corps, a common feature of military regimes elsewhere, have not occurred in Pakistan. Without many sticks, there is clearly a stark limit to how far the regime can motivate the military to do its bidding through building informal personalistic-alliances and providing economic incentives when the military is faced with a high cost to its corporate interests.

Regime Maintenance: An authoritarian military regime only seizes and remains in power by the use or threat of violence. Once its military becomes unwilling to repress on the new regime's behalf or takes other actions towards achieving a return to the barracks, it is committing an act of shirking essentially equal to the original coup. Furthermore, by illegally seizing power when the military's corporate interests were threatened, the regime itself has set a strong precedent for the military to do so again under such conditions.

While all of Pakistan's coups have been relatively bloodless, there is often a brief period afterward when the military is willing to crackdown for the new military regime in order to reestablish calm. Over time, however, the military becomes gradually wearier of performing widespread regime maintenance at the expense of its corporate interests. At the same time, the regime's efforts to achieve legitimacy often begin to backfire as political opposition revives and greater repression is required. The military begins to shirk in protecting the regime from domestic political crises and officers form a preference to return to the barracks.

ROLE OF INSTITUTIONS IN MILITARY-POLITICS RELATIONS

From the preceding sections, the military itself with its senior leadership and their vested interests can be seen as the prime reason for its continued role in politics in Pakistan.

Even without direct martial law, the military maintained its influence through its intelligence agencies (ISI's creation of IJI) and otherwise (e.g. as a mediator in the aforementioned political tussle between Ghulam Ishaq Khan and Nawaz Sharif). The role of other institutions that have helped the military with its rule emerges:

The first and foremost reason was a weak parliament. Pakistan was without a constitution of its own until 1956. This weakened the parliamentary system and democratic norms could not develop (PMs were appointed by the head of the state rather than people). Zia did not let any institution strengthen that could serve as a threat to his rule. He weakened the political parties and the 1985 elections were held on non-party basis. The freedom of expression of the Press, one of the pre-requisites of democracy, had always been curtailed during martial laws and censorship laws were enforced. This control over the press reached its limit when in

1982 three journalists were flogged by the martial law regime due to political reasons.

The judiciary was weak during martial law regimes and otherwise when dealing with generals. Several of its decisions have had political fallout. For example, the 1953 decision of Justice Munir upheld the dissolution of the Constituent Assembly and thus weakened the nascent democratic process in Pakistan. After the 1977 coup, the Supreme Court validated the martial law on the basis of "doctrine of necessity". Its role during the Presidential referendum and later during the hearing of the Junejo Government restoration case (decision influenced by the COAS) marred its reputation significantly. The civil bureaucracy has essentially felt comfortable with whomever is in power, provided it was given a security of service. Ayub Khan's Basic Democracy system was an instrument which made politicians redundant and gave the bureaucracy an outreach at the village level and helped ensure continuity of his regime. In the Yahya Khan marital law, the bureaucracy was given a diminished role in administration and it was fragmented with the dismissal of 303 civil servants. However, the Zia-ul-Haq martial law saw a revival of the bureaucracy's role and several bureaucrats were given key positions in governance such as Mr Agha Shahi as the Foreign Minister.

The United States, although not an institute, has been perceived as the most significant foreign player in Pakistan's politics. American aid, especially during the Ayub Khan era and as a result of the Afghan War during Zia-ul-Haq's regime, consolidated the dictators' rule. With their extensive military aid to Pakistan in the 50s and commencement of officer training in US military schools, they gave the Pakistan Army an image of a vibrant and elite force occupying important place in national affairs. Akmal Hussain and Mushahid Hussain claim that according to now-declassified US State Department reports, General Ayub Khan was recognised as the 'King-maker' in Pakistan's politics by the Americans. The Cold War entered a new phase with the Soviet invasion of Afghanistan in 1979 and Pakistan became a front-line state. For the United States, dealing with a military dictator was much easier in such times. US assistance to Pakistan was resumed in 1983 with a \$3.2

billion package. Even though America was opposed to Zia's continuation of Pakistan's nuclear programme, it continued to help him because of the Afghan war and hence helped enormously in the strengthening of his rule.

Conclusion

Today the combined numerical strength of Pakistan's Armed Forces stands at about 560,000 as compared to 137,000 in 1949. India managed to curtail the powers of the military right after partition while in Pakistan it was wooed by politicians from the start - six months after the creation of Pakistan, Liaqat Ali Khan, who was the Prime Minister and the Defence Minister, defended very high allocation for defence in the first budget debate in the constituent assembly.

Defence budget continues to devour national resources at an alarming rate. In 1994, Pakistan entered into a deal with France to acquire 3 Agosta Class Submarines at a cost of $1billion and the deal is suspect because of several press reports of heavy kickbacks accrued to politicians and certain naval officers.

Even though the government has more than two thirds majority in the Parliament, it cannot touch the 'sacred cow' by reducing the defence budget. The military has always had the final say regarding arms procurement and retains the veto over security-related decisions.

This must change. The defence budget and acquisition process must be made transparent; reports of kick-backs and commissions must be investigated and the culprits put to justice, be it Mr Asif Zardari in the submarine or proposed Mirage-2000 deal or the sitting Naval Chief Admiral Mansoor-ul-Haque. The initiative rests with the government: accountability must also include the military.

It would be premature to say whether the 13 amendment has truly strengthened democracy in Pakistan for all times to come. However, with the cold war having ended, a free press and a judiciary separate from the executive and a strong government in Pakistan, any general will have to think a hundred times before following in the footsteps of his ambitious predecessors. And whether the vested interests in the military like it or not, the government must hold meaningful talks with India and resolve the disputes: starting with Siachin and eventually Kashmir.

Because otherwise both the countries will keep trying to match each other tank for tank and plane for plane until both collapse of sheer exhaustion. Especially prone to this is Pakistan with its economy in dire straits; the debt-retirement scheme is just a stop-gap measure, the real solution to the crisis is to reduce the defence budget (bilaterally with India) and divert resources to developmental and social sectors.

5

The Pakistani Army: Order of Battle

The Pakistani army is organized into nine Corps and Force Command Northern Area. These contain 22 divisions, 15 independent brigades (6 armoured and 9 infantry), 9 Corps artillery brigades, 7 engineering brigades and 15 army aviation squadrons - including two of attack helicopters. In addition, the Pakistani army has 8 air defence brigades. It must be pointed out, however, that Pakistani brigades and divisions are somewhat smaller than their Indian counterparts. Again, this order of battle differs to a certain extent from that normally quoted. The order of battle is as follows:

Pakistan's two principal fighting formations are Army Reserve North (ARN) and Army Reserve South (ARS). These are an approximate equivalent to the Indian Strike Corps in terms of size and composition. These have, as in the case of their Indian counterparts, a nucleus of a single armoured division and up to two infantry divisions with numerous brigades:

STATUS OF COMBAT ARMS

Armour

As in the case of the Indian army, the Pakistani army possesses three armoured division and a number of armoured brigades. These operate almost 2,500 Main Battle Tanks of a bewildering variety and from various generations. The most recent acquisitions are 320 T-80 UD MBTs from the Ukraine. This deal has been mired in controversy because of Russia's refusal to supply spares, including gun barrels, and doubts over Ukraine's ability to provide spares and support.

The T-80UD is a major improvement over the existing Pakistani tank fleet. The most modern units, until the arrival of the T-80UDs, were license made Chinese T-85 II tanks. An indigenous MBT - the Al-Khalid - has failed to materialise. The rest of the fleet consists of over a thousand T-69/-59 tanks of Chinese origin, which have been upgraded with 105mm guns. The rest of the fleet is a mixture of 1950s & 1960s vintage M-47/-48A5 tanks. These, while serviceable, are not really a match for even older Indian armour. The Pakistani tank fleet lacks modern fire control equipment and advanced night-fighting capabilities. It can be expected that Pakistan will attempt to rectify this in the near future.

Artillery

As in the case of its Indian counterpart, Pakistan's Regiment of Artillery has undergone a tremendous re-organization and modernization programme. While substantial quantities of new equipment have been inducted, large numbers of completely obsolete artillery pieces - long since relegated to reserve/storage status in the Indian army - remain in service.

Pakistan created the subcontinent's first artillery division using a core component of two artillery brigades and an air defence unit. While Pakistan has far fewer artillery tubes than the massive Indian artillery park, it is interesting to note that it was responsible for this major organizational innovation. The most noteworthy feature of Pakistan's artillery is the number of 155 and 203mm self-propelled guns. This gives Pakistani armour an integral artillery capability that is currently lacking in Indian armoured units. Moreover, these guns are more easily operated in an NBC environment than towed guns.

Pakistan's artillery also comprises an assortment of older pieces, including some Second World War vintage 25 pounders. As in the case of the Indian artillery, considerable progress has been made in the introduction of fire control computers and other surveillance and target acquisition equipment. This, of course, dramatically enhances the efficacy of artillery - no matter how old the guns are.

Infantry

There is not much difference between Pakistani and Indian army infantry formations. Pakistan has not developed an organization equivalent to the Indian RAPIDS and has not attempted the massive modernization programme - in terms of modern night vision, target finding and anti-tank weaponry - that the Indian army has recently undertaken. The only really noteworthy aspect of the Pakistani infantry is the fact that it was the first to introduce mechanized units to the subcontinent. These mechanized infantry units are provided with over eight hundred M-113 armoured personnel carriers. While not as capable as India's BMP-2 units, these older APCs provide Pakistan's infantry with a reasonable degree of battlefield mobility. However, as far as NBC warfare is concerned, these older APCs offer somewhat less protection than the BMPs.

Air Defense

Unlike the Indian army, Pakistan lacks any medium self-propelled surface-to-air missiles and modern self-propelled air-defence guns. Pakistan's six air defence brigades are equipped with a wide variety of shoulder-launched SAMs and thousands of towed air defence guns. These are used with both Western and Chinese fire-control radar. It is not known if Pakistan intends to obtain any more advanced radar and target acquisition equipment. The Pakistani army air defence units remain constrained in their ability to obtain advanced self-propelled air-defence assets since Russia, the principal producer of these items, will not sell these items to Pakistan. Strangely enough, Pakistan does not seem to be making particularly vigorous efforts to rectify this shortcoming in their army air defences.

NBC Warfare

Both the Indian and Pakistani armies are extremely well trained. This is especially true up to brigade level. Both armies possess a high degree of tactical skill and pride themselves on their ability to perform their assigned tasks. Using a mixture of traditional methods and modern techniques and equipment, both armies are extremely capable. In the area of NBC warfare, however, a rather confusing picture emerges. Both countries frequently made mention of their ability to fight in NBC conditions, but little hard information is available on the degree of NBC readiness.

In the 1980s, the Indian army began some tentative preparations for NBC warfare. In the early part of that decade, a limited quantity of S6 respirators and No.1Mk.3 NBC suits - both of British origin - was purchased. A quantity of NBC equipment was imported from the USSR, but proved to be useless in Indian environmental conditions. Moreover, India's defence research organization, in 1987, produced prototypes of NBC suits, decontamination suits, facelets, overboots and NBC tents. This equipment has entered production and service with the Indian armed forces.

As regards training, from 1987 onwards, the Indian army, through its College of Military Engineering, began running familiarization courses in NBC warfare, while scientist conducted courses at brigade level. Moreover, a series of studies were undertaken to provide for both active and passive defence against nuclear attack for army combat formations.

As regards equipment, the Indian Ministry of Defence has obviously allocated high priority to the indigenous production of NBC gear.

This has also involved the participation of the private sector for the manufacture of both NBC suits and respirators. In addition, the Indian army has retained its old Second World War respirators - these are old, but would still offer significant protection. India would not find it particularly difficult to produce enough NBC personal gear - respirators and NBC suits - for its armed forces in a relatively short period of time - though this equipment might be placed in storage. Mention should also be made of the fact that a new decontamination vehicle has entered production.

While it is abundantly clear that NBC warfare has been accorded a much higher priority in the Indian army, it remains unclear as to the exact status of NBC preparedness and training in the Indian army. Attempts to contact senior military officers on this subject proved unsuccessful, though some retired officers offered some vague information that leads to the conclusion that some training is in progress.

It has become clear that India's Army Training Command has conducted detailed studies into NBC warfare. Indeed, given India's perception of its nuclear threat, it is not surprising that the Indian army schools of instruction and combat include NBC scenarios. Moreover, the publisher of the prestigious Indian Defence Review stated that the forces earmarked for use against Pakistan are well equipped to deal with NBC warfare.

It would be natural for India's Strike Corps to be the first to be fully equipped and prepared for NBC warfare and there are some indications of this beginning to occur. It is highly probable that at least one Corps is fully prepared - trained and equipped for NBC warfare.

The other formations would probably receive personal NBC gear - but will be allocated a lower priority for receiving decontamination and monitoring equipment. It should be pointed out that the RAPIDS require virtually no modifications for deployment in an NBC environment.

It can probably be assumed that the state of NBC warfare in Pakistan is in a similar state to that of India, except that Pakistan's industry is not yet capable of meeting all NBC needs and that the country lacks the massive R & D infrastructure of India. Indian sources assume that Pakistan has a nucleus of NBC trained personnel - with Chinese NBC gear.

One thing is clear, however, both countries have now made NBC warfare something of a priority and are making efforts - covertly - to train and equip themselves. Nonetheless, there may be a large gap between what the military wants and reality.

While there is some reference to NBC warfare and the necessity to fight under such conditions in both armies, there have never been any major NBC exercises conducted by either side. It is therefore not inconceivable that the principal focus of NBC training and equipment programs in both countries is more geared towards meeting an emergency that might arise after one side uses such weapons. This would involve stockpiling equipment and drafting rapid training instructions - aimed at rapidly familiarizing troops who have to enter an NBC contaminated area. It does not seem that either country intends to develop a tactical nuclear warfare doctrine.

One of the reasons for the lack of NBC exercises could be the extremely severe environmental conditions prevailing on the South Asian battlefield. These conditions range from the intense cold of the Siachen glacier to the blistering heat of the Thar desert. Under normal peacetime conditions these climates pose great difficulties for human endurance, if the troops were clad in full NBC gear and armoured vehicles 'buttoned-up', there would be more casualties from heat-stroke than from exposure.

This brings us to the other issue that needs to be considered - where on the South Asian battlefield could tactical nuclear weapons possibly be used ? The answer to this question will determine whether or not there is any battlefield use for nuclear weapons.

PAKISTAN ARMY MOVED INTO THE POLITICAL ARENA

Pakistan Army, throughout its 54 years of existence, has been involved in the administration of the country — often in augmentation of bureaucracy in purely civil jobs, occasionally in aid of civil power for maintenance of law and order and off and on in governing the country under Martial Law regimes. It has earned kudos and criticism depending on its aims and achievements in the assigned or assumed tasks. Escorting caravans of refugees, fighting floods, checking illegal trade, running steamers and trains, building roads or killing wild boars were all people friendly activities. Number of times troops were called out in aid of civil power for maintenance of public peace and imposition of the will of the government. Lahore (1953), Kalat (1958), Dir-Bajaur (1961), Balochistan (1974) are examples that fall in this category. These operations were constitutional and executed with efficiency and elan.

Three times 1958, 1969 and 1977 the whole country was placed under Martial Law. In 1999 when the mismanagement of a ruthless dictator had reached a new zenith the Army moved in and replaced the civilian government. Martial Law was not declared. The regime received its legitimacy from the Supreme Court. In all these cases, the purists have vehemently argued against assumption of civil power by the army.

According to them, problems of political adjustment and consensus could have been sorted out through the political process had it been allowed the time. Others make vigorous case in favour of the army leaders' actions and credit them with having saved the country at relevant times.

However, even by the standards of pro-military elements the glaring failure of army leadership to keep the country together in 1971, prevent estrangement of Balochistan in the wake of 1974 Marri-Bugti operations and thwart understated hostility in Sindh during the MRD movement (1983) are exceptions that cannot be glossed over lightly.

It must also be admitted that differences did exist in the perceptions of junior ranks and the leadership component on the role of the army in situations that were purely political. It goes to the credit of the institution and its leadership that the essential unity of the force has remained rock solid. For this compliments are due to the moral and mental prowess of the army commanders who at relevant times were able to convince the rank and file and indeed the whole country that army's actions were indeed in the defence and extension of supreme national interest. Part of credit must go to army's recruitment and training policies that emphasise loyalty under stress and willing subordination of the individual to the collective will of the institution.

Now back to history. The departing British rulers had initially not contemplated the division of the Indian Army. The Chiefs of Staff in London had 'hoped for a political settlement'. When the Quaid made it clear that he meant to see Pakistan a fully independent country with no binds on its sovereignty, the directive for the bifurcation of the Indian Army was issued. Liaquat Ali Khan echoed the Quaid and said that Pakistan without an army would collapse like a 'house of cards'. Muslim League was resolved to take over only when the incipient government of Pakistan had its army and under its own control.

A degree of emphasis is detectable. Why such a stance? Was it solely due to the external dangers that undoubtedly loomed large? Or did their concerns have an internal dimension also? Wasn't there an element of doubt in the mind of the two leaders about the capability of political institutions to control and ensure cohesion in the newly acquired state?

'Moth-eaten,' lamented the Quaid-e-Azam when he first saw the map of Pakistan. Implied was a cause to worry and a reason for speedy acquisition of strength to offset the diminished capability. Machinations of the Hindu bureaucracy in the Ministry of Defence ensured that Pakistan's Armed Forces are denied their rightful share of defence equipment.

The new state with no government machinery and infrastructure faced danger from two sides. An influx of refugees and a war in Kashmir in the east and claims to the Frontier province by Afghanistan in the west put Pakistan in a bind. However, despite meagreness in men and material, the Army proved to be the most effective, reliable and stable among the instruments of state power.

Colossal problems and chaos on one hand and proven effectiveness of the army on the other persuaded the early rulers to quickly 'starch the limp security apparatus' they had inherited. The Army claimed and received special patronage from the government. In view of what it could be asked to do in a situation of extreme uncertainty allocation of resources was perfectly justified.

Says Stephen Cohen in his treatise on Pakistan Army, 'There are armies that guard the nation's borders, there are those that are concerned with protecting their own position in the society, and there are those that defend a cause or an idea. The Pakistan Army does all three.' This is a tall order. Its successful fulfilment demands equal in size resources implying a position of pre-eminence in the financial and hence political scheme of things.

The task of maintenance of national unity and cohesion also fell to the lot of the army by default. Pakistan's political leadership was land based and parochial in make-up, approach and outlook. The top rung was always prone to suggestions, allurements and intimidation. In the absence of strong political programmes, parties aspiring for power made no appeal to the people. National politics was confined to the drawing rooms of the elite. Inevitably a permanent climate of instability, like that of monsoon weather alternating regularly between the fair and the cloudy was created.

Pakistan Peoples Party of 1967-71 was an exception but soon after its assumption of power it also became like any other grouping of the established classes. In good time the PPP became to be identified more as a disturber of social harmony and tranquillity than a proponent of a new social order.

Now go back in time again and witness displacements and degradations of governments. At provincial level changes started from the first day of independence. Dismissal of Dr. Khan Sahib ministry in the Frontier on the morrow of independence was followed sometime later by Khurro in Sindh and Mamdot in the Punjab. This points out to early fissures between the centres of power. In East Pakistan Mr. Nur ul Amin was defeated in elections by a student that went to highlight the gulf between the ruling party and popular sentiment.

At the centre a game of musical chairs started after the assassination of Liaquat Ali Khan in 1951. In such a scenario everything had to come to a stand still. After 9 years of impasse, a constitution was finally promulgated only to be abrogated two years later. By then, the politics of Pakistan had entered a dark phase. Sectarianism and parochialism had taken root. Occasionally riots were choreographed for show of force and intimidation. Leaders of political establishment, instead of focussing on the national level crises concentrated on games of power and pelf. The main political party, the Muslim League split up under such pressures.

The vacuum had to be filled in consonance with the laws of nature. The Army moved in on a very good logic. Political instability was affecting the integrity of the Army and hence the defence of the nation was jeopardised. The situation had to be put right. General Ayub Khan, first the Chief Martial Law Administrator, a little later the President, eagerly and competently filled the top leadership slot. He was a military man and had a clear mind but an authoritarian style. He had the Constitution of 1962 tailor made to his requirements. However, he ruled well and laid the foundations for the industrialisation of the country. He also laid the foundations of break up of Quaid-e-Azam's Pakistan.

He authorised a war over Kashmir soon after his victory against Miss Fatima Jinnah in the presidential election. Pakistan Army failed in its objectives in Kashmir (1965) but did succeed in defending the country against Indian invasion across international borders. The pointless war disillusioned people particularly in East Pakistan where they felt insecure, unprotected and exploited. By 1968 movement against Ayub government gathered tremendous momentum and in March 1969 he stepped aside handing over power to the Commander-in-Chief of the Army. Some observers point out that around that time the establishment led by Ayub Khan took the decision to let East Pakistan go its separate way. They point out that it was in conformity with that bias that General Ayub Khan handed over power to the Commander-in-Chief rather than to the Speaker of the National Assembly as was laid down in his own constitution. Theories that General Yahya Khan forced Ayub out are not convincing and are certainly not held out either by the character of Yahya Khan or by the events that followed.

Under General Yahya Khan came the East Pakistan tragedy. Thousands of innocent citizens were killed and the ensuing war resulted in the break of Quaid-e-Azam's Pakistan and emergence of Bangladesh. But was the Army as an institution to blame? Had not the political establishment coaxed, cajoled and encouraged the Army in its actions. Read again the first comment on the army action in Dacca on 26th March 1971 'Thank God, Pakistan has been saved'. It came from a political leader, Mr. Bhutto.

Mr. Bhutto, became the CMLA and the President before he became the first elected Prime Minister of Pakistan. Such was the influence of the military on a 'champion of democracy'. To remove a counterpoise, he quickly forced out General Gul Hassan Khan the incumbent C-in-C who according to many was instrumental in Mr. Bhutto's accession to power.

General Tikka Khan served loyally for four years. Then Mr. Bhutto in preference to a number of other equally competent officers selected General Zia-ul-Haq as the next Chief of Army Staff mainly because he believed the latter to be more reliable.

Events following the 1977 elections, created a crisis of huge proportions. The whole nation was in turmoil and the Army once again took over the administration of the country. True that the Army had intervened only when the country was on the verge of a civil war but equally true is the fact that there was a presence of highly ambitious officers among the top brass. Stephen Cohen mentions that Bhutto had been warned of the dangerous consequences of military crackdown in Balochistan as the middle ranks of Officer Corps were acquiring a taste for political power. Obviously, Mr. Bhutto ignored the warnings.

General Zia proceeded cautiously and read the whole situation carefully. He came up with a perfect solution. He realised that the Pakistani people could be easily rallied under the slogans of Islamisation. He promised Nizam-e-Mustafa leaving its definition in contemporary economic and political terms as vague. Under this scheme Zia acquired the brawn of the street in addition to the power of the state. With this intermixture of formal and informal power came a deeper penetration of the Army into politics. The army also assumed the role of the defender of the ideological borders of the state to the joy of a certain group.

Then in 1979 Soviet Union intervened in Afghanistan. Here the interests of Afghan Mujahideen, Pakistan, United States, China and other Muslim countries came to coincide. Pakistan supported Afghans and the Army trained Mujahideen guerrillas with American weapons. Mujahideen's success was a great plume in the hat of Pakistan Army but the country was left plagued with the fallout.

Zia's era ended in 1988. Some people draw a comparison between the regimes of Ayub and Zia. Although the two regimes lasted about the same number of years but Zia would have continued, had he not been killed in the air crash. Ayub Khan was a reformer who treaded on a number of toes in pursuit of a social agenda. Zia didn't commit that mistake. He brought about no reforms but preserved the status quo in the name of piety. As leader of the army also he was no patch on Ayub. Ayub's army was spick and span; straight, professional and exclusive. Zia transformed it beyond recognition to some of its old souls. It became 'awami' in culture, threw away its exclusivity, acquired hypocrisy, cultivated the art of compromise on standards and learnt the many unsavoury ways that were considered essential to ruling Pakistan.

After General Zia, came General Aslam Beg who now runs an NGO and a political party. He exercised political power through proxy. General Asif Nawaz, who was a little more forthright, created waves when he took on the MQM in Karachi although the party was a partner in the coalition at the centre. General Abdul Wahid was unobtrusive. However, when the occasion called, he exercised the power of his office in a most decisive manner and saw his constitutional bosses President Ghulam Ishaq Khan and Prime Minister Nawaz Sharif out of office. General Karamat was tolerable but towards the fag end of his tenure he was asked to resign over a non-issue. This highhandedness did not go well with the Army.

This was a period when a naval chief also had to go due to a corruption scandal. The overall image of the forces was badly smeared. Their former sheen and prestige had suffered. Their confidence and sharpness was reduced. They came to be treated like any other department of the Government of Pakistan and often assigned duties far removed from the business of warfare. Somewhere along the line they also picked up some of the tasteless peculiarities of their civilian counterparts and became poorer in self-regard.

In such a season of despair, General Pervez Musharraf took over as Chief of Army Staff. His first concern was restoration of the morale of the command. Kargil was an opportunity and he made the best of it. The soldiers found their mettle and were well on their way when the Prime Minister bungled. Victory won in the field was thrown away. Showing complete ignorance of the military system he began to conspire against his own Army Chief. A badly choreographed drama to sack the COAS rebounded with a force that knocked the Prime Minister from his perch.

Having taken over the country as a result of the consensual action by the army, General Pervez Musharraf is now striving for continuity. People have tentatively put their faith in the General and are hoping for results.

Mr.Nawaz Sharif like some of his predecessors had badly underestimated General Pervez Musharraf both as a leader of the army and leader of the country.

STRUCTURE OF THE PAKISTAN ARMY

The Structure of the Pakistan Army can be broken down two ways, administrative, and operational. Operationally the Pakistan Army is divided in 11 Corps having areas of responsibility (AOR) from mountainous regions of northern Pakistan to the desert and coastal regions of the south.

Administratively it is divided in different regiments. The General Headquarters (GHQ) of Pakistan Army is located in the garrison city of Rawalpindi in Punjab province. It is planned to be moved to the capital city of Islamabad.

Other Field Formations

- Division: An Army Division is an intermediate between a Corps and a Brigade. It is the largest striking force in the army. Each Division is headed by [General Officer Commanding] (GOC) in the rank of Major General. It usually consists of 15,000 combat troops and 8,000 support elements. Currently, the Pakistani Army has 29 Divisions including 20 Infantry Divisions, 2 Armoured Divisions, 2 Mechanized Divisions, 2 Air Defence Divisions, 2 Strategic Divisions and 1 Artillery Division. Each Division composes of several Brigades.
- Brigade: A Brigade generally consists of around 3,000 combat troops with supporting elements. An Infantry

Brigade usually has 3 Infantry Battalions along with various Support Arms & Services. It is headed by a Brigadier, equivalent to a Brigadier General in some armies. In addition to the Brigades in various Army Divisions, the Pakistani Army also has 7 Independent Armoured Brigades, 5 Independent Artillery Brigades, 3 Independent Infantry Brigades, and 3 Anti-Tank Brigades. These Independent Brigades operate directly under the Corps Commander.

- Regiment: A regiment is commanded by a Colonel.
- Battalion: A Battalion is commanded by a Lieutenant-Colonel and is the Infantry's main fighting unit. It consists of more than 900 combat personnel.
- Company: Headed by the Major/Captain, a Company comprises about 120–150 soldiers.
- Platoon: An intermediate between a Company and Section, a Platoon is headed by a Lieutenant or depending on the availability of Commissioned Officers, a Junior Commissioned Officer, with the rank of Subedar or Naib-Subedar. It has a total strength of about 30–36 troops.
- Section: Smallest military outfit with a strength of about 9–13 personnel. Commanded by a Non-commissioned officer of the rank of Havildar Major or Sergeant Major.

Regiments

There are several battalions or units associated together in an infantry regiment. The infantry regiment in the Pakistani Army is an administrative military organisation and not a field formation. All the battalions of a regiment do not fight together as one formation, but are dispersed over various formations, viz. brigades, divisions and corps. An infantry battalion serves for a period of time under a formation and then moves to another, usually in another sector or terrain when its tenure is over. Occasionally, battalions of the same regiment may serve together for a tenure.

Most of the infantry regiments of the Pakistani Army originate from the old British Indian Army and recruit troops from a region or of specific ethnicities. Regiments of the Pakistani Army include:

Special Forces

The Special Services Group (SSG) is an independent commando regiment/corps of the Pakistan Army. It is an elite special operations force similar to the United States Army Special Forces (Green Berets) and the British Army's SAS.

Personnel

According to the International Institute for Strategic Studies (IISS) the Pakistan Army has an active force of 725,000 personnel in 2013. In addition there were around 500,000 reserves bringing the total to 1,225,000.

Enlisted Ranks

Most enlisted personnel used to come from rural families, and many have only rudimentary literacy skills, but with the increase in the literacy level the requirements have been raised to Matriculate level (10th Grade). Recruits are processed gradually through a paternalistically run regimental training centre, taught the official language, Urdu, if necessary, and given a period of elementary education before their military training actually starts. In the thirty-six-week training period, they develop an attachment to the regiment they will remain with through much of their careers and begin to develop a sense of being a Pakistani rather than primarily a member of a tribe or a village. Enlisted men usually serve for eighteen years, during which they participate in regular training cycles and have the opportunity to take academic courses to help them advance.

Officer Ranks

Each year, about 320 men and women enter the Army bi-annually through the Pakistan Military Academy at Kakul in Abbottabad in the Khyber Pakhtunkhwa; a small number—like doctors and technical specialists—are directly recruited, and are part of the officer corps. The product of a highly competitive selection process, members of the officer corps have completed twelve years of education and spend two years at the Pakistan Military Academy, with their time divided about equally between military training and academic work to bring them up to a baccalaureate education level, which includes English-language skills.

Academic Institutions

The Army has twelve other training and educational establishments, including schools concentrating on specific skills such as infantry, artillery, intelligence, engineering, or mountain warfare. The National University of Sciences and Technology (NUST) has been established which has absorbed the existing colleges of engineering, signals, electrical engineering and medicine. At the apex of the army training system is the Command and Staff College at Quetta, one of the few institutions inherited from the colonial period. The college offers a ten-month course in tactics, staff duties, administration, and command functions through the division level. Students from foreign countries, including the United States, have attended the school but reportedly have been critical of its narrow focus and failure to encourage speculative thinking or to give adequate attention to less glamorous subjects, such as logistics.

The senior training institution for all service branches is the National Defence University, Islamabad. Originally established in 1971 at Rawalpindi, to provide training in higher military strategy for senior officers, the institution was relocated to Islamabad in 1995. It also offers courses that allow civilians to explore the broader aspects of national security. In a program begun in the 1980s to upgrade the intellectual standards of the officer corps and increase awareness of the wider world, a small group of officers, has been detailed to academic training, achieving master's degrees and even doctorates at universities in Pakistan and abroad.

Pakistani officers were sent abroad during the 1950s and into the 1960s for training in Britain and other Commonwealth countries, and the United States, where trainees numbering well in the hundreds attended a full range of institutions ranging from armoured and infantry schools to the higher staff and command institutions. After 1961 this training was coordinated under the International Military Education and Training (IMET) program, but numbers varied along with the vicissitudes of the United States-Pakistan military relationship. Of some 200 officers being sent abroad annually in the 1980s, over two-thirds went to the United States, but the cessation of United States aid in 1990 entailed suspension of the IMET program. In 1994 virtually all foreign training was in Commonwealth countries. However, after the 9/11 attacks, Pakistan again begun sending officers to US Army schools. Today there are more than 400 officers serving in foreign countries. Officers retire between the ages of fifty-two and sixty, depending on their rank.

Science and Technology

Apart from conducting military operations, exercises, and military ethics, the Pakistan Army maintains its own science and technology corps and organizations. Most notable science and engineering corps including Military Engineering Service (MES) Corps of Engineers, Corps of Electrical and Mechanical Engineering (EME), and Frontier Works Organisation. Its Army Strategic Forces Command served as the primary military organization in the matters of conducting and directing research on nuclear and space (such as military satellites). The cadets and officers of the Pakistan Army who wished to study science and technology are given admission at the College of Electrical and Mechanical Engineering (CEME) and the Military College of Engineering where the scientific and military education are taught. The admissions of engineering colleges are not restricted to civilians as they can also gain admission and graduate with engineering and science degrees.

Uniforms

Pakistan Army uniforms closely resemble those of the British Armed Forces. The principal colour is greenish brown. Dress uniforms were worn mostly on formal occasions. The service uniform was worn for daily duty. The service uniform for the ground forces was khaki (sand/tan) cotton. Officers purchased their uniforms, but enlisted personnel received a standard uniform issue, which consisted of service and field uniforms, fatigues, and in some cases, dress uniforms. The uniforms consisted of shirt, trousers, sweater, jacket or blouse, and boots. There is also a white dress uniform. The fatigues were the same for winter and summer. Heavy winter gear was issued as needed. Headgear included a service cap for dress and semi-dress and a field cap worn with fatigues. Army personnel also wear berets, usually worn in lieu of the service cap.

Brown and black and more recently former US BDU style camouflage fatigues are worn by army troop units. The uniform of a Pakistan army soldier exhibits much information i.e.

Pakistan Army has introduced pixilated arid camouflage pattern in uniform and resized qualification badges which are now colourless and service ribbons are no longer worn along with the ranks are now embroidered and are on chest. The name is embroidered and is on right pocket and the left pocket displays embroidered Pak Army. Flag of Pakistan is placed over the black embroidered formation sign on the left arm and adventure course insignias are put up as per ADR for khaki uniform, decorations & awards and the ranks.

Ethnic Composition

Traditionally, the army was a predominantly Punjabi force because of its dominant Population (Punjab is the most populous province of Pakistan, with approximately 45% of the country's total population). In British India, three districts: Jhelum, Rawalpindi, and Campbellpur (now Attock) dominated the recruitment flows. By 2007 the percentage representation in the Pakistan Army as a whole was approximate as follows:

Punjabis: 53.19%

Pashtuns: 21%

Sindhis: 13.5%

Kashmiris: 9.11%

Baloch: 3.2%.

Extensive efforts have been made to bring the Baloch and Sindhis on par with other ethnicities, presently the Army recruitment system is enlisting personnel district-wise irrespective of provincial boundaries. This decision has given a fair chance to every citizen of Pakistan to be part of the Pakistan Army as each district possesses a fixed percentage of seats in all branches of the army, as per census records. Large numbers of men from Sindh and Balochistan have joined the ranks of the army and have proved their commitment and bravery to the national cause in Kargil and the ongoing global war on terrorism.

Women and non-Muslim Pakistanis

Women have served in the Pakistan Army since its foundation. Currently, there is a sizeable number of women serving in the Pakistan Army. Most women are recruited in the Army to perform medical and educational work. There is also a Women's Guard section of Pakistan's National Guard where women are trained in nursing, welfare and clerical work and there are also women recruited in very limited numbers for the Janbaz Force. Only recently has Pakistan began to recruit women for combat positions and the Elite Anti-Terrorist Force in 2007, several female graduates were nominated to be Sky Marshals for Pakistan based airlines. In addition recently eight of the 41 cadets from the Pakistan Military Academy at Kakul became the first women guards of honour. Pakistan is the only country in the Islamic world to have female *Major Generals* in the Army. Major General Shahida Badshah was Pakistan's first female two-star general.

Non Muslim Pakistanis are allowed to sit in all examinations and serve in any part of the Pakistan Army.

There have been numerous Christians who have risen to the rank of Brigadier; and in the 1990 the first Christian promoted to the rank of Major General was Julian Peter who commanded the 14th Div in Okara Cantt. In 2009 brigadier Noel Israel Khokhar, was also promoted to rank of Major General. Capt. Hercharn Singh, the first Sikh as Commissioned Officer in Pakistan Army. He was commissioned in Baloch Regiment. Currently, he's serving as an ADC to a Corps Commander.

Recipients of Nishan-e-Haider

The Nishan-e-Haider (Sign of the Lion) is the highest military award given by Pakistan, ranking above the Hilal-i-Jur'at (Crescent of Courage). Nishan-e-Haider recipients receive an honorary title as a sign of respect: *Shaheed* meaning *martyr* for deceased recipients. As of 19 Sep 2013, all Nishan-e-Haider awards have thus far been given to the people engaged in battles with India.

MILITANT GROUP APPEALS TO PAK ARMY

The Pakistan Army is reported to have taken into custody one serving Brigadier and four Majors for having links with the Hizb-ut-Tehrir (Party of Liberation). On December 17,2010, the Pakistani chapter of the Hizb-ut-Tehrir had issued an open letter to the Pakistani armed forces, calling upon "sincere" Islamic soldiers to establish Khilafah (Islamic caliphate) in Pakistan.

The letter, titled *O Muslims! Deliver This Letter to All the Sincere Ones Whom You Know in Pakistan's Armed Forces* accused Pakistani rulers of bowing before the United States and India. The letter was published simultaneously in English and Urdu on Hizb-ut-Tehrir's website.

The letter said:

"You are leading the largest and most capable Muslim armed forces in the world. The Muslim armed forces alone have the material strength to establish the Khilafah. As such you are the successors of the noble Ansar, who gave the material support (Nussrah) to Sayyedenah Muhammad... [Peace be upon him] for the establishment of the Islamic state in Madinah [the Saudi city].

Moreover, you must move now to uproot Pakistan's traitor rulers. For even though the weaknesses of America and India are more evident than ever before, Pakistan's traitor rulers are racing to extend support to them, using the considerable resources of the Muslims to do so.

"O officers of Pakistan's armed forces!

"As for America, her economy is collapsing... America is afraid that her defeat in Afghanistan, known as the 'graveyard of empires,' would spell doom for her own capitalist empire. As such America is compelled to exhaust her resources in a quagmire, just like the Soviet and British empires before her.

"But rather than allowing America's occupation [of Afghanistan] to collapse, the traitor rulers [of Pakistan] are working to extend America's foothold in the region. Using the excuses of training and intelligence sharing, the rulers have granted America an unprecedented presence within Pakistan.

America has officers that walk through Pakistan Army's General Headquarters with their sleeves rolled up, making themselves at home. She has Marines in Baluchistan trying to secure the area adjacent to the Chaman border [along Afghanistan]. American intelligence directs operations, including drone attacks, whilst sitting in truck containers, with air-conditioning units visible in the summer.

"America's Air Force personnel have a permanent presence in [the Pakistani town of] Jacobabad. Her private military organizations fan fear within the people, through brutal attacks in the markets, streets and mosques. Her military and intelligence personnel are flooding into Pakistan through Dubai under an agreement with the traitor rulers. And these are just some of the examples, O brothers."

"[Pakistani] rulers have created a war-like situation, which is not between the kafir [infidel] American occupiers and the Muslims, as it should have been – but between Muslims, the Muslims of the tribal areas, and Pakistan's armed forces"

"Compensating for America's own troops' lack of bravery and her Western allies' withdrawal from the occupying forces, the traitor rulers ensure that the full burden of America's dirty and tough war is on your shoulders. You can witness how much America needs you from the fact that the [Pakistan Army's] delay in the North Waziristan operation, [as a means] to support America's operations in Kandahar, forced US President Barack Obama to announce a delay in America's limited troop withdrawal from Afghanistan.

"As yet another service to America, the traitor rulers use a mixture of deception, bribery and threats to persuade you to fight. The traitor rulers publicize that America can initiate the break up of Pakistan and threaten its nuclear arsenal, as pretexts to justify their continued support to America... it is their [i.e. Pakistani rulers'] very support that allowed America into the region, [and] supplies… [of] weapons and food [through Pakistani territory, which help] expand her presence within Pakistan.

"The traitor rulers publicise Western aid [for example,. for Pakistan flood victims] to say that beggars cannot be choosers and so Pakistan is compelled to assist America – even though loans from the Western capitalist colonialist have only ever come with conditions to ensure economic exploitation of resources, from Africa to Latin America, and even though this region's immense resource wealth is one of the factors that prompted America to invest billions in its war."

"O officers of Pakistan's armed forces!

"As for India, after over 60 years of oppressive and discriminatory Hindu rule, India is a fragile entity that is weaker than ever before, with a myriad of separatist movements working to tear her apart. Moreover, India lacks essential resources and is dependent on the Muslim Lands [unclear] for providing gas and oil as well as securing sea and land routes for mineral resources.

"But rather than working to end the oppressive Hindu rule, Pakistan's traitor rulers have worked to strengthen it, for the sake of America, who seeks to woo India into its influence, to counter China and any Khilafah that arises. The traitor rulers mobilize Pakistan's security forces to persecute and arrest the Kashmiri Mujahideen, granting the cowardly Hindu occupying forces a great gift, which they neither deserve nor could achieve for themselves.

"The [Pakistani] rulers assisted India in fencing the Line of Control, consolidating the Hindu occupation [of Kashmir]. And the traitor rulers protect the American occupation which established a foothold for India in Afghanistan, in the form of consulates, from which Indian intelligence launches mischief in Baluchistan and the tribal areas.

"O officers of Pakistan's armed forces!

"The traitor rulers are allying with the kuffar [infidels], as if this was the source of strength and well-being for the Muslims. In reality, alliance with the kuffar is a source of fragility, weakness, despair and humiliation. Allah… said, 'The parable of those who seek allies other than Allah is that of a spider who builds a house; but indeed, the weakest of houses is the spider's house – if they but knew' (Surah Al-Ankaboot 29:41).

"You must seize the traitor rulers and end their support of the Ummah's enemies. The situation is on your side, your enemies are faltering and you are strong. Your strength can be seen from the fact that you faced American- and Indian-backed mischief in the tribal areas and Baluchistan, whilst being tested simultaneously by floods and traitor rulers.

"Above all, you are a Muslim army that believes in victory and martyrdom, which multiplies your strength. The Islamic feelings run deep within you, so you witnessed no desertions when fighting the kuffar to defend Muslims in Kashmir, but you witnessed many when fighting Muslims in the tribal areas to defend America. It is these Islamic feelings that America fears and wants removed from you."

"O officers of Pakistan's armed forces!

"Some of you stand with the traitor rulers and the kuffar Americans, supporting them for worldly gains with full knowledge of the mischief that they do. Know that such people will be punished with the traitors at the hands of the Ummah when the Khilafah is established soon, Insha Allah [Allah willing]. And know that Allah's punishment... is greater than any suffering in this life. Allah... said, 'So, Allah made them taste the disgrace in the present life, but greater is the torment of the Hereafter if they only knew' (Surah Al-Zamar 39:26).

"Others of you are silent, squandering the strength that Allah... has bestowed upon you and about which you will be asked on the Day of all Days. Do you not see how the army of Fir'awn [i.e. Pharaoh, the evil hegemon] was punished along with the tyrant they obeyed? Does this life and its fleeting pleasures tempt you from the eternal bliss of Jannah [Heaven]?

"Allah... said, 'O you who believe! What is the matter with you, that when you are asked to march forth in the cause of Allah, you cling heavily to the earth? Are you pleased with the life of this world rather than the Hereafter? But little is the enjoyment of the life of this world compared to the Hereafter' (Surah at-Tawba 9:38).

POLITICAL-ARMY-INTEL WRITING PAK OBITUARY?

The assassination of Punjab Governor Salman Taseer followed by the killing of Federal Minister for Minority Affairs, Shabaz Bhatti for their liberal views and their support for expunging the Blasphemy law from the constitution are sending a shiver down the spine of those Pakistanis who aspire for a liberal, democratic and prosperous Pakistan. After all, Pakistan was once a country with the highest per capita GDP in South Asia. What happened? Shall we ask the late Pakistani Army Chief and President Gen. Zia-ul-Haq?

Following the assassination of Shabaz Bhatti, a Christian, on March 02, the Tehrik-e-Taliban Pakistan (TTP) warned that all those who oppose the Blasphemy law and insult Islam will meet the same fate. Who is the next target? Ms. Sherry Rehman who introduced the bill in the National Assembly to amend the Blasphemy law? Or will this extend to all minorities or "infidels" in Pakistan including the Ahmedias? According to Pakistani law Ahmedias are not Muslims, and they are a persecuted community. Despite their declared good intentions, the current government in Pakistan remains weak. This is precisely because the Army-ISI establishment calls the shots in strategic areas. The issue of terrorist/ jehadi groups in Pakistan is considered a very important issue. There have been no comments on the assassinations of Taseer and Bhatti from the army. They may hide behind the excuse that they do not interfere in governance and law and order issues. It is also intriguing that the army has not acted openly in the various militant attacks on it and the ISI's establishments in Lahore and Rawalpindi. Yet they operate at times in the tribal areas though selectively, and it is the army under President Musharraf that attacked the Lal Masjid in 2007, killing about two thousand or more. The critical issue then was that the mullahs had abducted some Chinese citizens allegedly for immoral activities, and Musharraf received a direct ultimatum from Chinese President Hu Jintao for their immediate release. Otherwise, Musharraf knew what exactly was happening in Lal Masjid and did nothing about it.

There is a perception that the Lal Masjid episode turned the Islamists against the entire establishment and catalyzed their growth. That may be partially but not entirely true. The roots go back to Zia's Islamization programme positing himself as the Caliph of Pakistan. He tried to Islamise in an obscurantist agenda every vein in Pakistan. And he portrayed India as an existential enemy which even Gen. Ayub Khan, a Westernized man, had ever thought of.

Since then Islamism-terrorism –India became a heady mix in Pakistan's politics and strategy, a combination which is very difficult to root out. Any hard line against religious ideology, and peace with India have become still born ideas.

Following his coup against Nawaz Sharif and his government in 1999, Musharraf had remarked that even if the Kashmir issue was resolved there will remain many other problems with India, meaning that Pakistan and India could never be friends. His successor, Gen. Asfaq Kayani is on record having stated in Brussels at a NATO conference, that there was no commonality between Pakistan and India – historically, culturally and religiously. He meant exactly what Musharraf had said. Musharraf used the Taliban in Afghanistan for strategic depth and reared and armed the Lashar-e-Toiba (LET), Jaish-e-Mohammad (JEI) and the Kashmiri separatists against India. Kayani has followed on the Musharraf path. He is on record to have stated that the terrorists were the Pakistan army's assets, and used these assets in attacks on the Indian embassy and other interests in Afghanistan. The policy of terrorism against India remains alive. Needless to state that in the November 2008 bloody Mumbai attack the ISI's hand was all too clear.

It is, therefore, an important question to revisit whether the back-channel exchanges between India and Pakistan would have ultimately resulted in a solution over Kashmir. Kashmir in another manner, is a golden goose for the Pakistani military intelligence establishment. Musharraf had pulled the carpet from under India's feet in Shimla.

Kayani has snuffed all overtures from President Asif Ali Zardari to mend fences with India. The central point here is the use of hard line and misinterpreted Islam of Wahabis and Salafis to execute state policies. The military establishment of Pakistan appears to be sanguine that they hold the control stick of the jihadists. This is a very dangerous game they are playing, unless they think they will be able to execute a jehadi nation among the comity of liberal nations.

It has been argued by many Pakistani leaders including Parvez Musharraf that the Islamists get only 2 percent or under votes in national elections and, hence, have no influence on the government and society.

If this is true, why did the Pakistani government buckle under the pressure of the Islamists, and Prime Minister Yusuf Raza Geelani had to declare that the government had no intention of amending the Blasphemy law? It is precisely because the Islamists terrorists enjoy strong support from the army and some political parties.

According to some international assessments Pakistan spends seven times more in its defence than on education. The economic struggle has been forcing parents to send their children to Madrassas for religious education where they receive at least two square meals a day. Unlike Madrassas in India and Bangladesh which have turned to general education, the Pakistani Madrassas which are growing in number through external fundings, continue to graduate jehadis.

What, however, is significant is that an increasing number of young people in Pakistan are leaning towards hard line "nationalist" and Islamic thought. The showering of Taseer's killer, Hassan Qadri, with rose petals, and almost one thousand lawyers volunteering to represent Qadri in court, tells a story. There is an argument that many more thousands of lawyers did not offer their services to Qadri. But the vocal Lawyers' community in Pakistan, who were instrumental in the ousting of President Parvez Musharraf, did not condemn Qadri nor offer to prosecute him. In ousting Musharraf, the lawyers had army Chief Gen. Kayani's support. In this case Kayani is plotting Zardari's ouster who is seen as friendly to the US and amenable to India.

This begs the question whether Army Chief Gen. Kayani and his adjutants supported the lawyers to oust Musharraf for his alleged move to reconcile the Kashmir issue with India? And now they signal the judiciary, which is otherwise proactive to counter the civilian government, not to act strictly against the terrorists. These moves are obvious to any elementary Pakistan watcher.

Following the Taseer and Bhatti assassinations, the liberal Pakistani English language media appear to be constricted. So is Pakistani liberal society. Many of them can migrate abroad, but they are holding back, (including those involved with art, music, films etc.). As the late Salman Taseer's daughter remarked recently, if there is an exodus of liberals they will be handing over the country to religious extremists.

The Indian government must examine these developments threadbare. On the one hand India's overtures to Pakistan makes clear that India means no hostility despite Pakistan giving all the opportunities. On the other, whatever the Pakistani government may do to prevent people-to-people exchanges with India, New Delhi must open the gates to Pakistani intellectuals, artistes, media persons and students what India is all about, and take the impressions back home. This is the only way, perhaps, that India can reach the hearts and minds of the Pakistani liberals and upcoming fledgling generation.

PAKISTAN ARMY STEPS INTO GOVERNMENT ROLE AMID POLITICAL CRISIS

Pakistan's army stepped into a political struggle between the country's embattled prime minister and the opposition on Thursday, signaling a possible end to a crisis that has destabilized the coup-prone nation.

Pakistan has been gripped by mass rallies for more than two weeks, with protesters led by cricketer-turned-politician Imran Khan and firebrand cleric Tahir ul-Qadri camped outside parliament demanding Prime Minister Nawaz Sharif resign.

Attempts to resolve the crisis through talks have failed, creating a deadlock and raising the specter of violence as thousands of increasingly impatient activists, some armed with sticks, massed in the heart of Islamabad despite intense heat.

Addressing the roaring crowd late at night, Qadri said the army had offered to mediate in the stand-off, a proposal he immediately endorsed.

"The army chief has asked us to give him 24 hours to solve the crisis," he told thousands of flag-waving supporters. Khan, speaking shortly after him, echoed his remarks.

"The army will compile and put together a package of our demands and make sure they are implemented," Qadri added.

The army's press wing tweeted that army chief General Raheel Sharif would meet both opposition leaders late on Thursday. No other official comment was immediately available.

Some officials in Sharif's administration have accused the army itself of orchestrating the protests as a way to weaken the prime minister, and many believe that the fate of the anti-government movement ultimately lies in the military's hands.

Pakistan, a nuclear-armed nation of 180 million, has been ruled by the military for half of its entire history and has repeatedly swung between democracy and military. Sharif himself was toppled in a coup in 1999 during his previous tenure.

THE TROUBLING EFFECTIVENESS OF AL-QAEDA'S PSYOP ON THE PAKISTANI ARMY

Going forward in the global conflict before us, it is important to acknowledge and understand that al-Qaeda is currently engaged in an Information Operation (IO) campaign inside Pakistan. This is in addition to its efforts to gain influence outside of Pakistan, particularly with Muslims in Europe, the Middle East and in the US.

The primary target of the Pakistan campaign is the Pakistani military and it is driven by al-Qaeda's accelerating insurgency inside Pakistan. Understanding how and why al-Qaeda has undertaken this effort allows decision makers greater understanding of al-Qaeda's aims and equips them with a 'lay of the land' required to counter al-Qaeda's message and objectives.

Usama bin Laden's latest recorded message is the third in just two weeks following three years of virtual silence from the al-Qaeda leader. In it, bin Laden calls on Pakistani Muslims to acknowledge that Musharraf's actions are examples of his loyalty to the United States and representative of his unbelief. For bin Laden and his compatriots, such unbelief marks Musharraf as 'kufr' and places the requirement on believers to make "armed rebellion against him." The misguided understanding that bin Laden and al-Qaeda have of Islam makes it obligatory to fight against those who rule outside of their interpretation of Islam, and its overly broad application of tawhid. Yet bin Laden crafts a different message for the Pakistani Army, whom he advises to "resign" from their jobs, "disassociate yourself from Pervez and his Shirk (polytheism)" and "enter anew into Islam."

Ayman al-Zawahiri's latest video message and bin Laden's audio message, released on the same day, mark as-Sahab's 77th and 78th propaganda productions this year alone. There is a clear shifting of gears in the al-Qaeda Information Operations, most notably within Pakistan as well as their international efforts surrounding the 6th anniversary of the September 11th attacks.

Before looking further into the al-Qaeda Pakistani IO campaign, we must address the al-Qaeda-Taliban insurgency actively ongoing in Pakistan.

Al-Qaeda in Pakistan-From Terrorism to Insurgency

There is, of course, no single agreed upon definition of terrorism. Terrorism is defined in the US Code of Federal Regulations as "...the unlawful use of force and violence against persons or property to intimidate or coerce a government, the civilian population, or any segment thereof, in furtherance of political or social objectives." (28 C.F.R. Section 0.85) For instance, terrorism is – among other things-a tactic employed to increase support for a group through inspiration while also decreasing effective resistance to the group through intimidation. An example of this type of terrorism would be the beheading of those deemed to be 'spies' for the Americans in South Waziristan, the multiple car bomb and rocket attacks, or the anti-aircraft assassination attempts on Musharraf. Additionally, the bombings that took place after the Pakistani government raid on Lal Masjid (the Red Mosque) are an example of the use of terror to gain influence. No matter the definition of terrorism being applied, al-Qaeda has clearly been a terrorist organization in Pakistan.

Beyond Pakistan, Al-Qaeda seeks to – in part-influence American foreign policy through terrorist means. But within Pakistan, al-Qaeda has clearly and by specific design transformed from being simply a dangerous international terrorist group *within* Pakistan to a full-fledged internal insurgency *against* it. This transformation is represented through the efforts of al-Qaeda to acquire the armored assets of a state Army and its nuclear weapons, as well as the pursuit of land holdings to be integrated into the larger objective of creating an Islamic state to be ruled by a successor to the Prophet, a Khalifa or Caliph, nearly 1350 years after the last of the 'rightly guided' rulers.

An insurgency is a movement with specific governmental designs on the host country. In *Countering Evolved Insurgent Networks*, Col. Thomas X. Hammes (USMC, Ret.) quotes Bard O'Neill to define an insurgency. O'Neill wrote, "Insurgency may be defined as a struggle between a nonruling group and the ruling authorities in which the nonruling group consciously uses *political resources* (e.g., organizational expertise, propaganda, and demonstrations) and *violence* to destroy, reformulate, or sustain the basis of one or more aspects of politics."

In more accessible terms, Terrorism-Research.com offers that the ultimate goal of an insurgency "is to challenge the existing government for control of all or a portion of its territory, or force political concessions in sharing political power."

Both aptly describe al-Qaeda's actions, operations and aims within Pakistan, a ready-made nuclear power which the terrorist group seeks to wrest complete control.

Perhaps the best way to describe al-Qaeda's Pakistan insurgency is to call it a "Death by a Thousand Cuts." They have openly sought not only the assassination of Pervez Musharraf, but also the demise – or reconfiguration – of the Pakistani national government. In a strategy that has been executed with remarkable patience, al-Qaeda has gained acknowledged control of several sizable territories in Pakistan's Federally Administered Tribal Areas.

After defeating Pakistani forces on the battlefield, the Taliban-al-Qaeda alliance have secured various 'peace accords' replete with concessions from the Musharraf government. Effective control of North Waziristan, South Waziristan, Bajour and Swat have been ceded to them and Pakistani forces were – upon agreement – effectively withdrawn from the areas handed the Taliban-al-Qaeda alliance through the accords. The accords, no matter how presented by the Musharraf government, represented abject defeat.

Al-Qaeda Insurgency: Destination-Islamabad

Domination in these territories has allowed al-Qaeda the haven necessary to rebuild its training and planning infrastructure as well as replenish its human resources. After a few short weeks of basic military training, Taliban conscripts are sent in waves across the border to battle US and Coalition forces in Afghanistan.

However, al-Qaeda has no designs on investing in regaining that territory. There are no resources for them there – and a more formidable, if reduced, military force to be reckoned with. One whose defeat of the terrorist group drove them into Pakistan's border regions to begin with. Al-Qaeda's designs are not back towards the west, but rather onward deeper into the heart of Pakistan.

While al-Qaeda's Pakistan insurgency has been largely waged in the FATA region, it's territorial aims are by no means limited to it. Rather, al-Qaeda seeks control of all of Pakistan, including its military, weapons and economic capabilities. Al-Qaeda has been executing this strategy one territory, one victory at a time. And it now closes in on Islamabad.

Indeed, an analysis by the Pakistani Interior Ministry warned Pakistani President Pervez Musharraf of precisely this. The *New York Times* reported that the 15-page internal Pakistani document warned Musharraf that "the influence of the extremists is swiftly bleeding east and deeper into his own country, threatening areas like Peshawar, Nowshera and Kohat, which were considered to be safeguarded by Pakistani government forces." The Interior Ministry document said that Peshewar endures the "highest number of terrorist incidents, including attacks on local police," and that in Bannu and Tank regions, police are "patronizing the local Taliban and have abdicated the role of law and order." It is important to note that Peshewar is the capital of the North West Frontier Province (NWFP). Much of the Pakistani government, non-Islamist educators, officials and police forces live inside heavily armed and walled communities in the NWFP, where they are more safe from al-Qaeda attack. The NWFP borders the Federally Administered Tribal Areas under direct Taliban-al-Qaeda control on one side and the Pakistani capital of Islamabad on the other. The rising violence is a clear indicator of the expansion of al-Qaeda's insurgency as it marches patiently but steadily toward Islamabad. As evidenced by bin Laden's latest message, that patience may be nearing an end.

Usama bin Laden's latest message implored the Pakistani public to take up arms against Musharraf and warned the army's soldiers to break ranks and fight Musharraf with al-Qaeda rather than serve him. This is a sign that al-Qaeda's patient approach to its Pakistan insurgency has run its course. There could be a maelstrom of events to follow in Pakistan.

AQ Targets Police for Violence and Army Soldiers for Influence

The al-Qaeda Information Operation (IO) is designed to support the insurgency's incremental march on Islamabad. The key to understanding the al-Qaeda IO and its insurgency goals is to understand how al-Qaeda primarily targets Pakistani Interior Ministry forces (police, constabularies and the Frontier Corps) for physical attack while targeting Pakistani regular army forces for influence and subversion.

The persistent mention of Pakistani police forces – rather than Pakistani Army forces – is expected in any Pakistani Interior Ministry report, as the Police forces fall under the Interior. But Pakistani police forces also decidedly bear the brunt of al-Qaeda's lethal attacks and not the Pakistani Army. It's not that al-Qaeda and their indigenous Taliban allies cannot attack the Pakistani Army with expectations of success. They most certainly can and have. With bin Laden's latest audio message delivering a combination invitation and ultimatum to Pakistani Army soldiers, al-Qaeda's designs for the Pakistani Army are more clearly visible. The reason for attacking Pakistani police forces is two-fold and – in this writer's view-also the most elusive and yet perhaps most important indicator of the ongoing al-Qaeda insurgency.

First, the Interior Ministry is widely regarded as the one segment of the Pakistani government with unwavering loyalty to Musharraf, whom al-Qaeda has sought to assassinate several times. Unlike the military and the military's intelligence arm (ISI), the Pakistani police forces, constabularies and Frontier Corps of the Interior Ministry do not have historical ties to Islamist groups such as Lashkar-e-Taiba, al-Qaeda and the Taliban. Interior Ministry loyalty to Musharraf makes their ranks logical targets for the Islamists who seek to kill and replace Musharraf atop an Islamist-run Pakistani government.

Secondly, and most importantly, al-Qaeda at the same time seeks to avoid open bloody conflict with the Army. Not because it fears the deadly consequences of such a confrontation, but rather because al-Qaeda senior leadership wants the Pakistani military intact – for themselves. Ideally, they do not want to ultimately find Musharraf killed or oustered only to have the military splintered internally between pro-government and pro-al-Qaeda commanders. Al-Qaeda is executing an insurgency to gain control, not to touch off a civil war.

In the end, al-Qaeda's design is also to co-opt an intact military in order to gain command of a military force with the assets of a state (aircraft, armor, etc.) and direct control of Pakistan's nuclear arsenal. Recent reports of defections of Pakistani military elements since bin Laden's latest message to them indicates a level of success in the al-Qaeda IO campaign targeting them.

Measuring al-Qaeda's PSYOP Success

Three weeks ago, well over 200 Pakistani Army soldiers surrendered to a much smaller number of fighters from the Taliban-al-Qaeda alliance without a shot fired. But the al-Qaeda IO campaign primarily targeting the Pakistani regular army forces has a spillover effect on other forces-and the general populace-as well. It is reported in Pakistan that many soldiers in the Pakistani Army, Frontier Corps paramilitary and police forces are refusing to fight or putting up little fight against their own countrymen inside the Federally Administered Tribal Area. It is difficult to dispute the success of al-Qaeda's Psychological Warfare efforts inside Pakistan. The message has been consistent for several years and al-Qaeda's patience and restraint in seeing it through are significant qualities of the terrorist organization turned insurgent group. With every message and in all their forms, al-Qaeda has sought to convince the Army soldiers that they are not al-Qaeda's enemy, rather that they are simply being misled by Musharraf. In bin Laden's latest message, he said of the Pakistani Army, "we see the armies becoming tools and weapons in the hands of the Kuffaar [unbeliever, referencing Musharraf and the US] against the Muslims."

This message resonates, as many Pakistanis are reluctant to take up arms against other Pakistanis, whether those they would confront are Taliban or al-Qaeda or not. It must also be considered that upwards of 30% of the Pakistani Army are, like the Taliban, ethnic Pashtuns. The vast majority of them are enlisted foot soldiers, as very few ethnic Pashtuns hold leadership positions, largely due to internal social and educational dynamics.

Even among the Pakistani police forces in the North West Frontier Province, many are said to have requested leave or simply deserted when faced with the outlook of deadly confrontations with fellow Pakistanis among the Taliban-al-Qaeda alliance. In other instances, including the Interior Ministry's report that specifically cited the Bannu and Tank regions, police are "patronizing the local Taliban and have abdicated the role of law and order."

Where True Power Lies...And Grows

This is an indication that fear is also a prime motivator among Pakistanis. In the North West Frontier Province capital of Peshawar, al-Qaeda's black banner of jihad can be seen displayed in the widows of many shops and flying in various places. This does not necessarily mean that there is explicit support in the hearts and minds of all Pakistanis there – even among those flying the al-Qaeda banner.

Though Peshewar and the rest of the NWFP are technically under Pakistani state control, this indicates a reflection among the populace of where the true power lies – outside the walled communities where many government employees and 'moderate' citizens take refuge. In many cases, the al-Qaeda banner may well be flown simply out of self-protection to avoid attack on their particular shops.

The police cannot protect everyone all the time, but al-Qaeda and the Taliban can attack at their choosing. And from a local's perspective, this is where the true power lies. And as more and more Pakistanis in the police forces, the Frontier Corps and the regular army begin to show a reluctance to do battle, the al-Qaeda power in these region grows, both in measurable means on the ground and within the minds of the Pakistani populace.

Such are the tangible gains of effective, persistent and robust al-Qaeda information operations, a classic PSYOP directed at both the Pakistani population writ large and also expressly directed at the Pakistani Army. As a result, Pakistani forces are engaging al-Qaeda and the Taliban less and less. In fact, President Musharraf announced that in 2008, there will be no Pakistani Army activity at all in al-Qaeda-held territory, deferring engagement to the less capable and less effective Frontier Corps and Pakistani police and constabularies.

6

Pakistani Military and The Taliban: Failed Peace Talks

Though it has flirted with peace deals with the militants, the army finds it impossible to meet the demands of the TTP and the TNSM. According to the late B. Raman, a noted counter-terrorism expert, these include the suspension of all military operations in the tribal areas; the withdrawal of army posts from the FATA; the release of all tribals arrested under the Anti-Terrorism Act; the release of Maulana Abdul Aziz Ghazi and tribal students arrested during the commando action in the Lal Masjid of Islamabad in July 2007; and, enforcement of the Sharia in the tribal areas.

Stung to the quick by a series of Taliban successes in "liberating" tribal areas and under pressure from the Americans to deliver in the "war on terror", in the initial stages the Pakistan army employed massive firepower to stem the rot.

Helicopter gunships and heavy artillery were freely used to destroy suspected terrorist hideouts. This heavy-handed firepower-based approach without simultaneous infantry operations failed to dislodge the militants but caused large-scale collateral damage and served to alienate the tribal population even further. Major reverses led to panic reactions including the hurried negotiation of "peace accords" that were invariably broken by the militants.

On September 5, 2006, the Government of Pakistan had signed a "peace accord" with the tribal leaders of Waziristan (and probably the Taliban as well, though the government denies this) in the

North Waziristan town of Miranshah. The salient points of this rather surprising agreement included the following:

- The Government agrees to stop air and ground attacks against militants in Waziristan.
- Militants are to cease cross-border movement into and out of Afghanistan.
- Foreigners (understood to mean foreign jihadists) in North Waziristan will have to leave Pakistan but "those who cannot leave will be allowed to live peacefully, respecting the law of the land and the agreement".
- Area check-points and border patrols will be manned by a tribal force. Pakistan army forces will withdraw from control points.
- No parallel administration will be established in the area. The law of the Government shall remain in force.
- The Government agrees to follow local customs and traditions in resolving issues.
- Tribal leaders will ensure that no one attacks law enforcement personnel or damages state property.
- Tribesmen will not carry heavy weapons. Small arms are allowed.
- Militants will not enter agencies adjacent to this agency (the agency of North Waziristan).
- Both sides will return any captured weapons, vehicles, and communication devices.
- The Government will release captured militants and will not arrest them again.
- The Government will pay compensation for property damaged and deaths of innocent civilians in the area.

The terms of the Miranshah peace accord were humiliating for a proud professional force to swallow. The accord is reported to have led to the payment of large amounts of money for "damaged property" – sums that went indirectly to the militants. The US and its NATO allies were taken completely by surprise by the accord that allowed the militants to make peace with the Pakistan army and gave them the freedom to use the NWFP and FATA areas close to the Afghan border as safe havens to attack the US and NATO forces. The militants soon broke the cease-fire as well as the peace accord. Other similar peace agreements were also signed. In October 2007, the Pakistan Government entered into a peace agreement with the terrorists in the Swat Valley as militancy there was spinning out of control. This accord too did not last long. All these accords clearly showed that the Pakistan army and the Musharraf-led government of the day had no clear strategy to counter the growing menace of Taliban-al Qaeda insurgency in the NWFP and FATA. The government and the army were groping in the dark and hoping that something would work out.

Frontier Corps

The far less capable and less well-trained and equipped Interior Ministry paramilitary force, the Frontier Corps, is being employed in direct fighting in the Waziristan agencies. However, it has failed to cope with the better armed and better motivated Taliban militants. Perhaps the use of the Frontier Corps instead of the Pakistan army made political as well military sense to the Pakistan GHQ. The Frontier Corps, which numbers about 60,000 men, is manned almost completely by Pushtuns who are naturally trained for mountain warfare, have far better knowledge of the terrain in FATA than the army and have cultural affiliations with the people residing there. The officers of the Frontier Corps are usually taken from the Pushtun cadre of Pakistani armed forces, which is also an advantage.

Raised by the government of the British Raj in the late 19th century, the Frontier Corps maintains control over the tribes in the FATA. It has always been responsible for manning the Pak-Afghan border along the Durand Line. The Pakistan army has put in considerable effort to train the Frontier Corps for counter-insurgency warfare with technical and material support from the United States. As the terrain is mostly mountainous, it is felt that lightly-armed Frontier Corps infantrymen can conduct operations effectively. In the long run, better trained and more suitably equipped Frontier Corps troops, combined with administrative and economic reforms, might well provide the answer to the problem of militancy in FATA.

UNDERSTANDING PAKISTAN'S MILITARY

A guided tour of Pakistan's Army, from its role within Pakistani nationalism, prospects of mutiny, and the relationship of the ISI to the Jihadi world, to hostilities with India, suggests that some key ways of defusing the situation may be being neglected

Voltaire remarked of Frederick the Great's Prussia that "Where some states have an army, the Prussian Army has a state." In view of the sheer size, effectiveness and wealth of the Pakistan military and associated institutions compared to the rest of the state, much the same could be said of Pakistan.

The Pakistani military is the only Pakistani state institution which works as it is officially meant to – which means that it repeatedly does something that it is not meant to, which is to overthrow what in Pakistan is called "democracy" and seize control of the state from other institutions. The military has therefore been seen as extremely bad for Pakistan's progress, at least if that progress is to be defined in standard western terms.

On the other hand, it has also always been true that without a strong military, Pakistan would most probably long since have disintegrated. That is more than ever true today, as the country faces the powerful insurgency of the Pakistani Taliban and their allies. The Taliban threat makes the unity and discipline of the Army of paramount importance to Pakistan and the world – all the more so because the deep unpopularity of US strategy among the vast majority of Pakistanis has made even the limited alliance between the Pakistani military and the US extremely unpopular in Pakistani society, and among many soldiers.

The Pakistani military owes its success as a modern institution to the fact that it has to a considerable extent separated itself from the political culture of the rest of the country, which revolves around kinship, factions, and patronage – which alas all too often shades over into corruption and even kleptocracy. Of course, corruption does exist within the military, but to nothing like the same extent as in the rest of society.

The military has been able to achieve this separation because of two deeply intertwined and mutually dependent factors: a collective ethos which promotes honest service to the military as an institution; and a *great deal of money.*Without the resources to reward the soldiers adequately and provide them with decent services, the collective ethos of service, honesty and discipline could not be maintained. On the other hand, without this collective ethos, many of the resources given to the military would simply be stolen, as they are in the rest of the state.

To put it another way, the military's success as an institution and its power over the state comes from its immunity to kinship interests and the corruption they bring with them; but it has only been able to achieve this immunity by turning itself into a sort of giant kinship group, extracting patronage from the state and distributing it to its members.

The scale of military spending has severely limited funds available for education, development, medical services and infrastructure. If continued, this imbalance risks eventually crippling the country and sending Pakistan the way of the Soviet Union – another country which got itself into a ruinous military race with a vastly richer power. On the other hand, the rewards of loyal military service have also helped to prevent military mutinies and coups by junior officers – something that would plunge Pakistan overnight into African chaos, and usher in civil war and Islamist revolt.

Our mad dog

As a Lt Colonel fighting the Pakistani Taliban told me in July 2009:

"The soldiers, like Pakistanis in general, see no difference between the American and the Russian presences in Afghanistan. They see both as illegal military occupations by aliens, and that the Afghan government are just pathetic puppets. Today also, they still see the Afghan Taliban as freedom-fighters who are fighting these occupiers just like the Mujahedin against the Russians. And the invasion of Iraq, and all the lies that Bush told, had a very bad effect – soldiers think that the US is trying to conquer or dominate the whole Muslim world. But as far as our own Taliban are concerned, things are changing.

Before, I must tell you frankly, there was a very widespread feeling in the Army that everything Pakistan was doing was in the interests of the West and that we were being forced to do it by America. But now, the militants have launched so many attacks on Pakistan and killed so many soldiers that this feeling is changing...

But to be very honest with you, we are brought up from our cradle to be ready to fight India and once we join the Army this feeling is multiplied. So we are always happy when we are sent to the LOC [the Line of Control dividing Pakistani and Indian Kashmir] or even to freeze on the Siachen. But we are not very happy to be sent here to fight other Pakistanis, though we obey as a matter of duty. No soldier likes to kill his own people. I talked to my wife on the phone yesterday. She said that you must be happy to have killed so many miscreants. I said to her, if our dog goes mad we would have to shoot it, but we would not be happy about having to do this."

Between 2004 and 2007 there were a number of instances of mass desertion and refusal to fight in units deployed to fight militants, though mostly in the Pathan-recruited Frontier Corps rather than in the regular Army. In these morally and psychologically testing circumstances, anything that helps maintain Pakistani military discipline cannot be altogether bad – given the immense scale of the stakes concerned, and the consequences if that discipline were to crack.

Fortunately, commitment to the Army, and to the unity and discipline of the Army, is drilled into every officer and soldier from the first hour of their joining the military. Together with the material rewards of loyal service, it constitutes a very powerful obstacle to any thought of a coup from below, which would by definition split the Army and would indeed very likely destroy it and the army altogether. Every military coup in Pakistan has therefore been carried out by the Chief of Army Staff of the time, backed by a consensus of the Corps Commanders and the rest of the High Command. Islamist conspiracies by junior officers against their superiors (of which there have been two over the past generation) have been penetrated and smashed by Military Intelligence.

Morally Superior

The Pakistani military therefore, more even than most militaries, sees itself as a breed apart, and devotes great effort to inculcating in new recruits the feeling that they belong to a military family different from (and vastly superior to) Pakistani civilian society. The mainly middle-class composition of the officer corps increases contempt for the "feudal" political class. The Army sees itself as both morally superior to this class, and far more modern, progressive and better-educated.

This belief is also widely present in Pakistani society as a whole, and has become dominant at regular intervals. It is sadly true that whatever the feelings of the population later, every military coup in Pakistan when it happened was popular with most Pakistanis, including the Pakistani media, and was subsequently legitimized by the Pakistani judiciary. As Hasan-Askari Rizviwrites, "the imposition of martial law was not contested by any civilian group and the military had no problem assuming and consolidating power."

It is possible that developments since 2001 have changed this pattern, above all because of the new importance of the independent judiciary and media, and the way that the military's role both in government and in the unpopular war with the Pakistani Taliban has tarnished their image with many Pakistanis.

However, this change is not proven yet, and depends critically on how Pakistani civilian governments perform in future. On that score, by the summer of 2009, only a year after Musharraf's resignation, many Pakistanis of my acquaintance, especially in the business classes, were once again calling for the military to step in to oust the civilian administration of President Zardari – not necessarily to take over themselves, but to purge the most corrupt politicians and create a government of national unity or a caretaker government of technocrats.

Military loathing for the politicians is strengthened by the fact that Pakistani politics is dominated by wealth and inherited status, whereas the officer corps has become increasingly socially egalitarian, and provides opportunities for social mobility which the Pakistani economy cannot, and a position in the officer corps is immensely prized by the sons of shopkeepers and big farmers across Punjab and the NWFP.

This allows the military to pick the very best recruits, and increases their sense of belonging to an elite. In the last years of British rule and the first years of Pakistan, most officers were recruited from the landed gentry and upper middle classes.

These are still represented by figures like former Chief of Army Staff General Jehangir Karamat, but a much more typical figure is the present COAS (as of 2010), General Ashfaq Kayani, son of an NCO. This social change reflects partly the withdrawal of the upper middle classes to more comfortable professions, but also the immense increase in the numbers of officers required.

Meanwhile, the political parties continue to be dominated by "feudal" landowners and wealthy urban bosses, many of them not just corrupt but barely educated. This increases the sense of superiority to the politicians in the officer corps – something that I have heard from many officers and which was very marked in General Musharraf's personal contempt for Benazir Bhutto and her husband.

I have also been told by a number of officers and members of military families that "the officers' mess is the most democratic institution in Pakistan, because its members are superior and junior during the day, but in the evening are comrades. That is something we have inherited from the British".

This may seem like a ludicrous statement, until one remembers that in Pakistan, saying that something is the most spiritually democratic institution isn't saying very much. Pakistani society is permeated by a culture of deference to superiors, starting with elders within the family and kinship group. Pakistan's dynastically-ruled "democratic" political parties exemplify this deference to inheritance and wealth; while in the Army, as an officer told me:

"You rise on merit – well, mostly - not by inheritance, and you salute the military rank and not the sardar or pir who has inherited his position from his father, or the businessman's money. These days, many of the generals are the sons of clerks and shopkeepers, or if they are from military families, they are the sons of havildars [NCOs]. It doesn't matter. The point is that they are generals."

Pakistani Nationalism

The social change in the officer corps over the decades has led to longstanding Western fears that it is becoming "Islamized", leading to the danger that either the Army as a whole might support Islamist revolution, or that there might be a mutiny by Islamist junior officers against the high command. These dangers do exist, but in my view only a direct and massive attack on Pakistan by the US could bring them to fruition.

It is obviously true that as the officer corps becomes lower middle class, so its members become less westernized and more religious – after all, the vast majority of Pakistan's population are conservative Muslims. They are many different kinds of conservative Muslim, and this is also true of the officer corps.

On the whole, by far the most important aspect of a Pakistani officer's identity is that he (or sometimes she) is an officer. The Pakistani military is a profoundly shaping influence as far as its members are concerned. This can be seen amongst other things from the social origins and personal cultures of its chiefs of staff and military rulers over the years. It would be hard to find a more different set of men than Generals Ayub, Yahya, Zia, Musharraf, Beg, Karamat and Kayani in terms of their social origins, personal characters and attitudes to religion. Yet all have been first and foremost military men.

This means in turn that their ideology was first and foremost Pakistani nationalist. The military is tied to Pakistan, not the universal Muslim ummah of the radical Islamists' dreams; tied not only by sentiment and ideology, but also by the reality of what supports the Army. If it is true, as so many officers have told me, that "No Army, no Pakistan", it is equally true that "No Pakistan, no Army".

In the 1980s General Zia did undertake measures to make the army more Islamic, and a good many officers who wanted promotion adopted an Islamic façade in the hope of furthering this. Zia also encouraged Islamic preaching within the army, notably by the Tabligh-e-Jamaat.

However, as the careers of the generals Karamat and Musharraf indicate, this did not lead to known secular generals being blocked from promotion; and in the 1990s, and especially under Musharraf, most of Zia's measures were rolled back. In recent years, preaching by the Tabligh has been strongly discouraged, not so much because of political fears (the Tabligh is determinedly apolitical) as because of instinctive opposition to any groups that might encourage factions among officers, and loyalties to anything other than the Army itself.

Of course, the Army has always gone into battle with the cry of *Allahu Akbar*(God is Great) – just as the old German army carried Gott mit Uns (God with Us) on its helmets and standards; but according to a moderate Islamist officer, Colonel (retd) Abdul Qayyum:

"You shouldn't use bits of Islam to raise military discipline, morale and so on. I'm sorry to say that this is the way it has always been used in the Pakistani army. It is our equivalent of rum – the generals use it to get their men to launch suicidal attacks. But there is no such thing as a powerful jihadi group within the army. Of course, there are many devoutly Muslim officers and jawans, but at heart the vast majority of the army are nationalists, and take whatever is useful from Islam to serve what they see as Pakistan's interests.

The Pakistani army has been a nationalist army with an Islamic look." However, if the Army is not Islamist, its members can hardly avoid sharing in the bitter hostility to US policy of the overwhelming majority of the Pakistani population. To judge by retired and serving officers of my acquaintance, this includes the genuine conviction that either the Bush administration or Israel were responsible for 9/11. Inevitably therefore, there was deep opposition throughout the Army after 2001 to US pressure to crack down on the Afghan Taliban and their Pakistani sympathizers.

"We are being ordered to launch a Pakistani civil war for the sake of America", an officer told me in 2002. "Why on earth should we? Why should we commit suicide for you?"

Mutineer Scenarios

In 2007-2008, this was beginning to cause serious problems of morale. The most dangerous single thing I heard during my visits to Pakistan in those years was that soldiers' families in villages in the NWFP and the Potwar region were finding it increasingly difficult to find high-status brides for their sons serving in the military, because of the growing popular feeling that "the Army are slaves of the Americans", and "the soldiers are killing fellow Muslims on America's orders."

By late 2009 the sheer number of soldiers killed by the Pakistani Taliban and their allies, and still more importantly the increasingly murderous and indiscriminate Pakistani Taliban attacks on civilians, seems to have produced a change of mood in the areas of military recruitment.

Nonetheless, if the Pakistani Taliban are increasingly unpopular, that does not make the US any more popular; and if the US ever put Pakistani soldiers in a position where they felt that honour and patriotism required them to fight America, many would be willing to do so.

The most dangerous moment in my visits to Pakistan since 9/11 came in August-September 2008, when on two occasions US forces entered Pakistan's Tribal Areas on the ground in order to raid suspected Taliban and Al Qaeda bases. On the second occasion, Pakistani soldiers fired in the air to turn the Americans back. On September 19th 2008 the Chief of the Army Staff, General Kayani, flew to meet the US Chief of the Joint Staffs, Admiral Mike Mullen, on the US Aircraft Carrier USS Abraham Lincoln, and in the words of a senior Pakistani general "gave him the toughest possible warning about what would happen if this were repeated".

Pakistani officers from Captain to Lt General have told me that the entry of US ground forces into Pakistan in pursuit of the Taliban and Al Qaeda is by far the most dangerous scenario as far as both Pakistani-US relations and the unity of the Army is concerned. As one retired general explained, drone attacks on Pakistani territory, though the ordinary officers and soldiers find them humiliating, are not a critical issue because they cannot do anything about them:

"US ground forces inside Pakistan are a different matter, because the soldiers can do something about them. They can fight. And if they don't fight, they will feel utterly humiliated, before their wives, mothers, children. It would be a matter of honour, which as you know is a tremendous thing in our society. These men have sworn an oath to defend Pakistani soil. So they would fight. And if the generals told them not to fight, many of them would mutiny, starting with the Frontier Corps."

At this point, not just Islamist radicals but every malcontent in the country would join the mutineers, and the disintegration of Pakistan would come a giant leap closer.

ARMY DEPLOYMENTS AND EXPERIENCE GAINED

As far as the regular army is concerned, it has moved several combat formations from the Corps facing India across the LoC and the international border in Jammu and Kashmir to the northwest, besides troops from the two western Corps at Peshawar and Quetta. Three brigades of 11 Corps based at Peshawar and two brigades of the Quetta-based 12 Corps are reported to have been moved to Pakistan's western border with Afghanistan. One brigade each has been deployed in the northwest from 30 Corps at Gujranwala and 31 Corps at Bahawalpur.

The internal crisis is considered so grave that even the Strike Corps have not been spared and a total of about nine brigades have been re-located to the west, though not all of these have been rushed headlong into counter-insurgency operations. These include two brigades from the Kharian-based 17 Infantry Division of 1 Corps, Pakistan's army Reserve North. However, this massive re-deployment at the risk of depleting combat strength on the eastern border with India has not really fetched the desired dividends. When fighting formations are pulled out from their operational roles and their primary areas of responsibility, to be employed for secondary tasks, the expectation is always that their absence will be for a limited duration and that they will be employed only to launch surgical strikes that will be followed by quick extrication. On the contrary, these formations are getting sucked deeper into a worsening quagmire on the western border.

While the Pakistan army has conducted a number of successful operations in the NWFP and FATA areas, it has not been consistent in its efforts and has failed to gain the upper hand. For example, the success at Bajaur in end-September 2008 came after several months of poor results in lackadaisical operations. The tactics, techniques and procedures adopted by the Pakistan army have not yielded results that are commensurate with the effort put in. The army's intelligence network is virtually non-existent as humint sources are proving difficult to cultivate. Its ability to undertake operations at night and in conditions of poor visibility is rather limited as it lacks suitable night vision devices, hand-held battlefield surveillance radars and other sensors. Its movements are ponderous and easy for the militants to spot as its columns follow the beaten track while the militants know every nook and cranny of the terrain over which they operate.

Many of the army's God fearing soldiers are not convinced that going after their fellow Muslims, even if they are anti-national militants, is a justifiable approach. Deep down in their hearts, many of them would much rather fight the US and NATO troops whom they see as occupiers and violators of their land, their faith and their culture. The army leadership has failed to address this emotive issue with any degree of success. Clearly, at present the army lacks the capacity to fight the insurgents effectively in the NWFP and FATA. It is also completely out of synch with the aspirations of the tribal people inhabiting these areas and is unable to win the battle of hearts of minds that is crucial to gaining popular support. While a few of the tribal chieftains are neutral in the fight between the army and the militants, most of them encourage their people to provide shelter and succour to the militants.

The senior leadership of the Pakistan army has so far been employing a heavy-handed approach to put down rumblings of discontent in Balochistan and the Northern Areas in the past. It has failed to understand that artillery barrages and helicopter and air force bombings of civilian villages and towns are inherently counterproductive. The field commanders must be taught to discriminate between innocent civilians and armed combatants and must demonstrate concern for senior citizens, women and children instead of treating them with disdain. Success will come only when the army begins to close in with the militants and clears them from key areas systematically while ensuring that sufficient combat units are left behind to prevent the militants from taking over the cleared territory again. One method that can be adopted is to establish an interlinked grid of company-sized 'posts' to dominate given areas, conduct patrolling and strike operations based on hard intelligence and, simultaneously, enable the civil administration to execute development projects and run schools, hospitals, a postal service and banks. And, army or para-military columns must be physically deployed to ensure rear area security and keep the arteries open for supplies and reinforcements. All this is, of course, infinitely more difficult than lobbing 500 kg bombs from the air combined with artillery barrages.

Lack of Integrated Approach to Counter-insurgency

The leadership of the Pakistan army is perturbed that a comprehensive effort is not being made at the national level to fight insurgency in the restive north-western areas. According to Lt Gen Asad Durrani, former DG ISI, "The army, employed on a number of IS/COIN duties, is more or less on its own. The part to be played by the political leadership and to an extent by the civil administration – vital to the entire effort – is mostly missing. In Swat and Waziristan for example, the army is still stuck with rehabilitation, reconstruction, and a large number of militants... Considering that the "others" have more or less abdicated their responsibility (refusing to take "ownership" in today's terminology), the army – after some initial hiccups – has not done too badly. Indeed, its ability is not limitless."

Another senior retired officer, who prefers to remain anonymous, echoes similar views: "The army's capability... has improved significantly during the last decade. A lot of valuable experience has been gained after conducting a number of large-scale operations. Aspects of 'will' and 'morale' are however equally crucial... Remaining embroiled indefinitely in an insecure environment, and sustaining casualties without undertaking focused time-bound operations is not good for morale. This factor is being mitigated through frequent rotation of units... The army has been conducting operations at the tactical and operational levels, but there has been a state of drift at the national level. It relates to the nation's inability to develop a common understanding on the nature of problem, to correctly understand the contributory internal and external dynamics, to craft a wholesome strategy and have the political will to implement it. If this is achieved, the army will willingly and perhaps effectively play its role. So, it is not the army's ability, rather the national integrated effort and political will that has been floundering. This is a complex problem, needing many elements of national power to play a cohesive and sustained role..."

During his election campaign, Prime Minister Nawaz Sharif had promised peace talks with insurgent groups like the TTP. However, perhaps after consultations with the leadership of the Pakistan army, he appears to be backing off. "Of course we want to try talks but they are a far off possibility," said a government official recently. "There is so much ground work that needs to be done. And when you are dealing with a group as diverse and internally divided as the Pakistani Taliban, then you can never be sure that every sub-group would honour talks." (Maria Golovnina and Mehreen Zahra-Malik, "Despite promises to talk, new Pakistan PM gets tough on insurgents" Reuters, July 23, 2013.)

PAKISTAN'S UNHOLY ALLIANCE THE MILITANTS

The heavily guarded, high-walled concrete structure right in the heart of Islamabad has no signboard. But everyone in the capital knows that the sprawling compound surrounded by barbed wire houses the Directorate for Inter-Services Intelligence (ISI). The spy agency has been the country's big brother. It is powerful, ubiquitous and has functioned with so much autonomy from the central government that it has almost become a state within a state.

It is not only responsible for intelligence gathering, but also acts as a determinant of Pakistan's foreign policy and a vehicle for its implementation. For every civilian and military government, control of the ISI was seen as crucial to maintaining a firm grip on power. The agency had been so powerful for so long that it played by its own rules. Its various heads had contrasting profiles, but emerged among the most powerful figures in the country's establishment. For years they ran semi-independent operations in Afghanistan and Kashmir and helped to form and topple civilian governments.

For more than two decades the ISI had sponsored Islamic militancy to carry out its secret wars. It was a crucial partner in the CIA's biggest covert operation ever, one that forced the Soviet Union to pull out of Afghanistan and served as a catalyst to the disintegration of the communist superpower. In Afghanistan, as well as Kashmir, the agency discovered the effectiveness of covert warfare as a method of bleeding a stronger adversary, while maintaining the element of plausible deniability. The ISI falls directly within Pakistan's military chain of command and had also served as an instrument for promoting the military's domestic political agenda and the guardian of its self-professed 'ideological frontiers' of the country.

Almost all ISI officers are regular military personnel, who are rotated in and out for a fixed tenure. However, there have been some exceptions. The export of jihad sponsored by the ISI had its blowback. It had allowed the Islamists a huge space for their activities. State patronage, in the form of an 'unholy alliance' between the military and the mullahs, resulted in an unprecedented rise of radical Islam. The ISI had helped to create much of the Islamic militancy and religious extremism that Musharraf was confronted with. That unholy alliance had been a major factor in the country's drift to Islamic fundamentalism. Founded in 1948 by a British army officer, Major-General R. Cawthome, then Deputy Chief of Army Staff in Pakistan, the agency was initially charged with performing all intelligence tasks at home and abroad. Its scope of operation extended to all areas related to national security. Until the 1960s, the ISI largely remained an obscure organization that confined itself to playing its specified role. But in the mid 1970s its scope was expanded to domestic politics. Ironically, it was a civilian leader, Zulfikar Ali Bhutto who created the ISI's internal wing which played a critical role in the ousting of his government a few years later. It was to cast its heavy shadow over the country's politics in later years.

A charismatic and populist leader, Bhutto took over a humiliated military and a brutally truncated Pakistan in search of a new identity, following the Indian-supported secession of East Pakistan (now Bangladesh), in 1971. The country had been dismembered by civil war and Indian military action. It was no longer the country created by Mohammed Ali Jinnah. The Pakistan that emerged from the ashes of defeat required a different geopolitical orientation. A revolt by young Turks in the army in the aftermath of a humiliating defeat in the war had forced the military ruler, General Yahya Khan, 3 to hand over power to Bhutto. His legitimacy was rooted in the country's first democratically held elections in 1970. Bhutto's socialist Pakistan People's Party had swept the fateful polls in the western wing of then-united Pakistan, trouncing the right-wing Islamic parties.

The scion of a feudal family of Sindh and a former foreign minister, Bhutto was seen as the savior of the new Pakistan. He successfully negotiated with India the release of 90,000 troops taken prisoner by Indian forces. He had come to power with the largest support base of any Pakistani leader since the inception of the country in 1947.

But he failed to sustain the confidence of the nation. Bhutto was ideally placed to put into practice the objective of social democracy and develop secular ideas and institutions. But it did not happen. Bhutto's strategy was to bring the disparate elements of this divided society together through a kind of Islamic nationalism, which was then supposed to create the cohesion and stability necessary for socialist economic reforms, but unfortunately all Bhutto succeeded in doing was to rehabilitate religious extremism. Under pressure from the religious parties whose cooperation they were courting, Bhutto's government increased the religious content in school syllabuses and, succumbing to pressure from Saudi Arabia as well as to the demands of religious parties, declared the Ahmedis, an Islamic sect, to be non-Muslim. This apparently minor action had long-term implications for the country as it fuelled Islamic zealotry and sharpened the sectarian divide. Bhutto's attempt to co-opt religious elements merely emboldened them, and eventually the clergy joined hands with their traditional ally, the military, to plot the overthrow of his government. Bhutto's attempt to establish an authoritarian rule led him to rely more and more on the coercive apparatus of the state and the intelligence agencies.

Bhutto did little to strengthen democratic institutions and to make the process of democratic reform irreversible. Instead, his entire effort was aimed at promoting a personalized rule. He did not trust anyone. Given his overwhelming paranoia and insecurity, Bhutto geared up the ISI to keep surveillance not only on his opponents, but also on his own party men and cabinet ministers. The agency kept dossiers on politicians, bureaucrats, judges and anyone else considered important. The collapse of democratic institutions and the Constitution's loss of sanctity created a vacuum of authority that provided a favourable condition for the Bonapartist generals. Bhutto's use of the army to crush the uprising in Pakistan's western province of Balochistan provided an opportunity to the military to reassert itself in the country's politics. Bhutto's politics of expediency and attempts to appease the country's religious lobby allowed the Islamists, who were routed in the 1971 elections, to revive themselves. A nationwide agitation, led by right wing Islamic parties in the aftermath of the controversial elections in 1977, shook his government. In a desperate attempt to appease the Islamists, Bhutto prohibited the sale and use of alcoholic beverages, banned gambling and closed down nightclubs. But the die had already been cast.

Bhutto had handpicked General Zia ul-Haq, a lesser-known officer, for the post of army chief in 1976 over the heads of half a dozen senior officers, believing he did not have any personal ambitions. General Zia was a devout Muslim and Bhutto thought he would never betray his trust. Once elevated to the top position, the General did not take much time to develop secret contacts with hardline religious groups and conspired with them to overthrow his benefactor. On 5 July 1977, a bloodless military coup brought an end to Bhutto's six-and-a-half-year civilian rule. There was a complete convergence of interests between the Islamists and the military leadership which had ousted the Bhutto government. Several accounts of Bhutto's last days in power revealed that Major-General Ghulam Jilani, Bhutto's handpicked chief of the ISI, played a key role in the coup plan. Two years later, in April 1979, Bhutto was hanged after a dubious trial on charges of murdering a political rival. A secularist, elected with an overwhelming mandate in 1970, Bhutto probably had the best chance of any leader of taking on the Islamists and winning. His inglorious demise can only fill Pakistan's current leader, attempting a similar task, with foreboding.

Bhutto's usurper, General Zia, came from a humble lowermiddle-class background. His father, a religious man, held a clerical government post during British rule in India. Despite his poverty, he provided his son with a decent education. Zia was educated at Delhi's most prestigious St Stephen's College before getting a commission in the Royal Indian Army in 1942. He was a captain at the time of the creation of Pakistan in 1947. He was a hard-working officer, but lacked brilliance. Many of his colleagues believed he was lucky to be promoted beyond Colonel. From a young age, Zia was actively involved with the popular religious movement, Tablighi Jamaat, 6 one of the most influential grassroots Islamic movements in the South Asian subcontinent, which had hardline traditionalist views on the role of Islam in modern society.

A short man with a thick moustache, Zia bore a strong resemblance to the British comedian, Terry-Thomas. But he was by no means a fool. He was shrewd enough to know how to make his way up. He convinced Bhutto of his absolute loyalty and more importantly of his incapacity to be otherwise. Zia was not only an authoritarian; he also aspired to turn Pakistan into an ideological state ruled by strict Islamic sharia laws. He was an unpopular and controversial leader, whose survival in power largely owed to the external factors that emerged after the invasion by Soviet forces of Pakistan's northern neighbour, Afghanistan, in 1979. Pakistan became a frontline state and a bulwark in the West's war against communism.

General Zia brought in his close confidant, Lt.-General Akhter Abdur Rehman, to head the ISI in 1979, as the spy agency became a crucial cog in the resistance against the Soviet forces. Its tentacles started to spread far and wide. An artillery officer, General Rehman 'had a cold, reserved personality, almost inscrutable, always secretive, with no intimates except his family.' His officers remembered him as a hard man to serve due to his brusque manner and reputation as a strict disciplinarian. 'That made him an ideal man for the job,' said Brigadier Mohammed Yousuf, a former ISI officer who served under him. General Rehman ran the organization until 1987.

He was not a radical Islamist, but a staunch Muslim nationalist. Under General Rehman, the ISI, in partnership with the CIA, conducted the biggest covert operation in modern history. The two organizations had secretly collaborated for years, yet General Zia was not prepared to give a free hand to the CIA. He laid down strict rules to ensure that the ISI would maintain control over contacts with Afghan mujahidin groups. No CIA operatives would be allowed to cross the border into Afghanistan. Distribution of weapons to the Afghan commanders would be handled only by the ISI. All training of mujahidin would be the sole responsibility of the ISI. While the CIA supplied money and weapons, it was the ISI that moved them into Afghanistan. The Americans relied almost entirely on the Pakistani service to allocate weapons to the mujahidin groups. The framework provided the Pakistani spy agency with almost total control over the covert operation inside Afghanistan. The decade-long secret war raised the organization's profile and gave it huge clout. With the active help of the CIA and Saudi Arabia, the ISI turned the Afghan resistance into Islam's holy war.

The decade-long conflict in Afghanistan gave the Islamic extremists a rallying point and a training field. Young Muslims around the world flocked to Afghanistan to fight against a foreign invader. Some 35,000 holy warriors joined the Afghan war from 1979 to 1989. The largest number came from the Middle East.

Some were Saudis, among whom was a young man called Osama bin Laden.

The 23-year-old son of a wealthy construction magnate said he arrived in Peshawar for the first time in 1980. He was a very shy person who had no experience of war and, as a fresh graduate from the King Abdul Aziz University, bin Laden had left the luxury of his home to help the mujahidin fighting jihad in Afghanistan. It was the beginning of his long association with Afghan and Pakistani Islamic radicals. By 1984 he was spending most of his time in Peshawar, sometimes with Abdullah Azzam, a Palestinian Islamic scholar and an ideologue who inspired the rush of foreign Muslims to fight in Afghanistan.

It was also during this period that he developed links with the ISI, which had become the main conduit for arms and training for the Islamic warriors. The Afghan war placed enormous resources at the agency's disposal.

Weapons provided by the CIA were channelled to Afghan fighters through the ISI. By the mid 1980s, every dollar given by the CIA was matched by another from Saudi Arabia. The funds, running into several million dollars a year, were transferred by the CIA to the ISI's special accounts in Pakistan. The backing of the CIA and the funnelling of massive amounts of US military aid helped the ISI develop into 'a parallel structure wielding enormous power over all aspects of government.' It became all-pervasive and there was an unprecedented expansion in the surveillance of political opponents.

Even those in the army were not spared. According to a former senior intelligence officer, part of the ISI's function was to keep a careful watch on the generals and ensure their loyalty to the regime. In the words of Brigadier Yousaf, 'So powerful had the ISI become that apprehension, even fear, of what the ISI could do, was real.' The Afghan war provided the agency with the public profile that it did not have before. Former ISI officials point out that the general expansion the agency underwent as a consequence of its Afghan role had a bearing on its overall functioning. While its role in supervising a successful covert operation in Afghanistan won the ISI international acclaim, at home it was a dreaded name.

The Afghan resistance was projected as part of the global jihad against communism. The ISI's training of guerrillas was integrated with the teaching of Islam. The prominent theme was that Islam was a complete socio-political ideology under threat from atheistic communists. The Afghan war produced a new radical Islamic movement. Besides the holy warriors from Islamic countries, thousands more joined madrasas set up with funding from Saudi Arabia and some other Muslim countries. More than 100,000 foreign Muslim radicals were directly influenced by the Afghan jihad. The military's involvement in the politics of religion, however, had started long before the Afghan jihad. General Zia not only ushered Pakistan into its longest period of military rule, but also tried to turn the country into an ideological state. He extended the army's role in domestic politics much further than defined by earlier military rulers. Previously, the military was seen as the ultimate guarantor of the country's territorial integrity and internal security. But Zia expanded its role as the defender of Pakistan's ideological frontiers as well.

Addressing army officers, Zia argued that, as Pakistan was created on the basis of the two-nation theory and Islamic ideology, it was the duty of the 'soldiers of Islam to safeguard its security, integrity and sovereignty at all costs, both from internal turmoil and external aggression'. He claimed the state was created exclusively to provide its people with the opportunity to follow 'the Islamic way of life.' Preservation of the country's Islamic character was seen to be as important as the security of the country's geographical frontiers. Zia's military rule differed by its very serious attempt to create an ideological basis for all areas of activities of the state and society. General Zia cleverly used Islam to consolidate his power and legitimize his military rule. The Islamization process became the most important feature of his eleven- year rule and its raison d'e^tre.

For General Zia, Pakistan was an Islamic ideological state and therefore politics could not be separated from religion. He believed that he had a divine obligation to establish an Islamic society ruled in accordance with the Qur'an and sharia. Afraid to face a free electorate and having no mandate to govern, the General turned to Allah. He introduced a rigid interpretation of Islamic sharia, thus empowering the clergy. The move to Islamize the state found ready allies among the religious parties, many of which already had close ties with the military. The Jamaat-i-Islami and other Islamic groups were co-opted by the government. For the first time in Pakistan's history, the Islamists occupied important government positions. Being in power helped Jamaat-i-Islami, the most influential and organized mainstream religious party, penetrate state institutions. Thousands of party activists and sympathizers were given jobs in the judiciary, the civil service and educational institutions. These appointments strengthened the hold of the Islamists on crucial state apparatuses for many years to come.

The process of the Islamization of the state and society took place on two levels. Firstly, changes were instituted in the legal system. Sharia courts were established to try cases under Islamic laws. For the first time, the government assumed the role of the collector of religious taxes. Secondly, Islamization was promoted through the print media, radio, television and mosques. Through a series of religious decrees, the government moved to Islamize the civil service, the armed forces and the education system. School textbooks were overhauled to ensure their ideological purity. Books deemed un-Islamic were removed from syllabuses and university libraries. It was made compulsory for civil servants to pray five times a day. Confidential reports of government officials included a section in which the staff were given marks for regularly attending prayers and for having a good knowledge of Islam. General Zia's move to Islamize the army carried the most critical implications. Pakistan's army, carved out of the British Indian army, inherited British traditions and remained a secular organization until General Zia tried to give it a new Islamic orientation. Islam was incorporated into the army's organizational fabric. For the first time Islamic teachings were introduced into the Pakistan Military Academy.

Islamic training and philosophy were made a part of the curriculum at the Command and Staff College. A Directorate of Religious Instruction was instituted to educate the officer corps on Islam. Islamic education also became a part of the promotion exams. The officers were required to read The Quranic Concept of War, a book written by a serving officer, Brigadier S. K. Malik. The officers were taught to be not just professional soldiers, but also soldiers of Islam. In his foreword to the book, General Zia wrote: 'The professional soldier in a Muslim army, pursuing the goals of a Muslim State, cannot become "professional" if in all his activities he does not take on "the colour of Allah".' To gain promotion an officer was required to be a devout Muslim. Scores of highly professional and secular officers were sidelined for not meeting the criterion of a 'good Muslim'. As a consequence of this policy, many conservative officers reached the senior command level. Radical Islamist ideology permeated the army with the free flow of religious political literature in the armed forces training institutions. Friday prayers at regimental mosques, a matter of individual choice in the past, became obligatory. Mullahs belonging to the Deobandi sect were appointed to work among the troops.

They were supposed to be the bridge for officers between the westernized profession and the faith. Units were required to take noncombatant mullahs with them to the front line. Soldiers were encouraged to attend 'Tablighi' gatherings. The purpose was to indoctrinate cadets and young officers with an obscurantist interpretation of Islam. Many of those cadets later rose to positions of power and took control of sensitive institutions, including the ISI. The change in the social composition of the officer corps also led to the ideological reorientation of Pakistan's army in the 1980s. The army officer corps, till the 1970s, was elitist in character and composition. But the trend changed. In the past, members of the upper class or the rural aristocracy had largely dominated the army ranks; now the new officers mostly came from the lower and middle social strata. The rank and file of junior officers since the 1970s had come, not from prosperous central Punjab, but from the impoverished and relatively backward northern districts where a fundamentalist religious ethos prevailed. Unlike their predecessors, the new officers did not come from elite English-language schools, but were the product of modest state-run educational institutions. The spirit of liberalism, common in the 'old' army, was practically unknown to them. They were products of a social class that, by its very nature, was conservative and easily influenced by Islamic fundamentalism. They were distinctively less westernized.

Their narrow nationalist orientation and education, professional training and culture made them very receptive to the influence of Islamic groups, particularly to the Jamaat-i-Islami (JI), which freely carried out propaganda work among the officers and circulated Islamic literature. Most importantly, the JI's propaganda among vast numbers of troops was officially sanctioned by commanding officers on the battalion level and above. That led to the evolution of a long-lasting alliance between the military and the mosque. The main objective of the JI was to penetrate the army and use it to seize state power. The practice introduced by General Zia of sending combat officers to universities in Pakistan, in which the JI often had pervasive influence, facilitated the party's objective. The influence of the JI was particularly visible among officers from rural and semi-urban backgrounds. They had a high level of religious intolerance and held extremist views regarding 'external enemies' and the threat to Islam.

The number of officers sporting beards for religious reasons had visibly risen. These young officers constituted the main base for General Zia's regime. According to a retired general, 25 to 30 per cent of the officers had Islamic fundamentalist leanings. Many of them regularly attended 'Tablighi' groups that propagated the faith. They would take time off to join missionary bands preaching a return to purist Islamic values and recruiting other Muslim men to join them. Thousands of soldiers and army officers would join the annual gathering of the TJ at Raiwind on the outskirts of Lahore. More than one million faithful from across the country and abroad attend this Muslim congregation, the largest after the Haj in Mecca. Even the liberals adopted the philosophy on issues like jihad and support for militancy in Kashmir. The humiliating military defeat by the Indian army in the 1971 war, coupled with the disintegration of the country, also had a very deep impact on the psyche of army officers. Many young officers turned to religion for solace and became born-again Muslims. Given this situation, it was not surprising that radical Islamic officers made unsuccessful coup attempts in the mid 1980s. They wanted to bring about an

Islamic revolution and establish a theocratic state. The fact that the attempts were crushed and the rebel officers were charged with treason indicated that, notwithstanding its Islamization, the state was not prepared to tolerate a theocratic rule.

The situation in Afghanistan provided inspiration to a whole generation of Pakistani Islamic radicals who considered it their religious duty to fight the oppression of Muslims anywhere in the world. It gave a new dimension to the idea of jihad, which till then had only been employed by the Pakistani state in the context of mobilizing the population against the arch rival – India. The Afghan war saw the privatization of the concept of jihad. Militant groups emerged from the ranks of traditional religious movements, who took the path of an armed struggle for the cause of Islam. The ISI's active role in the Afghan jihad brought Pakistani army officers into direct contact with the radical Islamists.

The handling of jihad also indoctrinated the military and intelligence officers. At least two former ISI chiefs – General Hamid Gul and General Javed Nasir – remained actively involved with Islamic radical movements. Both promoted pan-Islamism and strove for an Islamic revolution that would free Pakistan from perceived western, and particularly American, cultural and political influences. General Gul, who liked to call himself a 'Muslim visionary', succeeded General Rehman in 1987 when the Afghan resistance had entered its most critical juncture. The most charismatic of the ISI chiefs, he openly aligned himself with the hardline Afghan mujahidin leader, Gulbuddin Hekmatyar, and right-wing Pakistani Islamic parties. He would later take credit for dismantling the Soviet Union. General Gul had worked closely with the CIA, but turned anti-American after the Geneva Accord in 1987, which paved the way for the withdrawal of Soviet forces from Afghanistan. The Accord was signed by the Pakistani civilian government led by Prime Minister Mohammed Khan Junejo against the wishes of President Zia, who believed it deprived the Afghan mujahidin of the opportunity to take over Kabul. Resentment among the military and ISI officers deepened in 1990, just one year after the Soviets pulled out of Afghanistan and the US administration imposed sanctions on Pakistan for its nuclear programme. The CIA ended its support for the Afghan rebels and its links with the ISI went cold. It was a sudden end to the strong link between the two agencies. The military leadership accused the United States of dumping Pakistan after the collapse of the Soviet Union. Long before the Afghan war was over, General Gul had started organizing a new jihad front in Kashmir. 'It is the years of our work that has realized the armed uprising against the Indian forces in Kashmir,' he told me in early 1990 when he was commanding the country's elite armoured corps.

The death of General Zia ul-Haq in a mysterious air crash in August 1988 brought an end to Pakistan's longest-serving military government. It left the generals with the choice of either imposing martial law again or holding elections and transferring power to a democratically elected civilian government. They went for the second option, realizing that a perpetuation of military rule might provoke public resistance and exacerbate the turmoil in an already highly polarised society. However, the generals were not prepared to pull out completely and leave the political field solely to the politicians, particularly to the daughter of Zulfikar Ali Bhutto, Benazir Bhutto, who now led the Pakistan People's Party, which was certain to sweep the polls. To contain Benazir, the military cobbled together the Islamic Democratic Alliance (IDA), uniting all the right-wing parties under the leadership of Nawaz Sharif. General Aslam Beg, then Chief of Army Staff, and General Gul justified the move by saying it was necessary for the viable functioning of a democratic system.

The main objective, however, was to ensure the military's continued role in the new system, overseen by the generals. By creating a counterbalance in the form of the IDA, the generals constrained the new government of a political party that had led the resistance against military hegemony for ten years. The military-sponsored alliance comprised a mix of traditional power brokers, religious parties and politicians who had emerged on the scene during the 1980s under military patronage. General Zia's regime, needing a measure of legitimacy and a social base of support, had co-opted segments of Punjab's dominant socio-economic strata: influential landlords, industrialists and emerging commercial groups. The new leadership of the Pakistan Muslim League thus largely consisted of politicians who owed their political rise to the military's backing. The other important components of the alliance were the right-wing Islamic groups, including the Jamaat-i-Islami, which had been involved in the Afghan jihad against the Soviet forces and the separatist war in Indian-controlled Kashmir.

While the IDA, which carried General Zia's legacy, could not achieve any significant electoral gains in the 1988 elections in the three smaller provinces, it did relatively well in Punjab and prevented the PPP from winning an absolute majority in the National Assembly. The military reluctantly handed over power to Benazir at the centre, but prevented her party from forming the government in Punjab, the biggest and most important of Pakistan's four provinces, which was being ruled by Nawaz Sharif. Political manipulation by the ISI helped Sharif retain power in the province with the support of independent members. Benazir Bhutto's assumption of power, touted at the time as the dawn of a new democratic era, was in fact a transition from direct to indirect military rule. The formal restoration of civilian rule in 1988 did not reduce the ISI's clout. A return to the barracks did not mean that the military's structure of control and manipulation had been dismantled. The ISI still kept a close watch on civilian rulers. The strains in civil and military relationships remained the biggest obstacle to democracy taking root in Pakistan.

The Chief of Army Staff remained the power behind the scenes in alliance with the new President, Ghulam Ishaq Khan, who held sweeping powers under the Eighth Amendment in the constitution introduced by General Zia. For the army, the new political situation offered power without responsibility. The military continued to oversee Pakistan's policies on Afghanistan and India, managing relations with the USA and controlling the country's nuclear weapons programme. The army high command's decision to rest content with dominance, rather than direct intervention, was based on a careful calculation of the advantages and disadvantages of playing arbiter in Pakistan's highly polarized and conflict-ridden political scene. A hamstrung Benazir Bhutto found herself directly clashing with the army when she removed General Gul from the

ISI. The General, who was the architect of the IDA, had never reconciled himself to even restricted civilian rule. Benazir was never trusted by the establishment and many generals made it a point not to salute her. It was in February 1990 when I met General Gul in Multan, where he was posted as the commander of Pakistan's main strike corps, after being sacked from the ISI. It was the period when the army had just concluded a major war exercise called 'Zarb-i-Momin'. The General accused Prime Minister Benazir of trying to make peace with India and questioned her patriotism. 'By conducting the exercise we have blocked her designs to undermine Pakistan's defence,' he said.

It was apparent that the generals were looking for an opportune moment to remove Benazir from power. The clash came to a head when the Prime Minister tried to retire the Chairman of the Joint Chiefs of Staff Committee, Admiral Iftikhar Ahmed Sarohi, and gave a year's extension in service to Lt.-General Alam Jan Mehsud, a senior general believed to be close to her government. The army top brass saw this as blatant interference in the army's internal affairs. Eventually, on 6 August 1990, President Ghulam Ishaq Khan dismissed her government on charges of corruption and dissolved the National Assembly. President Khan, a former top bureaucrat, was the central pillar of General Zia's military rule and represented his legacy. Benazir's party met a humiliating defeat in the following elections, losing the government even in her home province and political stronghold, Sindh.

The military leadership did not want to take any chances that time. To ensure the IDA's electoral victory, the ISI financed the election campaign of many top Alliance leaders. The list, which was published in national newspapers, contained the names of some leading politicians, including Nawaz Sharif. Most of them later held important posts in the new government. In 1988, the long-simmering political discontent in Kashmir exploded into a popular uprising against Indian control. Thousands of young Kashmiris crossed over to the Pakistani side of the Line of Control to receive guerrilla training as the Indian authorities tried to crush the insurgency by brute force. Essentially an indigenous rebellion, it soon turned into an armed struggle against Indian forces.

Thousands of Kashmiri youths joined the separatist struggle, which was initially led by the independent nationalist organization, Jammu and Kashmir Liberation Front (JKLF)

The ISI used the extensive intelligence and militant network that it had built up during the Afghan war to support a new jihad against the Indian forces in Kashmir. In Afghanistan in the 1980s, jihadist cadres came from the ranks of motivated Islamists across the Muslim world who were prepared to die for the cause, as well as kill the 'communists'. The spirit saw its continuation in Kashmir, which became one of the world's hottest 'Islamic jihad' spots. The ISI's involvement increased further in the early 1990s when, in an attempt to sideline the JKLF, it started supporting the pro-Pakistani Hezb-ul Mujahideen. The move divided the Kashmiri struggle and led to internecine battles. The mid 1990s saw the increasing role of Pakistani-based militant groups. That was when Harkat-ul-Mujahideen (HuM), Lashkar-e-Taiba (LeT) and later Jaish-e-Mohammed (JeM) emerged as the main guerrilla forces in the disputed state. Those hardline Islamic groups changed the complexion of the struggle.

CHALLENGES FROM AFGHANISTAN

The fallout of the draw-down of the US-led NATO-ISAF forces by the end of 2014, will pose the most complex challenge to the new government and the Pakistan army as it is an external security threat with internal security linkages. The security vacuum that will be created by the departure of foreign troops from Afghan soil is likely to lead to Taliban resurgence that the Afghan National Security Forces (ANSF – army plus the police) will be incapable of stemming.

The Karzai government is seen as an obstacle to the realisation of Pakistan army's key objectives in Afghanistan due to its steady rejection of Pakistan's overtures, including the use of its good offices for reconciliation negotiations with the Taliban. India's commitment to a strong and stable Afghanistan and its US$ 2 billion investment in the country's reconstruction are a cause for concern in Pakistan, particularly among the security agencies. The army resents Afghan calls for military aid from India due to fears of military encirclement – even though the Pakistan army appears to have realised the folly of seeking 'strategic depth' in Afghanistan in military terms. To counter the perceived attempts at encirclement, the Pakistan army and the ISI have begun to reach out to members of the erstwhile Northern Alliance.

Another bone of contention is Pakistan's accusation that insurgent groups like the TNSM of Mullah Fazlullah, are operating out of secure bases in Afghanistan. At present the Pakistan army lacks the capacity to fight these groups across the Durand Line. However, it may have no option but to attempt to do so in case these groups step up their attacks post-2014 and the Afghan government is powerless to stop them. Such a scenario could even lead to state-on-state conflict in the worst case.

There are approximately 2.0 million Afghan refugees in Pakistan today. Most of them are Pushtoons. Besides being an economic burden, they are seen as a national security threat as the Afghan government does not recognise the Durand Line as the boundary with Pakistan. Though the Pushtoons in Khyber-Pakhtoonkhwa are fairly well integrated with the national mainstream, separatist tendencies can come to the fore again. If the post-2014 security situation deteriorates into a civil war four to five years later – a probability that cannot be ruled out – Pakistan will be deluged with hundreds of thousands of additional refugees, further exacerbating the problem. Pakistan is hesitant to back Mullah Omar's Taliban fully because it is unsure of getting its unfettered support if the Taliban comes back to power sometime in the future.

According to Ahmed Rashid, a perceptive observer of the developments in the Af-Pak region, it is necessary "to ensure that Pakistan, which gives sanctuary to the Taliban leadership, cooperates rather than sabotages the transition and the peace process, and allows the Taliban to hold talks with Kabul on their own terms rather than on terms that Pakistan may impose." The Army is unlikely to give up its quest to attempt to exercise full control over a Taliban-dominated Afghan government.

- The need to appease Pakistani Pashtun opinion and prevent more Pashtuns joining the Islamist revolt within Pakistan;

- The fear that if the Afghan Taliban come to full power, they will support the Pakistani Taliban and try to recreate the old Afghan dream of recovering the Pashtun areas of Pakistan, but this time led by the Taliban and under the banner of jihad;
- The belief that the Taliban are by far the most powerful force among Afghan Pashtuns;
- The belief that Pakistan needs powerful allies within Afghanistan to combat Indian influence and that the Afghan Taliban and their allies in the Haqqani network and Gulbuddin Hekmatyar's Hizb-e-Islami are the only ones available;
- The assumption that sooner or later the present US-backed state and army in Afghanistan will break down, most probably along ethnic lines;
- Pakistan's economic dependence on the USA and on the World Bank and IMF;
- Pakistan's strategic dependence on China, which regards Pakistan as an important ally, but which has also acquired potentially very large economic assets of its own in Afghanistan, and which certainly does not favour Islamist extremism.

Conclusion

There can never be a purely military or a purely political solution to an insurgency. A successful counter-insurgency strategy is a dynamic but balanced mixture of aggressive offensive operations conducted with a humane touch and socio-economic development.

Political negotiations to address the core issues of alienation of the population and other political demands must also be conducted with the local leadership simultaneously. The tribal culture prevailing in the NWFP and FATA, with its fierce ethnic loyalties and its diffused leadership, makes the task of the army and the government more difficult. The need to follow an integrated approach at the national level is unquestionable. The management of governance, development and security must proceed along parallel lines if the root causes of insurgency are to be successfully addressed in the long-term.

At present the Pakistan army falls short of being truly combat worthy for the nature of sub-conventional warfare that circumstances have forced it to wage in the NWFP and FATA. It needs to address the doctrinal, structural and organisational issues that are hampering its efforts. Shortcomings in morale and motivation also need to be overcome as these form the bedrock of counter-insurgency operations along with tactics, techniques and procedures.

The army would do well to understand, analyse and learn from the counter-insurgency doctrine that the Indian army has so successfully followed for 20 years in Jammu and Kashmir and over half a century in India's north-eastern region. On its part, the Indian army must also study the counter-insurgency campaign of the Pakistan army and learn the right lessons so as to carefully avoid the hazards and pitfalls that the Pakistan army has encountered as insurgencies and terrorism are not going to end quickly in Southern Asia.

TALIBAN-US-PAKISTAN RELATIONS AND THE INDIAN THREAT

In this chaos a group of young Afghan religious students, many of them former fighters from the resistance, calling themselves Taliban (in Pushto language Taliban means students), swept through the country with popular support to establish their rule. Interested to keep their presence alive, the Americans maintained contacts and supported them, ignoring their orthodox beliefs, their harsh rule and even the presence of Al Qaeda in their midst. This continued until it was time for the Americans to overthrow their government in order to serve the changing American interests.

While the Taliban government was in control, Pakistan too maintained friendly relations with them in the interest of keeping its western border secure, extending whatever support it could. The ISI played a role through the contacts it had developed during war against the Soviets.

In the wake of 9/11 things began to change. Having invaded Afghanistan in the name of war on terror, branding Taliban as brutes and their resistance as terrorism, the Americans wanted the Pakistan army and the ISI to join the war.

This posed a serious security concern for Pakistan. It could destabilize the Pak-Afghan border and strain relations with the Pashtun tribes on both sides of the Durand Line, the British drawn boundary that cut through the Pashtun region to divide British India and Afghanistan and which Pakistan had inherited. The fact that Pakistan's border region, called Federally Administered Tribal Areas (FATA) is autonomous where the writ of the Pakistan Government does not prevail made matters more complex.

Pakistan's military doctrine is based primarily on meeting the main threat from India on its eastern border while maintaining a peaceful border with Afghanistan in the west. A direct conflict with the Taliban would have forced Pakistan to divert its military assets from eastern to the western front, thus thinning out its defenses against India. This was the last thing Pakistan wanted to do because of its unfavorable ratio of 1:4 against India in terms of conventional forces. Understandably, President Musharraf was unwilling to do the American bidding.

U.S. projection of its military failures onto Pakistan

There always is a problem with powers that begin to act in imperialistic fashion. Their vision of the world becomes colored. They tend to believe that pursuit of their imperialist designs takes precedence over the national interests of those who cannot stand up to them, even if that means compromising their own national and security interests.

America had also been behaving as one such imperial power and treated its smaller allies more like colonies. President Musharraf was threatened that in case of noncompliance with America's wishes, "Pakistan would be bombed into the stone-age". Musharraf was coerced into conceding to American demands.

Despite the state-of-the-art surveillance equipment and military hardware, the US and NATO forces failed to stop the Taliban fighters from moving back and forth into the unmarked Pak-

Afghan border that passes through a treacherous mountainous region to regroup and strike on the invading foreign troops. The American commanders reacted by demanding that the Pakistan army engage these fighters and seal the border. Those with even the slightest knowledge of the area would know that the Americans were asking for the moon. This was physically impossible.

Pakistan army's operations failed. In the process it earned a severe backlash from the local tribes who resented army's action against their kinsmen from across the border who sought refuge in their area, as it violated the old tribal custom of providing sanctuary to any one who asked for it, even it was an enemy. The Pakistan army paid a heavy price. More soldiers died in this action than the combined number of casualties that the US and NATO troops have suffered in Afghanistan so far.

President Musharraf under advice of his army commanders and the intelligence community called off the action and resorted to persuasion instead. Through jirgas (assembly of tribal elders) effort was made for the tribesmen to voluntarily stop the influx of Taliban fighters. It didn't succeed either. This was not to the liking of the American commanders. They blamed the ISI for working against their interests.

Washington accuses the ISI of complicity with insurgents

Washington and the American media frequently alleged that elements within ISI were maintaining contacts with the Taliban and attributed the failure of American troops in combating the Taliban to these contacts. Such allegations were also found to be part of the raw, unverified and even fabricated field reports 'leaked' in Afghanistan recently and splashed in the western media. The Americans have in the past also described the ISI to be out of control and demanded of the Pakistan government to purge the agency of Taliban sympathizers.

This is ridiculous. Firstly, ISI is a military organization operating under strict organizational control and discipline where officers are rotated in the normal course. It functions according to a defined mandate, unlike armed forces in some other countries and unlike the CIA which is known to be an invisible government on its own.

Above all, Pakistan and its military are committed to weeding out religious extremism as a matter of state policy.

Secondly, if the American troops are so incapable of overcoming a rag tag army of Taliban and if the complicity of ISI with the Taliban can be instrumental in changing the course of the American war, then it is a sad day for America as a super power and the strength of NATO forces becomes questionable.

Thirdly, in the world of intelligence, contacts are kept even with the enemy and at all times. CIA keeps contacts within Russia and other hostile countries. Israel, the great American ally, spies on America itself. It is common for all intelligence agencies to do this in the security interests of their countries. Why then should America expect an exception to be made in case of ISI? Why should contacts that ISI developed with the mujahedeen and the Taliban earlier, and which if it does still maintain, become a source of such great concern for the American administration?

Demanding that the ISI subordinate Pakistan security to U.S. interests. It is strange that America expects ISI to serve the American agenda instead of Pakistan's interests first. One cannot forget that the Americans have a long history of abandonment of friends and allies and when they repeat this in Afghanistan citing their own national interest, despite their promises to the contrary, why should Pakistan be expected to be caught with pants down? Why Pakistan's military and the intelligence agency should be expected to abdicate their duty and not do what is necessary to ensure Pakistan's security in the long term?

It has often been argued that America expects Pakistan to be actively engaged in the Afghan war in return for the military assistance it provides. The answer is quite simple. The American establishment is doing all that needs to be done in support of its own war and not for the love of Pakistan. The war is theirs, not Pakistan's. Pakistan should do and is doing what is necessary and feasible, without jeopardizing its own security.

As for the assistance, bulk of the $10 billion that America gave in the past and was branded as "aid" was in fact the reimbursement of expenses that Pakistan had already incurred in supporting the war effort. The rest was to meet Pakistan's needs for operations in the border areas and for fighting terrorism that arose out of the war. The Americans still owe $35 billion to reimburse the losses Pakistan has incurred due to this war. As for the F16s that Pakistan is getting from the US, it pays for them, despite strict restrictions over their usage.

The Indian-Israeli attempt to destabilize Pakistan

While Americans had their issues with ISI, the Indians and Israelis began having their own. The agency exposed the growing Indian and Israeli confluence in Afghanistan to destabilize Pakistan. This happened right under the nose of the Americans and obviously not without their knowledge and consent. India having deployed its troops in the name of infra-structure development in league with Karzai government and with American funding and having established seven consulates along the sparsely populated Pak-Afghan border was engaged in heavily bribing the influential but ignorant and susceptible tribal leaders to spread disaffection among the local tribesmen against Pakistan.

Evidence was also unearthed by ISI about how the Indians bought the loyalties of Tehrik-e-Taliban Pakistan (TTP), a grouping of Pakistani tribesmen from FATA and Uzbek fighters from previous wars who settled in the region. The TTP were influenced by the same orthodox religious beliefs as the Taliban in Afghanistan and were active in propagating them in their own areas.

They were recruited to launch terror activities in the urban centers of Pakistan, including the capital Islamabad, and were funded, trained and equipped in Afghanistan jointly by the Indian, Israeli and Afghan intelligence agencies.

A group from amongst them managed to gain control of Swat area adjoining FATA through coercion of the local population, which was later cleared by the Pakistan army after a major surgical intervention. The ISI also laid bare strong physical evidence of Indian involvement in supporting insurgency in Balochistan by way of funding, training and equipping misguided and disgruntled Baloch elements grouped under various names including the Balochistan Liberation Army that was led by the fugitive grandson of the notable Bugti tribal chief – Akbar Bugti.

His comings and goings in the Indian consulate at Kandahar and the Indian intelligence HQ in Delhi were photographed and his communications intercepted. Numerous training camps in the wilderness of Balochistan were detected where Indian trainers imparted training in guerilla warfare and the use of sophisticated weapons, which otherwise could not be available to the Baloch tribesmen. Flow of huge funds from Afghan border areas to the insurgents was detected that was traced back to the Indian consulates.

7

Approach to the War on Terror in Pakistan

Although Pakistan has been a frontline state in the war on terror since the tragic events of September 11, 2001, there is no doubt that General Musharraf initially cast his lot with the United States mainly as a result of deep fears about what U.S. enmity might imply for Pakistan's long-standing rivalry with India, its efforts at economic revival, its nuclear weapons program, and its equities in the conflict over Kashmir.

Desirous of protecting Islamabad's interests in these areas and to avoid Pakistan becoming a target in the campaign against terrorism, Musharraf reluctantly cut loose Islamabad's ties with the Taliban— a force it had nurtured, trained, and equipped for almost a decade in its effort to secure control over Afghanistan— and stood aside as the U.S.-led coalition assisted its detested antagonist, the Northern Alliance, to rout its own clients and their al- Qaeda accomplices and seize power in Kabul.

Because the al- Qaeda elements in Afghanistan during the 1990s were never directly dependent on the Pakistani Inter-Services Intelligence Directorate (ISID) for their success (despite maintaining a significant liaison relationship), the ejection of their Arab, African, and Central Asian mercenaries was viewed with fewer misgivings than the flight of the Pashtun- dominated Taliban, who were tied to Pakistan directly in terms of both patronage and ethnicity.

Islamabad's ties to the Taliban were so strong and so important that throughout the initial phase of Operation Enduring Freedom,

General Musharraf and his cohort implored the United States to desist from decisively destroying Mullah Muhammad Omar's regime in Afghanistan. When this objective could not be secured, Pakistani leaders argued against all coalition military operations that would result in ejecting the Taliban's foot soldiers from their traditional bases in the southeastern provinces of the country. When these entreaties were also disregarded by the United States and the comprehensive defeat of the Taliban appeared inevitable as a result of joint U.S. and Northern Alliance military operations, Islamabad responded by covertly exfiltrating its army and intelligence personnel seconded to the movement— along with some key Taliban operatives, if Indian intelligence sources are accurate— while permitting the defeated stragglers to cross over to safety across the frontier and into Pakistani territory.

Taliban forces and their al- Qaeda guests thus found their way across the highly porous Afghanistan- Pakistan border into the FATA. While Pakistani border patrols concentrated their efforts against the latter group, resulting in the seizure of numerous low-level al- Qaeda elements, these operations nonetheless were never rigorous or watertight enough and were, in any event, frustrated by other factors: the old tribal tradition of extending succor to strangers who ask for protection; the region's history of providing foot soldiers, first, for the anti- Soviet jihad and, later, for the war against the Northern Alliance in Afghanistan; the absence of a strong Pakistani state presence in this area; and the utterly hostile topography consisting of remote and difficult mountain terrain with poor lines of communication, all of which combined to bestow on the defeated remnants a substantial measure of sanctuary and assistance.

The U.S. inauguration of the "global war on terror" soon compelled General Musharraf to make good on his "principled" decision to join the U.S.-led coalition. This inevitably required Musharraf to confront the sources of terrorism that had developed internally in Pakistan, most of which ironically resulted from his own army's previous decisions to nurture radical Islamist organizations because of their utility to Islamabad's military campaigns in Kashmir and Afghanistan.

Four different terrorist groupings were implicated in this regard. The first were the domestic sectarian groups like the Sunni Sipah- e- Sahaba and its offshoot the Lashkar- e- Jhangvi and the Shia Tehrik- e- Jafria Pakistan and its offshoot the Sipah- e- Muhammad, which were engaged in violent bouts of bloodletting within the country. Although many of these groups had enjoyed the support of the Pakistani government, the military, and the intelligence services previously, their unexpected growth in power over time had become not only an embarrassment to their sponsors but also a serious challenge to domestic order.

As Christine Fair has summarized it, "The scale of sectarian violence in Pakistan is staggering, with hundreds of people killed or injured in such attacks each year." The New Delhi–based Institute for Conflict Management has documented sectarian violence alone as claiming close to 5,000 lives in Pakistan since 1989, with incidents involving everything from targeted killings of high-profile civilians, to bombings of mosques and drive- by shootings of innocents, to pitched gun battles in major population centers. In one incident, for example, sectarian hostility in the town of Parachinar in the Kurram Agency involved a five- day war, where small arms, mortars, rocket launchers, and antiaircraft missiles were all used in a convulsive spasm that claimed hundreds of lives and injured many more.

Confronted by such challenges to the writ of his state, Musharraf was only too happy to exploit the opportunities offered by the war on terror to crack down on these groups and suppress them once and for all. He did so, however, only selectively. Focusing the government's energies primarily on those Deobandi and Shia groups whose objectives were out of sync with the military's perception of the national interest, he targeted Sunni groups such as the Lashkar- e- Jhangvi, the Sipah- e- Sahaba Pakistan, the Harkat- ul- Mujahideen al- Alami, the Jundullah, and to a much lesser degree the Harkat- ul- Jihad- e- Islami, as well as Shia threats such as the Sipah- e- Muhammad, primarily because they were engaged in "anti- national" jihadi violence within Pakistan rather than in support of Islamabad's external ambitions vis-à- vis India and Afghanistan.

Using the entire panoply of coercive state capabilities, these entities were therefore put down with a heavy hand through arrests, targeted assassinations, and aggravated intergroup massacres. Although many of the tools used to defeat these perpetrators of sectarian violence were often unconstitutional, Musharraf shrewdly judged that the aggressive dismemberment of these groups would not evoke either domestic or international condemnation. He was right.

Using the opportunities therefore afforded by the global war on terror, the Pakistani security services systematically eliminated many sources of sectarian violence within two years of the campaign's initiation, even though they have been unable to conclusively eradicate the cancer of sectarian bloodshed within Pakistan itself. In part, this is due to the selectivity of Musharraf's antisectarian campaign. But the continuing fragmentation of these violent groups; their links to the wider networks of international terrorism now resident in Pakistan, various foreign sponsors abroad, and the flourishing madaris within the country; and the continuing utility of their gun- toting membership to different political parties and occasionally to governmental organs themselves imply that sectarian threats will be impossible to extinguish so long as "state policies of Islamisation and [the] marginalization of secular democratic forces" continue to persist in Pakistan.

The second set of groups, the terrorist outfits operating with Pakistan Army and ISID support against India in Kashmir, was treated in a remarkably different way compared with the anti-national sectarian militants inside Pakistan. These groups, such as the Lashkar- e- Toiba, the Jaish- e- Muhammad, and the Harkat-ul- Mujahideen, for example, were the long lances in the Pakistani campaign to wrest the disputed state of Jammu and Kashmir from India. Since the late 1980s, the Pakistani military has financed, trained, armed, and launched these cadres on their murderous missions into Kashmir and elsewhere inside the Indian union. Because the struggle for control over the disputed Himalayan state was fully under way by the time the global war on terror was inaugurated, these terrorist groups were more or less exempted from Musharraf's domestic campaign against violence and extremism.

This exclusion was justified both on the strategic rationale that Pakistan's participation in the war on terror was intended, among other things, to protect its freedom of action in Kashmir and on the repeated, though fraudulent, assertion that these groups, far from being terrorists, only personified the legitimate Kashmiri struggle for self- determination against India. In fact, of all the Pakistani- sponsored Deobandi terrorist groups operating against India in Kashmir and elsewhere, only one entity— the Hizbul Mujahideen— began life as an indigenous Kashmiri insurgent group; the others, including the most violent organizations such as the Lashkar- e- Toiba, the Jaish- e- Muhammad, and the Harkat-ul- Mujahideen, are all led, manned, and financed by native Pakistanis. This reality notwithstanding— and perhaps because of it— Islamabad continued to sustain the operations of these groups against India but, in an effort to maintain the consistency of its commitments to the global war on terror, now began to emphasize that its support took only the form of moral, and not material, encouragement.

This charade was rudely interrupted by the December 13, 2001, terrorist attack on India's parliament when, in response to New Delhi's subsequent military mobilization, Pakistan was compelled by U.S. diplomacy to initiate a series of measures to restrict the activities of its terrorist clients. The implementation of these actions, however, was at best halfhearted and inconsistent. Far from seeking to extirpate these terrorist groups permanently, Musharraf sought mainly to defang India's threats of military action and to alleviate Washington's fears of an inconvenient Indo-Pakistani war. His overarching objective consisted of protecting these terrorist assets to the extent possible because they represented national investments— a "strategic reserve"—in Islamabad's subconventional war against New Delhi. Consequently, to this day, Musharraf has not sought to eliminate the Deobandi terrorist groups operating against India in Kashmir and elsewhere; he has instead sought only to modulate their activities, depending on the extent of satisfaction he derives from the prevailing state of diplomatic relations with New Delhi and the progress secured in the ongoing Indo- Pakistani peace process.

Although the Pakistani- supported infiltration of terrorist groups into Kashmir— but not into the rest of India— appears to have abated in recent years, most observers conclude that this phenomenon is linked either to Musharraf's desire not to provide India with any excuses to abandon the generally fragile peace process or to domestic crises within Pakistan. In any event, it is agreed that Musharraf simply has not made the decisive decision to abandon or eliminate the terrorist groups operating against India in the manner witnessed, for example, in the case of the more virulent anti- national sectarian entities operating within Pakistan.

The third group relevant to the Pakistani decision to join the U.S.-led coalition against terrorism consisted of the Taliban, that is, the Pashtun remnants of the regime ejected from power in Kabul as a result of the initial success of Operation Enduring Freedom. After their defeat at the hands of the Northern Alliance, the Taliban cadres hastily returned to the regions whence they originated. Many in the rank and file withdrew to their villages in the southern Afghan provinces of Helmand, Kandahar, Oruzgan, and Zabol as well as along the border areas on the western side of the Durand Line separating Afghanistan from Pakistan, that is, in the eastern Afghan provinces of Paktika, Paktia, Khowst, Nangarhar, and Konar.

Given their significance as high- value targets, the core Taliban leadership— along with those Pakistani Pashtuns who had joined their movement— crossed over the Afghanistan-Pakistan border into the relative safety of the FATA. Because most of the Taliban's fighters originally mobilized by the Pakistani ISID were drawn from the Ghilzai confederation of Pashtuns, which dominates eastern and southeastern Afghanistan, and from the other Pashtun tribes inhabiting the FATA, their return to these ancestral lands was not surprising. In fact, all the evidence relating to the incidence of terrorist attacks since 2001 suggests strongly that the war- fighting cadres of the Taliban continue to remain bivouacked in these areas.

The exact location of the supreme leadership of the Taliban movement, however, cannot be established with any self- evident clarity. Irrespective of where the rahbari shura (leadership council) centered on Mullah Omar and his closest associates found shelter in the immediate aftermath of their defeat, Afghan military and civilian intelligence officials as well as NATO commanders today believe that this coterie eventually found refuge in Quetta, the largest city and capital of Pakistan's Baluchistan Province, from where they continue to operate to this day.

As Col. Chris Vernon, NATO's chief of staff for southern Afghanistan, declared forthrightly, "The thinking piece of the Taliban [operates] out of Quetta in Pakistan. It's the major headquarters— they use it to run a series of networks in Afghanistan." These networks, in turn, are judged to be directed by four subsidiary shuras based in Quetta, Miran Shah, Peshawar, and Karachi: the first three actually control or coordinate most of the ongoing terrorist operations occurring, respectively, along the southern, central, and northern "fronts" in Afghanistan, whereas the fourth is believed to connect the Taliban with the logistics, financial, and technical assistance conduits emanating from the wider Islamic world. The pattern of terrorist attacks occurring in Afghanistan from 2002 to 2007, again corroborates this judgment.

Because the Pakistani state was most intimately involved in the creation of the Taliban before their fall, Musharraf's antiterrorism campaign after September 11, 2001, deliberately avoided any concerted targeting of this group and, in particular, its senior leadership. No other explanation is consistent with the fact that, although Pakistani military, intelligence, and paramilitary forces apprehended scores of al- Qaeda operatives, including numerous key individuals in the al- Qaeda hierarchy, the senior Taliban leaders killed or captured in southern Afghanistan or in the FATA have numbered literally a handful in comparison. This asymmetry in seizures is all the more odd because, prior to Operation Enduring Freedom, Pakistani military and ISID liaison elements were deeply intertwined with all levels of the Taliban mand structure and its war fighters in the field. In contrast, the Pakistani intelligence relationship with al- Qaeda in Afghanistan was more tenuous, yet Pakistan's military forces were able to apprehend far more al- Qaeda cadres than Taliban operatives.

These successes in regard to al- Qaeda have invariably been attributed by Pakistanis, including General Musharraf, to the fact that it was always easier to identify the ethnically alien al- Qaeda elements along the frontier in comparison with the Taliban who, being ethnically Pashtun, were able to disguise their identities by assimilating into the larger tribal population.

While this explanation is only partly true— non- native fighters have lived in and become amalgamated into the social structures of the Afghan- Pakistani frontier since at least the anti-Soviet jihad of the 1980s— it is also disingenuous because the Pakistani ISID was not only deeply involved in the recruitment, training, arming, and operations of Taliban fighters at multiple bureaucratic levels, but it also maintained an intense liaison relationship with the Ghilzai tribes whose population has been disproportionately represented in the Taliban. Since protecting these relationships was deemed to be especially critical for Pakistan's national security interests in the aftermath of the Northern Alliance victory in Kabul, the large number of Taliban foot soldiers who made their way into the FATA were largely ignored by Pakistani counterterrorism operations so long as they did not engage in any untoward activities that either called attention to their presence or magnified the troubles confronting the Pakistani state. All told, then, the Taliban network, just like the Pakistani- aided terrorist groups operating in Kashmir and elsewhere in India, was deliberately permitted to escape the wrath of General Musharraf's counterterrorism operations in the initial phase of the war on terror.

Such an approach, however, could not be extended to the fourth group, al-Qaeda, which had also taken up sanctuary in the FATA, particularly in South Waziristan initially. Although al- Qaeda continued to have sympathizers within the extreme fringes of Pakistani society even after the terrible events of September 11 were conclusively attributed to its operations, the Pakistani military establishment did not enjoy the luxury of slackening its campaign against this target because of the consequences for U.S.-Pakistani relations at a time when bilateral ties were just recovering after a decade of U.S. disfavor and when Washington had just embarked on a ferocious campaign against al- Qaeda worldwide. Most senior

Pakistani military officers at the corps command level were also genuinely horrified by the destruction that al- Qaeda wreaked in New York and Washington and, fearing for their country's own future in the face of the monster now present in their midst, supported Musharraf's decision to engage and destroy this terrorist organization of global reach.

Pakistan's military, accordingly, began to prosecute the war against al- Qaeda with great vigor, if not always with finesse, through multiple instruments. These included providing the United States and its military with facilities and access for the prosecution of Operation Enduring Freedom in Afghanistan, and conducting various law enforcement and internal security operations (sometimes in cooperation with their U.S. counterparts) aimed at interdicting terrorist financing and apprehending and rendering terrorist targets for prosecution abroad. Most important, however, the Pakistani military initiated Operation Al Mizan, a large- scale effort that involved moving major military formations from the Army's XI Corps and elite Special Services Group (SSG) battalions into the FATA, an area where regular army units had not ordinarily been deployed for decades. These infantry forces joined the Frontier Corps regiments— the paramilitary formations usually located in the region— as a show of force in order to both reassert the strong state presence that historically was lacking and apprehend the al-Qaeda elements that had taken shelter within the area.

This military campaign, which took the form of a gigantic cordon- and- search operation, had several consequences. First, it resulted in the capture of numerous al- Qaeda and other extremist operatives— some 700 at last count— who have since been turned over to the United States. Because these individuals are mostly foreigners— non–South Asian arrivals living in what are essentially Pashtun lands— detecting their presence, while not easy because of the local support they receive from the natives for ideological reasons and sometimes simply out of greed or fear, was certainly easier.

Second, it forced some though by no means all senior al-Qaeda operatives— for example, Khalid Sheikh Muhammad and Ramzi Binalshibh— to leave the relatively secure FATA sanctuary and disperse further inward into Pakistan, where their insertion into less ideologically congenial surroundings and their need to rely on more complex means of communication increased their susceptibility to detection and arrest.

Third, the dramatic irruption of the Pakistani state into the FATA, through a significant military presence of the kind not seen in more than a century, resulted in making conditions sufficiently inhospitable for al- Qaeda such that its senior leadership and cadres were compelled to relocate under fire from South to North Waziristan and beyond, where they operate to this day. This forced displacement, which unfortunately remains at continuous risk of reversal, nonetheless had the beneficial effect of disrupting many planned terrorist operations, but the dispersal of the organization's leadership in the northern FATA, especially in the Bajaur Agency where the terrain is inhospitable, the population is violently pro-Taliban, and the presence of the Pakistan Army is thin, has inadvertently made the task of destroying the al- Qaeda core all the more difficult.

In any event, these outcomes suggest that although Pakistan began as a reluctant entrant into the global war on terrorism, it has since become an active participant in the struggle. More than 85,000 Pakistani troops remain garrisoned along the Afghanistan-Pakistan border— a deployment that predates the initiation of the global war on terror. A significant fraction of these forces, however, is engaged today in counterterrorism operations in the border areas, and more than 600 soldiers have already sacrificed their lives in this effort. Further, Islamabad itself has now become a victim of terrorism as a variety of groups, ranging from those previously nurtured and now discarded by the Pakistani state, such as the al-Alami faction of the Harkat- ul- Mujahideen, to more distant beneficiaries of past Pakistani policies, such as al-Qaeda, seek to wreak an orgy of revenge against institutions and individuals whom they had previously counted among their sponsors and friends.

That Pakistan has made significant contributions to defeating various terrorist groups is therefore undeniable, yet its larger campaign against terrorism has also been conspicuously selective and perhaps self- serving. While it has secured major gains in eradicating some domestic anti- national sectarian terrorist groups and has contributed disproportionately to the ongoing campaign against al- Qaeda, it has been much more reluctant to conclusively eliminate those terrorist entities operating against India in Kashmir and elsewhere and against Afghanistan both in the FATA and in transit back and forth to the southern and eastern Afghan provinces. Further, the protection of the terrorist infrastructure that supports these groups has produced undesirable blowback because the actors traditionally involved in perpetrating terrorism in Kashmir increasingly either coordinate with or directly assist the Taliban and al- Qaeda in operations against not only Afghanistan but also the United States and even Pakistan itself.

Clearly, strategic and geopolitical calculations play an important part in accounting for this segmented Pakistani response. Islamabad, for example, has long viewed the terrorist groups operating in Kashmir and now in other Indian states as useful instruments for executing its policy of "strategic diversion" against New Delhi. For this reason, Pakistan has been reluctant to target and eliminate these groups conclusively, preferring instead to alternately tighten and loosen control over their operations depending on how much satisfaction it receives from India at any given moment.

The decision to avoid targeting the Taliban was born of similar calculations. Initially, it was owed simply to the inclinations of senior Pakistani military commanders who were just not prepared to add insult to injury by physically eliminating the very forces they had long invested in, especially because they had now suffered the ignominy of having to consent to their client's defeat. Over time, however, the reasons for protecting the Taliban only grew stronger: India's growing prominence in Afghan reconstruction, its increased influence and presence in Afghanistan more generally, the weakening of the Hamid Karzai government in Kabul, the progressive souring of Pakistani- Afghan relations (including those between Karzai and Musharraf personally), and the disquiet about a possible U.S. exit from Afghanistan (a prospect inferred from the mid-2005 announcement that the United States would divest full command of Afghan combat operations to NATO) once again increased Pakistan's paranoia about the prospect of a hostile western frontier. It was exactly the desire to avert this outcome that led to the initial Pakistani decision to invest in sustaining the Taliban. And with fear of the wheel turning full circle gaining strength in Islamabad since at least 2005, the temptation to hedge against potentially unfavorable outcomes in Kabul— by protecting the Taliban as some sort of a "force- in- being"—only appeared more and more attractive and reasonable to Pakistan.

Although Pakistan's discriminative approach to fighting terrorism was shaped and implemented by General Musharraf in his dual capacity as president and previously chief of army staff, it would be erroneous to conclude that this prevailing strategy is owed simply to the whim of one man. This is particularly relevant today when Musharraf's hold on power has become progressively weaker and the future of his political status and effectiveness increasingly clouded. Rather, Musharraf's decisions in regard to counterterrorism strategy since 2001, although publicly perceived as personal dicta, invariably reflected the consensus among the corps commanders of the Pakistan Army and, hence, represent the preferences of Pakistan's military- dominated state. In other words, even if Musharraf were to suddenly exit the Pakistani political scene at some point, Islamabad's currently disconsonant counterterrorism strategy would still survive so long as the men on horseback continue to be the principal guardians of national security policy making in Islamabad. Because it is unreasonable to expect that the uniformed military will give up its privileges in this regard anytime soon— even if a civilian regime were to return to the helm in the future— the internally segmented counterterrorism policy currently pursued by Pakistan will likely persist for some time to come.

Even if it could be imagined that a civilian dispensation could wrest some control of Pakistan's national security policy from the military, it is not at all certain that the current strategic direction would change dramatically: a civilian regime would probably have greater incentives to combat all sectarian terrorist groups more evenhandedly, but that too is uncertain. After all, both the

Pakistan People's Party led by the late Benazir Bhutto and the Pakistan Muslim League led by Nawaz Sharif have had problematic Islamist political allies in the past and, depending on the political exigencies of the moment, could harbor incentives to give even sectarian or otherwise radical entities a breather from prosecution, although that would likely be justified as only a temporary expedient. Both civilian parties historically also permitted the Pakistani military and intelligence services to aid, abet, and arm the terrorist groups operating in Kashmir and elsewhere in India, sometimes because they were simply powerless to prevent it but at other times with their full knowledge and consent. It also ought not to be forgotten that even a radically atavistic Islamist group such as the Taliban was raised, promoted, and unleashed by the civilian government of the late Benazir Bhutto (during her second term in office from 1993 to 1996) with the full collaboration of the Pakistani military and intelligence services— and that the Taliban continued to receive complete moral and material support under her civilian successor, the then prime minister, Nawaz Sharif.

Both the principal civilian political alternatives in Pakistan would likely continue to prosecute the current antiterrorist operations against al- Qaeda because there seems to be a fragile consensus among Pakistani political elites that this group remains a grave threat to both their country and the international community. This fact, however, only underscores the continuity that is likely to persist in Pakistan's approach to counterterrorism even if a civilian government were to ascend to power in Islamabad. Although there are likely to be differences in style, nuance, and emphasis, the weaknesses of Pakistan's moderate political parties, Islamabad's enduring interests vis- à- vis Afghanistan and India, and the likely inability of any civilian government to exercise comprehensive control over the Pakistani military and intelligence services all combine to suggest that dramatic changes in attitude and performance toward the Taliban and the terrorist groups operating on Indian soil may not be forthcoming. And, although sectarian groups within Pakistan may be pursued more uniformly and hopefully just as resolutely as the war against al- Qaeda, the net deviation from Musharraf's currently segmented antiterrorism policies may be either too subtle or too insignificant to really matter.

Ironically, the Bush administration itself bears some responsibility for reinforcing Musharraf's original instincts and entrenching what has now become the enduring Pakistani calculus. Although President Bush affirmed in the aftermath of the September 11 attacks that his war on terrorism would be total and that states supporting terrorist groups would be required to divest themselves of these entanglements decisively or face America's wrath, his own government never implemented his stirring vision in regard to Pakistan. Rather, during the Indo- Pakistani crisis of 2001–2002—a key moment of truth for Pakistan and its future course in the war on terror— successive U.S. intermediaries visiting the subcontinent pursued an approach that only permitted Islamabad to conclude that the war on terrorism was in fact eminently "divisible." By not pressing Pakistan to relinquish all its terrorist clients once and for all during that crisis— as Washington had previously compelled Islamabad to forsake the Taliban on September 13, 200136—the United States lost a momentous opportunity to help Pakistan rid itself of its long addiction to terror. Instead, the administration's diplomacy, by declining to hold Musharraf accountable for breaching his serial promises to end Pakistani support for terrorism, enabled Islamabad to infer that so long as operatives belonging to "terrorist groups of global reach"—meaning al- Qaeda— were being regularly apprehended by Pakistan, the ISID's links to, and protection of, other regional terrorist organizations would not become a critical liability in U.S.-Pakistan relations.

The liberties thus afforded Pakistan in regard to sustaining its ties with local Kashmiri terrorist groups during the initial phase of the global war on terror consequently reinforced Pakistan's inclination to treat the Taliban remnants similarly. This blunder had few consequences as long as the Taliban movement was in remission, but it has proved to be a most costly lapse on the part of the United States because the sanctuary afforded by Pakistan to the Taliban— and especially its leadership— since 2002 has only permitted the group to rejuvenate and, once again, to begin offensive operations in Afghanistan that, in effect, threaten to undo the gains secured by the early victories in Operation Enduring Freedom.

The U.S. neglect of the early Pakistani decision to ignore the Taliban as a target of counterterrorism operations can be explained only by the administration's single- minded concentration on the war with al- Qaeda. This obsession was no doubt justified at the time, but its inadvertent consequences have now come back to haunt the United States, NATO, Afghanistan, and the ongoing military operations associated with Operation Enduring Freedom more generally. By failing to recognize that the early immunity provided to the Taliban would eventually complicate the effort to defeat al- Qaeda— if for no other reason than that these two groups remain geographically commingled and because Taliban endurance in southern and eastern Afghanistan and in the FATA is an essential precondition for al- Qaeda's survival— the administration lost an opportunity to consolidate its political and military gains in Afghanistan while simultaneously compelling Pakistan to hasten its march away from extremism.

The Bush administration has now begun to press Musharraf to actively interdict the Taliban— an issue that did not become the subject of high- level U.S. demarches before 2005–2006—but it is not certain that, even if responsive Pakistani counterterrorism actions were to be mounted today, they would be as effective as they could have been had they been pursued in the administration's first term. This is because Pakistan's own current intelligence capabilities with respect to the Taliban are probably not as strong as they were when Mullah Omar and his associates were first ejected from Kabul.

Although it is certain that Pakistani information about the Taliban and their leadership is still better than that possessed by other intelligence agencies, including those of the United States, the probable atrophy of Islamabad's connections during the past several years of the war on terror, the strong and growing antagonism within Pakistan toward Musharraf's counterterrorism policies in the FATA, and the increasing opposition from Pakistan's fundamentalist political parties and their social bases of support toward Musharraf's domestic and foreign policies all viciously interact to increase the risk that belated Pakistani actions against the Taliban, including its leadership, may end up being far less successful than they otherwise might have been if executed a few years earlier. And that, in turn, implies not only that the challenges of defeating the Taliban are from a historical perspective rooted in fateful U.S. decisions to treat the Kashmiri terrorists differently when the administration should have done otherwise, but also that Washington ignored the Taliban until it was too late.

THE WEB OF TERROR: EROSION & ENCIRCLEMENT

The primary focus and target of the armies of *mujahiddeen*, and their suicidal hard core, the *fidayeen*, who pour out of the *madrassas* and Pakistani terrorist training camps, at present, is the Indian State of Jammu & Kashmir (J&K). The leadership of the terrorist movement in J&K passed out of the hands of local militants, and to groups created by and based in Pakistan as far back as in 1993, when the most powerful terrorist group indigenous to the State, the Jammu & Kashmir Liberation Front (JKLF) led by Yasin Malik, chose to give up arms and seek a 'political solution' to its grievances. The JKLF still demands Kashmiri 'Independence', and is strongly opposed to any amalgamation with Pakistan. The Pakistan-based groups, quite naturally, are far more amenable to a merger with that country.

Terrorist groupings enjoyed substantial mass support, particularly in the Kashmir Valley, as long as the movement for secession remained indigenous. Progressively, however, a process of disillusionment with the activities of Pakistan sponsored militants has combined with exhaustion to diminish this base, and terrorism is now sustained purely on inputs – ideologies, material, and increasing numbers of men – from across the border. The currently most active terrorist groups in the State are each headquartered in Pakistan, and include the Hizb-ul-Mujahiddeen (HuM) , linked to the JEI in Pakistan; Lashkar-e-Toiba (LeT), the armed wing of the Markaz-ad-Da'awa-wal-Irshad; the Harkat-ul-Jehad-e-Islami (HuJI) and the Harkat-ul-Mujahiddeen (formerly the Harkat-ul-Ansar), linked to the JUP, the Pakistan Tablighi

Jamaat and to the Hizb-e-Islami of Afghanistan; al Badr; and the recently formed Jaish-e-Muhammad (JeM). There are another score of minor and dormant groupings, also located in Pakistan. The umbrella Muttahida Jehad Council coordinates the activities of 13 of the most prominent terrorist factions (14 till the HuM was expelled for declaring a brief unilateral ceasefire in July 2000).

The years 1997, 1998 and the first half of 1999 had seen a gradual decline in violence and fatalities in J&K, but there was a radical escalation after the Kargil War of May-July 1999. The trends underwent a further deterioration after two ceasefires – the first announced unilaterally by the Hizb-ul-Mujahiddeen in July 2000, and the second, again unilaterally, by the Indian Prime Minister, A.B. Vajpayee, in November 2000 – as the possibility of an emerging peace process threatened the entrenched interests and ideological ambitions of the extremist Islamist groups in Pakistan, and of their official sponsors there. A total of 26,226 persons have died in this conflict between 1988 and 2000. These include 10,285 civilians, 12,375 terrorists, and 2,566 security force (SF) personnel. Among the civilian fatalities, 8,712 (nearly 85 per cent) have been Muslims.

The conflict in Kashmir has been substantially documented in the context of Pakistan's strategy and "overriding interest... to achieve internal security by provoking instability among its neighbors." There is, however, comparatively little understanding of the extremist or pan-Islamic agenda in the rest of South Asia, and of its integral links to the strategies and tactics that prepared the ground for terrorism in Kashmir.

As with much of South Asia, the culture and religious practices of the Muslims of Kashmir had little in common with the rigid and distorted version of Wahabbi Islam – with its ideological source in Saudi Arabia – that is the dominant ideological force among contemporary extremist Islamists. Kashmiri Islam was seeped with the mysticism and values of the devotional Sufi order, and the Kashmir Valley was, indeed, held up as a unique and inspirational example of secular values at the time of Partition and Independence, and in the decades that followed. The emergence of terrorism in the State was preceded by decades of religious mobilization and reorientation centered primarily in the mosques in the Valley, and when terror broke out in the late 1980s, it was the mosques and the *madrassas* that provided the motivation, the moral sanction, and the initial impetus, not only to the violence, but to the near complete ethnic cleansing of the Valley of its Kashmiri Pandit minority. It is interesting that, among the priority targets of the terrorists was the network of secular school, most of which were shut down under threat, especially in rural areas, progressively forcing the children into the only surviving 'educational' institution – the *madrassa* – the 'schools of hate' that created new 'supply lines' for *Jihad*.

There is, today, a sustained effort – with mixed results – to replicate these processes of religious mobilization and an extremist Islamist reorientation throughout South Asia. In India, while there have been several political factors and events contributing to higher levels of communal polarization, general communal conflict – expressed in the incidence of communal riots – has been on a decline. Political parties are yet to abandon the electoral strategy of exploiting religious sentiments and insecurities, but the mass base and credibility of those who seek to do so has suffered steady erosion. Nevertheless, the intent and strategy of Pakistan's covert agencies and extremist religious groupings is increasingly apparent in a wide range of activities intended to provoke communal confrontations, engineer terrorist incidents, and recruit soldiers for a pan-Islamic *Jihad* in pockets of Muslim populations across India. This is compounded by a process of 'encirclement' and massive demographic shifts that deepen the danger, particularly along India's Eastern borders.

During a three-day annual congregation of the members of the Markaz-ad-Da'awa-wal-Irshad at Muridke near Lahore on February 6, 2000, the Amir (head) of the Markaz, Hafiz Mohammad Saeed, declared that Kashmir was a 'gateway to capture India' and that it was the aim of the Markaz and its military wing, the Lashkar-e-Toiba, to engineer India's disintegration. Saeed added that his organization's campaign in Hyderabad (Andhra Pradesh) and Junagadh (Gujarat) were among the highest priorities. Abdul Rahman Makki, the LeT's ideologue, expanded on this theme, proclaiming that the group had opened a new unit in Hyderabad to liberate the Indian city from "un-Islamic Indian rule". These declarations are, at once, an expression of the pan-Islamic ambitions shared by all extremist Islamist groups operating in the region, and a reiteration of Pakistan's larger strategy of destabilization beyond the scope of the supposed 'core issue' of Kashmir.

Within this larger design was a series of 13 bomb blasts in various churches in Andhra Pradesh, Karnataka and Goa between May and July 2000, executed by an obscure Islamic sect created in 1924, the Deendar Anjuman. The Anjuman is headed by Zia-ul-Hassan, the son of its founder, who is based in Peshawar, Pakistan, where the sect goes by the name Anjuman Hizbullah. Hassan is also said to have floated a militant organization, the Jamat-e-Hizb-ul-Mujahiddeen in Pakistan, in order to 'capture India and spread Islam'. Intelligence sources indicate that Hassan is bankrolled by the ISI, and the Indian Union Home Minister stated in Parliament that linkages between the Deendar Anjuman and Pakistan's covert intelligence agency had been established by investigators. Investigations have exposed a network of the Anjuman's subversive activities extending across several small towns and urban centres, including Nuzvid, Atmakur, Kurukunda, Palem, Vijayawada, Khammam and Nandyal in Andhra Pradesh; and Batakurki, Ramdurg and Hubli in Karnataka.

Another series of 19 explosions had earlier, on February 14, 1998, left over 50 dead and more than 200 injured in the Coimbatore district of Tamil Nadu. While the Al Umma group, founded by S.A. Basha, investigations and subsequent arrests exposed the involvement of a wide network of extremist Islamist organization across South India, including the Indian Muslim Mohammadi Mujahideen, the Tanzim Islahul Muslimeen, the Jihad Committee in Tamil Nadu; and the Islamic Sevak Sangh, subsequently banned and revived as the People's Democratic Party (PDP), headed by Abdul Nasser Madani. ISI agents, including Azam Ghauri (who was subsequently shot dead in an encounter with the police at Jagityal, Karimnagar District, Andhra Pradesh, on April 6, 2000), Saleem Junaid, Farooq Ahmed and Mohammad Mansoor. By far the most dramatic serial blasts engineered by the ISI took place in Bombay on March 12, 1993, and these revealed a unique pattern of operation that has gradually consolidated itself over the years – the use of organized criminal networks to execute terrorist strikes. Nearly 1,800 kilograms of RDX and a large number of detonators and small arms had been smuggled through the West coast of India prior to these blasts, which killed over 300 persons and targeted critical commercial infrastructure, including the country's largest stock exchange at Dalal Street. The explosions were executed by the notorious D-Company headed by Dawood Ibrahim. Ibrahim now lives in Karachi, and runs India's largest criminal empire through aides located outside India, and primarily in the Middle East.

India's Northeast is another interesting area of emerging Islamist militancy, and here it combines with major demographic shifts that hold significant dangers for the future. Illegal migration on a large scale across the border from Bangladesh is the most potent single factor in the destabilisation of this region. In November 1998, the Governor of Assam, Lt. Gen. (Retd.) S.K. Sinha, submitted a report to the Indian President which estimated the total volume of this infiltration at six million people. Most of this increase was concentrated in a few areas, with a dramatic impact on the local demography and, hence, politics. According to the report, four districts of Assam – Dhubri, Goalpara, Barpeta, Hailakandi – had been transformed into Muslim majority districts by 1991 as a result of this mass infiltration. Another two districts – Nagaon and Karimganj – would have had a Muslim majority since 1998 and yet another district, Morigaon, is fast approaching this position. This demographic destabilization, combined with the widespread violence and political instability in the region has created a unique recruiting ground for the Islamists, and there has been a veritable efflorescence of Muslim terrorist groups operating along India's borders with Bangladesh in the Northeast. In Assam alone, there are over 15 terrorist groups operating under an Islamic banner, and the ISI's role in funding and arming these groups has now been fairly well documented.

Serial bombings and overt terrorist movements, however, cannot be a measure of the penetration that has been achieved by the extremist Islamists and their state sponsors. Acts of terror – especially on a large scale – represent the culmination of years of preparation that are reflected in motivation, mobilization and organizational development. Evidence of these processes is mounting throughout India, and is reflected in the number, both of fundamentalist and of subversive groups in existence, and the geographical spread of their activities. The most prominent of these include the Jamaat-e-Islami Hind (JEI Hind), the All India Milli Council (AIMC), All India Jihad Committee (AIJC), the People's Democratic Party (PDP, formerly the Islamic Sewak Sangh), All India Muslim Federation (AIMF), Muslim United Front (MUF), Tamil Nadu Muslim Munnetra Kazhagam (TNMMK), National Development Front (Kerala), Tabligh Jamaat, Students Islamic Movement of India (SIMI), Students Islamic Organisations (SIO), Al Umma, Al Jihad, and the Muslim Sena Sanghathan, Ikhwan-ul-Muslameen, Islami Inqalabi Mahaz, Tanzim Isla-ul-Muslameen, and the Minorities United Front, among others.

Each of these organizations runs one or more non-governmental organization (NGO), many of which have offices abroad. Very substantial funds are received, and a range of interactions, including frequent 'Tablighi conferences' with foreign delegations, are organized. The flow of funds is primarily through what are known as *hawala* (illegal) channels, and while Pakistan largely defines the patterns of use and the beneficiaries, the preponderance of such transfers originate in Saudi Arabia, Kuwait, United Arab Emirates, Qatar and Oman. Thus, very substantial transfers of foreign funds generated under the pretext of providing relief to the Coimbatore riot victims are believed to have been used for the Coimbatore blasts.

The range, the volume and the persistence of such subversive activity throughout the country is more a measure of Pakistan's tenacity and the intensity of the extremist Islamist vision, than it is of the present impact these activities have had on the larger Muslim community in India. The tragic loss of life, the wasted human and developmental resources, and the atmosphere of fear and suspicion that sporadic incidents of terrorism generate notwithstanding, India has the flexibility, the resilience and the political space to absorb a level of subversive and extremist Islamist activities significantly higher than the present. Nevertheless, the sheer lethality of weaponry and explosives, the possibility of an escalation to a new generation of Chemical and Biological Weapons, and the inherent uncertainty of the politics of a complex society characterized by immense religious and cultural diversity, make the existing risks and levels of activity unacceptable. These risks are even greater and less acceptable in countries where such space is wanting, where political instability is at higher levels, and where the roots of democracy are yet to take firm hold of the soil.

Islamist subversion threatens peace and regime stability more immediately in neighboring Bangladesh, where religious extremism has emerged as a major threat to the prevailing political order and to internal security. There are grave and immediate dangers to peace and stability in Bangladesh: the revival of the activities of the Jamaat-e-Islami, the return to Bangladesh and its politics of Pakistan-backed elements who collaborated closely with the genocidal campaign of 1971 in what was then East Pakistan, the rising rhetoric of Islamic *Hukumat* (rule), and the deepening linkages between militant Bangladeshi groups and the extremist Islamists in Pakistan, Afghanistan and West Asia. Here again, the pattern of funding, subversion and mobilization through the mosque and the *madrassa* is clearly in evidence. Prior to Independence, there were 1,467 *madrassas* in Bangladesh. Their number has currently risen to over 6,500, with more than 90,000 teachers and about 1.8 million students. A large number of these institutions have been established as a result of massive foreign aid, primarily from Gulf countries, and largely unmediated by official channels. Bangladesh's *madrassas* are the chief recruiting ground for Islamic militant groups, including several that are linked to Pakistan and also to Osama Bin Laden's *Al Qaida*. The latter category includes the Harkat-ul-Jehad-e-Islami, which was established by Shawkat Osman, alias Sheikh Farid in 1992 with Bin Laden's backing, and which has an estimated strength of about 15,000. The Harkat maintains six camps in the hilly areas of Chittagong, where the cadres are given arms training. Several hundred recruits have also been trained in Afghanistan. The cadres, recruited mainly from among students of various *madrassas*, style themselves as the 'Bangladeshi Taliban.' Reports suggest that foreign-aided religious fanatics are actively conspiring to establish 'Islamic *hukumat*' by waging war and killing progressive intellectuals, as well as various minority groups and 'heretical' sects, such as the Ahmadiyas.

In addition to the JEI, the prominent fundamentalist Islamist political parties in Bangladesh include the Muslim Leagure, Tabligh Jamaat, Jamaat-e-Tulba and Jamaat-ul-Muderessin. One significant pro-Iranian group, the Islamic Shasantantra Andolan (Movement for Islamic Constitution), is also active. The subversive activities of the ISI and foreign extremist Islamist agencies in Bangladesh increased radically after Sheikh Hasina's broadly secular Awami League came to power in June 1996, and this has contributed to an upsurge in militant and fundamentalist political activity. Superimposed over a history of military coups, a politics dominated by the rhetoric of Islam, and increasing international linkages, including networks with insurgent groups operating in India's Northeast, extremist Islamic militancy constitutes the most serious existing internal security threat in Bangladesh.

The security agencies of the infant democracy of Nepal are also being challenged by rising extremist Islamist activity, despite the fact that Muslims constitute a bare three percent of the population. Such activity is, presently, primarily directed against India, but its linkages with organized criminal operations and the destabilization of pockets of Muslim concentrations in the Terai region bordering India are a cause of increasing concern for Kathmandu. A succession of recent reports has documented increasing activities of the ISI and by the Pakistan Embassy at Kathmandu involving strong organized criminal networks and prominent political leaders in a range of activities targeting India and reinforcing the Islamist agenda within Nepal. The Muslim pockets of the Terai, especially Bardiya, Banke, Rupendehi and the Parsa-Morang belt have seen increasing '*Tablighi*' activities, and the construction of mosques and *madrassas* with financial flows from Pakistan – often directly from the Embassy at Kathmandu – from Saudi Arabia and from a range of pan-Islamic organizations.

Over the past two decades, more than 275 mosques and *madrassas* have been built in just the four districts of Rupandehi, Banke, Kapilvastu and Bardiya. There are some 15 major *tablighi/* fundamentalist organizations in Nepal, and at least five of these are well within the ambit of Pakistan's influence and control. These include the Jamaat-e-Millat-e-Islamia; the Nepal Islamic Yuba Sangh; the Nepal Muslim League; the Nepal Muslim Ekta Sangh; and the Democratic Muslim Welfare Association. Nepal is, consequently, emerging as an important 'staging post' for Pakistan's strategy of erosion and encirclement against India, and is increasingly the preferred route for terrorists movements to various areas of low-intensity conflict in J&K and the Northeast.

In Sri Lanka, the Muslim community and emerging fundamentalist forces have generally aligned themselves with the interests of the government. The Island nation's Muslim population is mainly Tamil, but has been driven out of the ethnically cleansed northern areas controlled by the Liberation Tigers of Tamil Eelam (LTTE), and is now concentrated along the eastern coast, the north-west coast, Kandy and suburban Colombo. Islamic fundamentalist mobilization in Sri Lanka began after a succession of attacks on the Muslims by the LTTE in the early 1990s, after which the government decided to arm the Muslim youth for self-defence. The conflict between Hindu and Muslim Tamils resulted in the polarization of mindsets on the issue of religious identity. There are, today, nearly a dozen Muslim fundamentalist organizations in Sri Lanka who are funded by foreign countries, primarily Saudi Arabia, with at least two political parties drawing significant support from Iran.

THE GLOBAL WAR ON TERROR

Using the opportunities therefore afforded by the global war on terror, the Pakistani security services systematically eliminated many sources of sectarian violence within two years of the campaign's initiation, even though they have been unable to conclusively eradicate the cancer of sectarian bloodshed within Pakistan itself. In part, this is due to the selectivity of Musharraf's antisectarian campaign. But the continuing fragmentation of these violent groups; their links to the wider networks of international terrorism now resident in Pakistan, various foreign sponsors abroad, and the flourishing madaris within the country; and the continuing utility of their gun- toting membership to different political parties and occasionally to governmental organs themselves imply that sectarian threats will be impossible to extinguish so long as "state policies of Islamisation and [the] marginalization of secular democratic forces" continue to persist in Pakistan.

The second set of groups, the terrorist outfits operating with Pakistan Army and ISID support against India in Kashmir, was treated in a remarkably different way compared with the anti-national sectarian militants inside Pakistan. These groups, such as the Lashkar- e- Toiba, the Jaish- e- Muhammad, and the Harkat-ul- Mujahideen, for example, were the long lances in the Pakistani campaign to wrest the disputed state of Jammu and Kashmir from India. Since the late 1980s, the Pakistani military has financed, trained, armed, and launched these cadres on their murderous missions into Kashmir and elsewhere inside the Indian union. Because the struggle for control over the disputed Himalayan state was fully under way by the time the global war on terror was inaugurated, these terrorist groups were more or less exempted from Musharraf's domestic campaign against violence and extremism.

This exclusion was justified both on the strategic rationale that Pakistan's participation in the war on terror was intended, among other things, to protect its freedom of action in Kashmir and on the repeated, though fraudulent, assertion that these groups, far from being terrorists, only personified the legitimate Kashmiri struggle for self- determination against India. In fact, of all the Pakistani- sponsored Deobandi terrorist groups operating against India in Kashmir and elsewhere, only one entity— the Hizbul Mujahideen— began life as an indigenous Kashmiri insurgent group; the others, including the most violent organizations such as the Lashkar- e- Toiba, the Jaish- e- Muhammad, and the Harkat-ul- Mujahideen, are all led, manned, and financed by native Pakistanis. This reality notwithstanding— and perhaps because of it— Islamabad continued to sustain the operations of these groups against India but, in an effort to maintain the consistency of its commitments to the global war on terror, now began to emphasize that its support took only the form of moral, and not material, encouragement.

This charade was rudely interrupted by the December 13, 2001, terrorist attack on India's parliament when, in response to New Delhi's subsequent military mobilization, Pakistan was compelled by U.S. diplomacy to initiate a series of measures to restrict the activities of its terrorist clients. The implementation of these actions, however, was at best halfhearted and inconsistent.

Far from seeking to extirpate these terrorist groups permanently, Musharraf sought mainly to defang India's threats of military action and to alleviate Washington's fears of an inconvenient Indo- Pakistani war. His overarching objective consisted of protecting these terrorist assets to the extent possible because they represented national investments— a "strategic reserve" —in Islamabad's subconventional war against New Delhi.

Consequently, to this day, Musharraf has not sought to eliminate the Deobandi terrorist groups operating against India in Kashmir and elsewhere; he has instead sought only to modulate their activities, depending on the extent of satisfaction he derives from the prevailing state of diplomatic relations with New Delhi and the progress secured in the ongoing Indo- Pakistani peace process.

Although the Pakistani- supported infiltration of terrorist groups into Kashmir— but not into the rest of India— appears to have abated in recent years, most observers conclude that this phenomenon is linked either to Musharraf's desire not to provide India with any excuses to abandon the generally fragile peace process or to domestic crises within Pakistan. In any event, it is agreed that Musharraf simply has not made the decisive decision to abandon or eliminate the terrorist groups operating against India in the manner witnessed, for example, in the case of the more virulent anti- national sectarian entities operating within Pakistan.

The third group relevant to the Pakistani decision to join the U.S.-led coalition against terrorism consisted of the Taliban, that is, the Pashtun remnants of the regime ejected from power in Kabul as a result of the initial success of Operation Enduring Freedom. After their defeat at the hands of the Northern Alliance, the Taliban cadres hastily returned to the regions whence they originated.

Many in the rank and file withdrew to their villages in the southern Afghan provinces of Helmand, Kandahar, Oruzgan, and Zabol as well as along the border areas on the western side of the Durand Line separating Afghanistan from Pakistan, that is, in the eastern Afghan provinces of Paktika, Paktia, Khowst, Nangarhar, and Konar. Given their significance as high- value targets, the core Taliban leadership— along with those Pakistani Pashtuns who had joined their movement— crossed over the Afghanistan-Pakistan border into the relative safety of the FATA.

Because most of the Taliban's fighters originally mobilized by the Pakistani ISID were drawn from the Ghilzai confederation of Pashtuns, which dominates eastern and southeastern Afghanistan, and from the other Pashtun tribes inhabiting the FATA, their return to these ancestral lands was not surprising. In fact, all the evidence relating to the incidence of terrorist attacks since 2001 suggests strongly that the war- fighting cadres of the Taliban continue to remain bivouacked in these areas.

The exact location of the supreme leadership of the Taliban movement, however, cannot be established with any self- evident clarity. Irrespective of where the rahbari shura (leadership council) centred on Mullah Omar and his closest associates found shelter in the immediate aftermath of their defeat, Afghan military and civilian intelligence officials as well as NATO commanders today believe that this coterie eventually found refuge in Quetta, the largest city and capital of Pakistan's Baluchistan Province, from where they continue to operate to this day.

As Col. Chris Vernon, NATO's chief of staff for southern Afghanistan, declared forthrightly, "The thinking piece of the Taliban [operates] out of Quetta in Pakistan. It's the major headquarters— they use it to run a series of networks in Afghanistan."

These networks, in turn, are judged to be directed by four subsidiary shuras based in Quetta, Miran Shah, Peshawar, and Karachi: the first three actually control or coordinate most of the ongoing terrorist operations occurring, respectively, along the southern, central, and northern "fronts" in Afghanistan, whereas the fourth is believed to connect the Taliban with the logistics, financial, and technical assistance conduits emanating from the wider Islamic world. The pattern of terrorist attacks occurring in Afghanistan from 2002 to 2007, again corroborates this judgment.

Because the Pakistani state was most intimately involved in the creation of the Taliban before their fall, Musharraf's antiterrorism campaign after September 11, 2001, deliberately avoided any concerted targeting of this group and, in particular, its senior leadership. No other explanation is consistent with the fact that, although Pakistani military, intelligence, and paramilitary forces apprehended scores of al- Qaeda operatives, including numerous key individuals in the al- Qaeda hierarchy, the senior Taliban leaders killed or captured in southern Afghanistan or in the FATA have numbered literally a handful in comparison.

This asymmetry in seizures is all the more odd because, prior to Operation Enduring Freedom, Pakistani military and ISID liaison elements were deeply intertwined with all levels of the Taliban mand structure and its war fighters in the field. In contrast, the Pakistani intelligence relationship with al- Qaeda in Afghanistan was more tenuous, yet Pakistan's military forces were able to apprehend far more al- Qaeda cadres than Taliban operatives.

These successes in regard to al- Qaeda have invariably been attributed by Pakistanis, including General Musharraf, to the fact that it was always easier to identify the ethnically alien al- Qaeda elements along the frontier in comparison with the Taliban who, being ethnically Pashtun, were able to disguise their identities by assimilating into the larger tribal population.

While this explanation is only partly true— non- native fighters have lived in and become amalgamated into the social structures of the Afghan- Pakistani frontier since at least the anti-Soviet jihad of the 1980s— it is also disingenuous because the Pakistani ISID was not only deeply involved in the recruitment, training, arming, and operations of Taliban fighters at multiple bureaucratic levels, but it also maintained an intense liaison relationship with the Ghilzai tribes whose population has been disproportionately represented in the Taliban. Since protecting these relationships was deemed to be especially critical for Pakistan's national security interests in the aftermath of the Northern Alliance victory in Kabul, the large number of Taliban foot soldiers who made their way into the FATA were largely ignored by Pakistani counterterrorism operations so long as they did not engage in any untoward activities that either called attention to their presence or magnified the troubles confronting the Pakistani state.

All told, then, the Taliban network, just like the Pakistani-aided terrorist groups operating in Kashmir and elsewhere in India, was deliberately permitted to escape the wrath of General Musharraf's counterterrorism operations in the initial phase of the war on terror.

Such an approach, however, could not be extended to the fourth group, al- Qaeda, which had also taken up sanctuary in the FATA, particularly in South Waziristan initially. Although al- Qaeda continued to have sympathizers within the extreme fringes of Pakistani society even after the terrible events of September 11 were conclusively attributed to its operations, the Pakistani military establishment did not enjoy the luxury of slackening its campaign against this target because of the consequences for U.S.-Pakistani relations at a time when bilateral ties were just recovering after a decade of U.S. disfavor and when Washington had just embarked on a ferocious campaign against al- Qaeda worldwide.

8

Terrorism and Pakistani Intelligence Agency

INTRODUCTION

Pakistan's intelligence agency, the Inter-Services Intelligence (ISI), has long faced accusations of meddling in the affairs of its neighbors. A range of officials inside and outside Pakistan have stepped up suggestions of links between the ISI and terrorist groups in recent years. In autumn 2006, a leaked report by a British Defense Ministry think tank charged, "Indirectly Pakistan (through the ISI) has been supporting terrorism and extremism—whether in London on 7/7, or in Afghanistan, or Iraq." In India, Mumbai's police chief has claimed to have proof that the ISI planned the July 2006 bombing of the Indian city's commuter rail system, which was carried out by the Kashmir-based militant group Lashkar-e-Taiba. After massive bombings marred former Prime Minister Benazir Bhutto's October 2007 return to Pakistan, some of her supporters blamed the ISI; Bhutto herself called for the sacking of the country's intelligence chief.

In a September 2006 BBC interview, President Pervez Musharraf underscored the importance of his nation's role: "Remember my words: if the ISI is not with you and Pakistan is not with you, you will lose in Afghanistan." In a later appearance on NBC's "Meet the Press," Musharraf acknowledged some retired ISI operatives could be abetting the Taliban insurgency in Afghanistan. But Pakistan's government denies allegations of supporting terrorism, citing as evidence its cooperation in the "war on terror," in which it has taken significant losses, politically and on the battlefield.

Does ISI Support Terrorists?

"The ISI probably would not define what they've done in the past as 'terrorism,'" says William Milam, former U.S. ambassador to Pakistan. Nevertheless, experts say the ISI has supported a number of militant groups in the disputed Kashmir region between Pakistan and India, some of which are on the State Department's Foreign Terrorist Organizations list. Though the level of assistance to these groups has varied, Kathy Gannon, who covered the region for decades for the Associated Press, says previous support consisted of money, weapons, and training.

Though Pakistani officials deny any current support for the Taliban—which the State Department does not deem a terrorist group—the ISI certainly has supported Afghan insurgents in the past. ISI's first major involvement in Afghanistan came after the Soviet invasion in 1979, when it partnered with the CIA to provide weapons, money, intelligence, and training to the mujahadeen fighting the Red Army.

At the time, some voices within the United States questioned the degree to which Pakistani intelligence favoured extremist and anti-American fighters. Following the Soviet withdrawal, the ISI continued its involvement in Afghanistan, first supporting resistance fighters opposed to Moscow's puppet government, and later the Taliban.

Pakistan stands accused of allowing that support to continue. Afghan President Hamid Karzai has repeatedly said Pakistan trains militants and sends them across the border. In May 2006, the British chief of staff for southern Afghanistan told the Guardian, "The thinking piece of the Taliban is out of Quetta in Pakistan. It's the major headquarters." Speaking at the Council on Foreign Relations in September, President Musharraf responded to such accusations, saying, "It is the most ridiculous thought that the Taliban headquarters can be in Quetta." Nevertheless, experts generally suspect Pakistan still provides some support to the Taliban, though probably not to the extent it did in the past. "If they're giving them support," Gannon says, "it's access back and forth [to Afghanistan] and the ability to find safe haven."

How much Control does Pakistan's political Leadership have over the ISI?

Experts say Musharraf exercises firm control over his intelligence agency. "I do not accept the thesis that the ISI is a rogue organization," Milam says. "It's a disciplined army unit that does what it's told, though it may push the envelope sometimes." With a reported staff of 10,000, ISI is hardly monolithic: "Like in any secret service, there are rogue elements," says Frederic Grare, a South Asia expert and visiting scholar at the Carnegie Endowment. He points out that many of the ISI's agents have ethnic and cultural ties to Afghan insurgents, and naturally sympathize with them.

President Musharraf's admission that retired ISI agents may be helping Taliban fighters suggests his government knows of at least some unsanctioned Pakistani support for the Afghan insurgency. Experts note Musharraf's acknowledgement also gives him plausible deniability of any sanctioned assistance Pakistan may also be providing. Marvin G. Weinbaum, an expert on Afghanistan and Pakistan at the Middle East Institute, says Pakistan has sent "retired" ISI agents on missions the government could not officially endorse. Some observers believe Pakistan's duplicity is deliberate: "Musharraf's been playing with us since day one," Grare says.

What has Pakistan done to Combat Terrorism?

Pakistan has arrested scores of al-Qaeda affiliates, including Khalid Sheikh Mohammed, the alleged mastermind of the 9/11 attacks. The ISI and the Pakistani military have worked effectively with the United States to pursue the remnants of al-Qaeda. Pakistan also stationed 80,000 troops in the troubled province of Waziristan near the Afghan border.

Hundreds of Pakistani soldiers died there in resulting clashes with militants, which Musharraf told a recent CFR meeting "broke the al-Qaeda network's back in Pakistan." Though Pakistan has effectively battled al-Qaeda, Weinbaum says it has largely ignored Taliban fighters on its soil. "There are extremist groups that are beyond the pale with which the ISI has no influence at all," he says. "Those are the ones they go after."

What is Pakistan's Interest in aiding the Taliban?

Pakistan does not enjoy good relations with the current leadership of Afghanistan, partly because of rhetorical clashes with Afghan President Hamid Karzai, and partly because Karzai has made strong ties to India. Some experts say Pakistan wants to see a stable, friendlier government emerge in Afghanistan. Though the raging insurgency certainly doesn't serve this goal, increased Taliban influence, especially in the government, might. Supporting the Taliban also allows Pakistan to hedge its bets should the NATO coalition pull out of Afghanistan. Not everyone agrees with this analysis. According to Weinbaum, Pakistan has two policies. One is an official policy of promoting stability in Afghanistan; the other is an unofficial policy of supporting jihadis in order to appease political forces within Pakistan. "The second [policy] undermines the first one," he says.

Pakistan's interest in aiding Kashmiri Militants

Throughout its existence, Pakistan has viewed India as its enemy. Though Islamabad has a real interest in fostering better relations with New Delhi, little love is lost between the nations. Some experts say the Kashmiri militants keep pressure on the Indian government, though others point out the militants' actions have sparked tense showdowns between the two nuclear-armed states in the past. While Pakistan has a formidable military presence near the Indian border, Gannon says the militant groups there serve as "their second line of defense and offence."

British and Indian Charges against Pakistan

Experts are skeptical. Indian officials claim to have evidence that the ISI planned the July bombing of the Mumbai commuter trains, but the charges seem unlikely to some observers of the long, difficult India-Pakistan relationship. The two nations have a history of finger-pointing, and while some of the allegations hold water, there is a tendency to exaggerate. Furthermore, endorsing an attack on India would undermine Musharraf's own policy. "Pakistan is genuinely trying to open up relations with India," Gannon says.

In Weinbaum's view, the British report—which London insists is not a statement of policy—makes "too broad a statement." Though Pakistan does offer safe haven to Kashmiri groups, and perhaps some Taliban fighters, the suggestion that the ISI is responsible for the 7/7 bombings of London's mass transit system is "a real stretch," Gannon says.

Pakistan's Relationship with the Tribal Leaders in its Northwestern Provinces

Despite President Musharraf's claims of success in Pakistan's three-year military incursion into Waziristan, the region remains problematic. Local tribesmen are the traditional power brokers, and over the last two decades, they have earned large sums of money offering safe haven to Taliban and foreign fighters. At the outset of the U.S.-led war in Afghanistan, many militants fled across the border into Waziristan, putting pressure on the Pakistani government to address the situation.

ISI officials met resistance when they asked local leaders to hand over foreign militants. Pakistan deployed troops to the area, though reports suggest that they took as many casualties as their adversaries. Unable to make military progress, Pakistani officials negotiated a peace deal with the local tribesmen, which was seen by many as a capitualtion to tribal influence in the area.

INTELLIGENCE AGENCIES IN THE 2008 ELECTORAL DEBATE

If the documents made public by the political parties when they were in opposition are a reliable indication of their actual agendas, reforming the intelligence agencies should indeed be a priority of the new government. The "Charter of Democracy," signed by former prime ministers Nawaz Sharif and Benazir Bhutto in May 2006 in London, states in Article 32 that: [T]he ISI, MI and other security agencies shall be accountable to the elected government through the Prime Minister Secretariat, Ministry of Defense, and Cabinet Division respectively. Their budgets will be approved by DCC after recommendations are prepared by the respective ministry. The political wings of all intelligence agencies will be disbanded. A committee will be formed to cut waste and bloat in the armed forces and security agencies in the interest of the defense and security of the country. All senior posting in these agencies shall be made with the approval of the government through respective ministry.

Similarly, the 2008 Pakistan Peoples Party election manifesto included a provision indicating that "all security agencies, including ISI and MI, will be answerable to the elected Prime Minister." As the date of the elections approached, criticism regarding the actual and potential involvement of the ISI increased and became an issue in the campaign. Asad Rehman, from Aurat Foundation Legislative Watch, declared, for example, that "the ISI role in facilitating negotiations with the Pakistan Peoples Party amounts to pre-poll rigging and the ISI is trying to protect the army's role in politics."

The real debate about reform started in October 2007, when Benazir Bhutto demanded the restructuring of the ISI, arguing that the reconciliation process was being destroyed by the ruling Pakistan Muslim League and the intelligence agencies. The then-PPP chairperson remained very cautious, though. She implicitly accused the agency of promoting vested interests and religious extremism but insisted that she was not blaming the ISI as an institution "because there [are] a lot of good people in it" but maintained that the ISI was getting a bad name because "a handful of people had been conspiring against civilian rulers and strengthening the hands of religious fundamentalists." Observing that the agencies have "failed to confine themselves to their legitimate role," she also insisted that the head of the IB should be a serving police official and not a retired bureaucrat or army officer.

In a context of growing domestic terrorism, Bhutto's argument was real but politically convenient. She was arguing that an intelligence agency that would not spend its time and resources keeping an eye on the political opposition, hounding government critics and dissenters, and keeping the media in check would do a better job of carrying out its actual responsibilities. But introducing the reform of the intelligence agencies to the political debate was not simply politically expedient.

Controlling the agencies was a real concern for the former prime minister, not least because she had twice been the victim of their manipulations and she had often discussed the issue in private. Yet, the debate remained limited to two issues only: the nominations of the agencies' heads and the dismantling of the so-called political wing of the ISI.

This last demand became itself a matter of debate when Chaudhry Shujaat Hussain, former interim prime minister and president of the PML-Q, the main political support of Pervez Musharraf, declared that the "political cell" of the ISI should continue to work because "it keeps a watch on political parties and reports their anti-government and anti-state activities." In the process, Hussain attacked his political opponents, in particular Nawaz Sharif, and exposed at once the depth of his democratic conviction and his own links with the agencies. The PPP retorted by reiterating its "demand for the end of the ISI role in the political process," accusing the MI of intimidation and abduction of PPP activists and candidates.

Postelection Adjustments

Before the February 18, 2008, elections, during the process of relative depoliticization of the army started by the new COAS, Parvez Kayani, it was briefly expected that the army would withdraw its officers from the ISI. The rumor was denied by the Inter-Services Public Relations director general, Major General Athar Abbas, who maintained that the army's presence in the agency was necessary.

In May 2008, after the formation of the new government, the press reported that the intelligence agencies had been instructed to report to Prime Minister Yousuf Raza Gilani and no longer to Pervez Musharraf. It was also announced that major structural changes were being made, some of which involved the ISI political wing's being made part of the MI. Neither announcement has been confirmed thus far, nor is it clear what democratic benefit the shift of the ISI political wing to the MI would bring. Later in May 2008, the PPP announced that it would soon take legislative action to disband political wings of all intelligence agencies.

Until the end of July 2008, reform seemed to be limited to changes at the head of the main agencies, reflecting the new power structure in Pakistan. As president and COAS, Pervez Musharraf had concentrated the control of the IB, ISI, and MI in his own hands, the latter by virtue of his position as COAS. He had further reinforced this control by nominating family members or staunch loyalists to leading positions. Brigadier Ejaz Shah, a close friend, was heading the IB; Musharraf's nephew, Lieutenant General Nadeem Taj, was director general of the ISI; and Lieutenant General Nadeem Ejaz was director general of the MI.

Pervez Musharraf lost control of MI to his successor when he resigned his position as COAS. The new head of the military, Parvez Kayani, soon appointed his own man, Lieutenant General Mohammad Asif. Nadeem Taj remained director general of the ISI for a few more months, even after Musharraf's departure from power. He was later replaced by Lieutenant General Shuja Pasha. The nomination signaled no more than a gradual assertion of power by the COAS. The IB is now headed by Tariq Lodhi, close to Asif Ali Zardari, leader of the PPP. Other controversial intelligence officials, such as Sindh operational head of the ISI, Brigadier Tariq Huda, have also been removed from their positions. Considered the de facto chief minister of Sindh, Huda was said to have been in charge of, among other things, the May 12, 2007, operation to block the entry into Karachi of Chief Justice Iftikhar Muhammad Chaudhry, a decision that resulted in the deaths of dozens of people.

More interesting, however, was Parvez Kayani's decision to dismantle the so-called political wing of the ISI on November 25, 2008. Such a decision had been a recurrent demand—without any success whatsoever—of the PPP both in opposition and in government. The situation changed in the fall of 2008 when Pakistan suddenly found itself under strong international pressure to rein in the ISI following the attack on the Indian embassy in Kabul, for which the entire international community held the intelligence agency responsible. It then became convenient to eliminate a structure whose function could easily be performed outside any formal mechanism. Parvez Kayani thus diminished international pressure by trying to persuade the international community that the ISI had effectively withdrawn from politics and that the civilian government was in charge. Thus, the civilian government was designated as responsible for a security policy over which it still had no control. Fundamentally, however, the system changed only marginally.

Prospects for Reform

In such a situation, the need for reform appears increasingly urgent, but its prospects are limited. The civilian government seems to be trying to make the ISI more accountable and has taken several steps to reduce its power. The agency budget is now discussed by Parliament. The government also holds regular security briefings involving not only cabinet members and intelligence officials but also the entire security apparatus. The intention is to assert control over the intelligence agencies by building a national consensus through Parliament. The forthcoming elections to the various parliamentary committee chairmanships will be decisive in this regard.

It would have been naïve, however, not to expect strong resistance from an organization that has never accepted democracy. The series of terrorist attacks that have taken place inside and outside Pakistan (in Kashmir, Afghanistan, and the Federally Administered Tribal Areas of Pakistan) in which responsibility of the ISI is increasingly acknowledged can be interpreted as evidence of its willingness to increase the vulnerability of the democratic government.

The tension between the two institutions is already obvious, as demonstrated by an incident on July 26, 2008. On that date the prime minister's office made a surprise announcement that the ISI and the IB would immediately be placed under the administrative, financial, and operational control of the Interior Ministry, headed by Rehman Malik. The decision was, however, reversed less than 24 hours after it was announced. The government's Press Information Department issued a statement saying the government had meant only to reemphasize "coordination between the Ministry of Interior and the ISI in relation to the war on terror and internal security." Similar terms were used by the entourage of Pervez Musharraf.

However, the Pakistani press reported on July 28, 2008, that the prime minister, then in London, was informed by a phone call in the middle of the night "that the Army, and especially the ISI, was trying its best to stay out of politics for the past many months but his decision to place the ISI under the control of Rehman Malik would be seen as an attempt to again politicize the ISI for achieving certain political objectives."

That the government had actually tried to confront the ISI in such a way is surprising. Putting the agency under the Interior Ministry made no sense, although some analysts suggest that "the move would have opened up the ISI's finances and operations to scrutiny," as asserted by Ayyesha Siddiqua Agha. The risk of a coup would have been real. The government explanation of a miscommunication seems, therefore, plausible. But it seems also likely that the government was trying to remind the intelligence agency that it had to conform to government direction and coordinate its operations with the Interior Ministry.

The fact that opposition senator Mushahid Hussain of the PML-Q denounced the attempted shift of ISI management as politicization and argued that putting the ISI under the Interior Ministry would "seriously undermine national security" shows that the ISI will also use politics to resist any attempt by the civilian government to control it.

The story immediately became an embarrassment for the prime minister, who was seen as unable to assert his control over the agency. He could not ignore what seems to have been a veiled, nevertheless real, threat from the army. The incident showed publicly that the agencies were running contrary to the government's policies and, despite the Pakistani constitution, the power of the prime minister over the ISI remained nominal. The episode may have further weakened the chances of actual reform of the ISI.

Western Dilemmas

The cooperation between Western intelligence agencies and the ISI could also prove a considerable obstacle to reform. Although this cooperation has always proved deeply frustrating, most ISI partners prefer flawed cooperation to no cooperation at all. Partners keep interacting directly with the ISI, depriving the Pakistan government of its leverage but putting pressure on it to deliver high-value targets who are either under ISI control or who would have to be identified and arrested by the ISI. If there are legitimate questions about the ability of the government to assert its control over the ISI in the future, the current policy carries its own contradiction.

Western governments may not be willing to gamble on the ability of the current government to increase its authority, but the security of the region, and by extension the security of the West, requires civilian ownership of Pakistan's foreign and security policies. There is no good answer to the dilemma, but policies whose undesired impact is to diminish the authority of the elected government are counterproductive and could become an impediment to the implementation of much needed reforms.

PAKISTAN'S INTER-SERVICES INTELLIGENCE (ISI)

The intelligence community of Pakistan, which was once described by the "Frontier Post" of Peshawar (May 18,1994) as its "invisible government" and by the "Dawn" of Karachi (April 25,1994) as "our secret godfathers" consists of the Intelligence Bureau (IB) and the ISI. While the IB comes under the Interior Minister, the ISI is part of the Ministry of Defence (MOD). Each wing of the Armed Forces has also its own intelligence directorate for tactical MI.

The IB is the oldest dating from Pakistan's creation in 1947. It was formed by the division of the pre-partition IB of British India. Its unsatisfactory military intelligence (MI) performance in the first Indo-Pak war of 1947-48 over Jammu & Kashmir (J & K) led to the decision in 1948 to create the ISI, manned by officers from the three Services, to specialise in the collection, analysis and assessment of external intelligence, military and non-military, with the main focus on India.

Initially, the ISI had no role in the collection of internal political intelligence except in Pakistan-Occupied Kashmir (POK) and the Northern Areas (NA—Gilgit and Baltistan). Ayub Khan, suspecting the loyalty and objectivity of the Bengali police officers in the Subsidiary Intelligence Bureau (SIB) of the IB in Dacca, the capital of the then East Pakistan, entrusted the ISI with the responsibility for the collection of internal political intelligence in East Pakistan.

Similarly, Z.A.Bhutto, when faced with a revolt by Balochi nationalists in Balochistan after the liberation of Bangladesh in 1971, suspected the loyalty of the Balochi police officers of the SIB in Quetta and made the military officers of the ISI responsible for internal intelligence in Balochistan.

Zia-ul-Haq expanded the internal intelligence responsibilities of the ISI by making it responsible not only for the collection of intelligence about the activities of the Sindhi nationalist elements in Sindh and for monitoring the activities of Shia organisations all over the country after the success of the Iranian Revolution in 1979, but also for keeping surveillance on the leaders of the Pakistan People's Party (PPP) of Mrs.Benazir Bhutto and its allies which had started the Movement for the Restoration of Democracy (MRD) in the early 1980s. The ISI's Internal Political Division had Shah Nawaz Bhutto, one of the two brothers of Mrs.Benazir Bhutto, assassinated through poisoning in the French Riviera in the middle of 1985, in an attempt to intimidate her into not returning to Pakistan for directing the movement against Zia, but she refused to be intimidated and returned to Pakistan.

Even in the 1950s, Ayub Khan had created in the ISI a Covert Action Division for assisting the insurgents in India's North-East and its role was expanded in the late 1960s to assist the Sikh Home Rule Movement of London-based Charan Singh Panchi, which was subsequently transformed into the so-called Khalistan Movement, headed by Jagjit Singh Chauhan. A myriad organisations operating amongst the members of the Sikh diaspora in Europe, the US and Canada joined the movement at the instigation and with the assistance of the ISI.

During the Nixon Administration in the US, when Dr.Henry Kissinger was the National Security Adviser, the intelligence community of the US and the ISI worked in tandem in guiding and assisting the so-called Khalistan movement in the Punjab. The visits of prominent Sikh Home Rule personalities to the US before the Bangladesh Liberation War in December, 1971, to counter Indian allegations of violations of the human rights of the Bengalis of East Pakistan through counter-allegations of violations of the human rights of the Sikhs in Punjab were jointly orchestrated by the ISI, the US intelligence and some officials of the US National Security Council (NSC) Secretariat, then headed by Dr.Kissinger.

This covert colloboration between the ISI and the US intelligence community was also directed at discrediting Mrs.Indira Gandhi's international stature by spreading disinformation about alleged naval base facilities granted by her to the USSR in Vizag and the Andaman & Nicobar, the alleged attachment of KGB advisers to the then Lt.Gen.Sunderji during Operation Bluestar in the Golden Temple in Amritsar in June, 1984, and so on. This collaboration petered out after her assassination in October,1984.

The Afghan war of the 1980s saw the enhancement of the covert action capabilities of the ISI by the CIA. A number of officers from the ISI's Covert Action Division received training in the US and many covert action experts of the CIA were attached to the ISI to guide it in its operations against the Soviet troops by using the Afghan Mujahideen, Islamic fundamentalists of Pakistan and Arab volunteers. Osama bin Laden, Mir Aimal Kansi, who assassinated two CIA officers outside their office in Langley, US, in 1993, Ramzi Yousef and his accomplices involved in the New York World Trade Centre explosion in February, 1993, the leaders of the Muslim separatist movement in the southern Philippines and even many of the narcotics smugglers of Pakistan were the products of the ISI-CIA collaboration in Afghanistan.

The encouragement of opium cultivation and heroin production and smuggling was also an offshoot of this co-operation. The CIA, through the ISI, promoted the smuggling of heroin into

Afghanistan in order to make the Soviet troops heroin addicts. Once the Soviet troops were withdrawn in 1988, these heroin smugglers started smuggling the drugs to the West, with the complicity of the ISI. The heroin dollars have largely contributed to preventing the Pakistani economy from collapsing and enabling the ISI to divert the jehadi hordes from Afghanistan to J & K after 1989 and keeping them well motivated and well-equipped.

Even before India's Pokhran I nuclear test of 1974, the ISI had set up a division for the clandestine procurement of military nuclear technology from abroad and, subsequently, for the clandestine purchase and shipment of missiles and missile technology from China and North Korea. This division, which was funded partly by donations from Saudi Arabia and Libya, partly by concealed allocations in Pakistan's State budget and partly by heroin dollars, was instrumental in helping Pakistan achieve a military nuclear and delivery capability despite its lack of adequate human resources with the required expertise.

Thus, the ISI, which was originally started as essentially an agency for the collection of external intelligence, has developed into an agency adept in covert actions and clandestine procurement of denied technologies as well.

The IB, which was patterned after the IB of British India, used to be a largely police organisation, but the post of Director-General (DG), IB, is no longer tenable only by police officers as it was in the past. Serving and retired military officers are being appointed in increasing numbers to senior posts in the IB, including to the post of DG.

In recent years, there has been a controversy in Pakistan as to who really controls the ISI and when was its internal Political Division set up. Testifying before the Supreme Court on June 16,1997, in a petition filed by Air Marshal (retd) Asghar Khan, former chief of the Pakistan Air Force, challenging the legality of the ISI's Political Division accepting a donation of Rs.140 million from a bank for use against PPP candidates during elections, Gen. (retd) Mirza Aslam Beg, former Chief of the Army Staff (COAS), claimed that though the ISI was manned by serving army officers and was part of the MOD, it reported to the Prime Minister and not to the COAS and that its internal Political Division was actually set up by the late Z.A.Bhutto in 1975.

Many Pakistani analysts have challenged this and said that the ISI, though de jure under the Prime Minister, had always been controlled de facto by the COAS and that its internal Political Division had been in existence at least since the days of Ayub Khan, if not earlier.

The ISI is always headed by an Army officer of the rank of Lt.Gen., who is designated as the Director-General (DG). The present DG is Lt.Gen.Mahmood Ahmed. He is assisted by three Deputy Directors-General (DDGs), designated as DDG (Political), DDG-I (External) and DDG-II (Administration). It is divided into the following Divisions:

* The Joint Intelligence Bureau (JIB)—Responsible for all Open Sources Intelligence (OSINT) and Human Intelligence (HUMINT) collection, inside Pakistan as well as abroad.
* The Joint Counter-Intelligence (CI) Bureau: Responsible for CI inside Pakistan as well as abroad.
* The Joint Signals Intelligence Bureau (JSIB): Responsible for all communications intelligence inside Pakistan and abroad.
* Joint Intelligence North (JIN): Responsible for the proxy war in Jammu & Kashmir and the control of Afghanistan through the Taliban. Controls the Army of Islam, consisting of organisations such as Osama bin Laden's Al Qaeda, the Harkat-ul-Mujahideen (HUM), the Lashkar-e-Toiba, the Al Badr and Maulana Masood Azhar's Jaish-e-Mohammad (JEM). Lt.Gen.Mohammad Aziz, presently a Corps Commander at Lahore, is the clandestine Chief of Staff of the Army of Islam. It also controls all opium cultivation and heroin refining and smuggling from Pakistani and Afghan territory.
* Joint Intelligence Miscellaneous (JIM): Responsible for covert actions in other parts of the world and for the clandestine procurement of nuclear and missile technologies. Maj Gen (retd) Sultan Habib, an operative of

this Division, who had distinguished himself in the clandestine procurement and theft of nuclear material while posted as the Defence Attache in the Pakistani Embassy in Moscow from 1991 to 93, with concurrent accreditation to the Central Asian Republics (CARs), Poland and Czechoslovakia, has recently been posted as Ambassador to North Korea to oversee the clandestine nuclear and missile co-operation between North Korea and Pakistan. After completing his tenure in Moscow, he had co-ordinated the clandestine shipping of missiles from North Korea, the training of Pakistani experts in the missile production and testing facilities of North Korea and the training of North Korean scientists in the nuclear establishments of Pakistan through Capt. (retd) Shafquat Cheema, Third Secretary and acting head of mission, in the Pakistani Embassy in North Korea, from 1992 to 96. Before Maj.Gen. Sultan Habib's transfer to ISI headquarters from Moscow, the North Korean missile and nuclear co-operation project was handled by Maj.Gen.Shujjat from the Baluch Regiment, who worked in the clandestine procurement division of the ISI for five years. On Capt.Cheema's return to headquarters in 1996, the ISI discovered that in addition to acting as the liaison officer of the ISI with the nuclear and missile establishments in North Korea, he was also earning money from the Iranian and the Iraqi intelligence by helping them in their clandestine nuclear and missile technology and material procurement not only from North Korea, but also from Russia and the CARs. On coming to know of the ISI enquiry into his clandestine assistance to Iran and Iraq, he fled to Xinjiang and sought political asylum there, but the Chinese arrested him and handed him over to the ISI. What happened to him subsequently is not known. Capt.Cheema initially got into the ISI and got himself posted to the Pakistani Embassy in North Korea with the help of Col.(retd) Ghulam Sarwar Cheema of the PPP.

* Joint Intelligence X (JIX): Responsible for administration and accounts.

* Joint Intelligence Technical (JIT): Responsible for the collection of all Technical Intelligence (TECHINT) other than communications intelligence and for research and development in gadgetry.
* The Special Wing: Responsible for all intelligence training in the Armed Forces in the Defence Services Intelligence Academy and for liaison with foreign intelligence and security agencies.

Since 1948, there have been three instances when the DG,ISI, was at daggers drawn with the COAS. The first instance was during the first tenure of Mrs.Benazir Bhutto as Prime Minister (1988 to 1990). To reduce the powers of the ISI, to re-organise the intelligence community and to enhance the powers of the police officers in the IB, she discontinued the practice of appointing a serving Lt.Gen, recommended by the COAS, as the DG, ISI, and, instead appointed Maj.Gen. (retd) Shamsur Rahman Kallue, a retired officer close to her father, as the DG in replacement of Lt.Gen.Hamid Gul in 1989 and entrusted him with the task of winding up the internal intelligence collection role of the ISI and civilianising the IB and the ISI. Writing in the "Nation" of July 31,1997, Brig.A.R.Siddiqui, who had served as the Press Relations Officer in the army headquarters in the 1970s, said that this action of hers marked the beginning of her trouble with Gen.Beg, the then COAS, which ultimately led to her dismissal in August,1990. Gen.Beg made Maj.Gen.Kallue persona non grata (PNG), stopped inviting him to the Corps Commanders conferences and transferred the responsibility for the proxy war in J & K and for assisting the Sikh extremists in the Punjab from the ISI to the Army intelligence directorate working under the Chief of the General Staff (CGS).

The second instance was during the first tenure of Nawaz Sharif (1990-93), who appointed as the DG,ISI, Lt.Gen.Javed Nasir, a fundamentalist Kashmiri officer, though he was not recommended by the COAS for the post. Lt.Gen.Asif Nawaz Janjua, the then COAS, made Lt.Gen.Nasir PNG and stopped inviting him to the Corps Commanders conferences. Despite this, Lt.Gen.Janjua returned to the ISI the responsibility for the proxy war in J & K and for assisting the Sikh extremists.

During her second tenure (1993-96), Mrs. Bhutto avoided any conflict with Gen.Abdul Waheed Kakkar and Gen. Jehangir Karamat, the Chiefs of the Army Staff in succession, on the appointment of the DG,ISI. Her action in transferring part of the responsibility for the operations in Afghanistan, including the creation and the handling of the Taliban, from the ISI to the Interior Ministry headed by Maj.Gen. (retd) Nasirullah Babar, who handled Afghan operations in the ISI during the tenure of her father, did not create any friction with the army since she had ordered that Lt.Gen. Pervez Musharraf, then Director-General of Military Operations, should be closely associated by Maj.Gen.Babar in the Afghan operations.

However, sections of the ISI, close to Farooq Leghari, the then President of Pakistan, had Murtaza Bhutto, the surviving brother of Mrs.Benazir, assassinated outside his house in Karachi in September,1996, with the complicity of some local police officers and started a disinformation campaign in the media blaming her and her husband, Asif Zirdari, for the murder. This campaign paved the way for her dismissal by Leghari in November,1996.

The third instance was during the second tenure of Nawaz Sharif (1997-99) when his action in appointing Lt.Gen. Ziauddin, an engineer, as the DG,ISI, over-riding the objection of Gen.Musharraf led to the first friction between the two. Gen.Musharraf transferred Lt.Gen.Mohammad Aziz, the then DDG,ISI, on his promotion as Lt.Gen. to the GHQ as the CGS and transferred the entire Joint Intelligence North (JIN), responsible for covert actions in India and Afghanistan to the Directorate-General of Military Intelligence (DGMI) to be supervised by Lt.Gen.Aziz. It is believed that the JIN continues to function under the DGMI even after the appointment of Lt.Gen.Mahmood Ahmed as the DG, ISI, after the overthrow of Sharif on October 12,1999. Gen.Musharraf, as the COAS, made Lt.Gen.Ziauddin PNG and stopped inviting him to the Corps Commanders' conferences. He kept Lt.Gen.Ziauddin totally out of the picture in the planning and implementation of the Kargil operations. After the Kargil war, Nawaz Sharif had sent Lt.Gen.Ziauddin to Washington on a secret visit to inform the Clinton Administration officials of his concerns over the continued loyalty of Gen.Musharraf. After his return from the US, Lt.Gen.Ziauddin went to Kandahar, as ordered by Sharif, to pressurise Mullah Mohammad Omar, the Amir of the Taliban, to stop assisting the anti-Shia Sipah Sahaba Pakistan and to co-operate with the US in the arrest and deportation of bin Laden. On coming to know of this, Gen. Musharraf sent Lt.Gen.Aziz to Kandahar to tell the Amir that he should not carry out the instructions of Lt.Gen.Ziauddin and that he should follow only his (Lt.Gen.Aziz's) instructions.

These instances would show that whenever an elected leadership was in power, the COAS saw to it that the elected Prime Minister did not have effective control over the ISI and that the ISI was marginalised if its head showed any loyalty to the elected Prime Minister.

In their efforts to maintain law and order in Pakistan and weaken nationalist and religious elements and political parties disliked by the army, the ISI and the army followed a policy of divide and rule. After the success of the Islamic Revolution in Iran in 1979, to keep the Shias of Pakistan under control, the ISI encouraged the formation of ant-Shia Sunni extremist organisations such as the Sipah Sahaba. When the Shias of Gilgit rose in revolt in 1988, Musharraf used bin Laden and his tribal hordes from the North-West Frontier Province (NWFP) and the Federally-Administered Tribal Areas (FATA) to suppress them brutally. When the Mohajir Qaumi Movement (MQM—now called the Muttahida Qaumi Movement) of Altaf Hussain rose in revolt in the late 1980s in Karachi, Hyderabad and Sukkur in Sindh, the ISI armed sections of the Sindhi nationalist elements to kill the Mohajirs. It then created a split between Mohajirs of Uttar Pradesh origin (in Altaf Hussain's MQM) and those of Bihar origin in the splinter anti-Altaf Hussain group called MQM (Haquiqi—meaning real). In Altaf Hussain's MQM itself, the ISI unsuccessfully tried to create a wedge between the Sunni and Shia migrants from Uttar Pradesh.

Having failed in his efforts to weaken the PPP by taking advantage of the exile of Mrs.Benazir and faced with growing unity of action between Altaf Hussain's MQM and sections of Sindhi nationalist elements, Musharraf has constituted a secret task force in the ISI headed by Lt.Gen.Mahmood Ahmed, the DG, and consisting of Lt.Gen.(retd) Moinuddin Haider, Interior Minister, and Lt.Gen.Muzaffar Usmani, Deputy Chief of the Army Staff, to break the PPP, the MQM and the Sindhi nationalists.

This task force has encouraged not only religious political organisations such as the Jamaat-e-Islami (JEI) of Qazi Hussain Ahmed, the Jamiat-ul-Ulema Islam (JUI) of Maulana Fazlur Rahman etc, but also sectarian organisations such as the Sipah Sahaba and the Lashkar-e-Jhangvi of Riaz Basra, living under the protection of the Taliban and bin Laden in Kandahar in Afghanistan, to extend their activities to Sindh.

These organisations have now practically got out of the control of the ISI. Instead of attacking the PPP, the MQM and the Sindhi nationalists and bringing them to heel as Musharraf had hoped they would, they have taken their anti-Shia jehad to Sindh and have been recruiting a large number of unemployed Sindhi rural youth for service with the Taliban. Sindh, which was known for its Sufi traditions of religious tolerance, has seen under Musharraf a resurgence of the street power of the JEI and the JUI, which had been practically driven out of the province in the 1980s, by the PPP, the MQM and the Sindhi nationalists, and has seen in recent months anti-Shia massacres of the kind used by Musharraf in Gilgit in 1988. Over 200 Shias have been gunned down, including 30 doctors of Karachi, and the latest victims of the sectarian Frankenstein let loose by Musharraf in Sindh have been Shaukat Mirza, the Managing Director of Pakistan State Oil, and Syed Zafar Hussain Zaidi, a Director in the Research Laboratories of the Ministry of Defence, located in Karachi, who were gunned down on July 28 and 30,2001, respectively. The Lashkar-e-Jhangvi has claimed responsibility for both these assassinations.

As a result of the policy of divide and rule followed in Sindh by the ISI under Musharraf, one is seeing in Pakistan for the first time sectarian violence inside the Sunni community between the Sunnis of the Deobandi faith belonging to the Sipah Sahaba and the Lashkar-e-Jhangvi and the Sunnis of the more tolerant Barelvi faith belonging to the Sunni Tehrik formed in the early 1990s to counter the growing Wahabi influence on Islam in Pakistan and the Almi Tanzeem Ahle Sunnat formed in 1998 by Pir Afzal Qadri of Mararian Sharif in Gujrat, Punjab, to counter the activities of the Deobandi Army of Islam headed by Lt.Gen.Mohammed Aziz, Corps Commander, Lahore.

The Tanzeem has been criticising not only the Army of Islam for injecting what it considers the Wahabi poison into the Pakistan society, but also the army of the State headed by Musharraf for misleading the Sunni youth into joining the jehad against the Indian army in J & K and getting killed there in order to avoid the Pakistani army officers getting killed in the jehad for achieving its strategic objective. The ISI, which is afraid of a direct confrontation with the Barelvi organisations, has been inciting the Sipah Sahaba and the Lashkar-e-Jhangvi to counter their activities.

This has led to frequent armed clashes between rival Sunni groups in Sindh, the most sensational of the incidents being the gunning down of Maulana Salim Qadri of the Sunni Tehrik and five of his followers in Karachi on May, 18,2001, by the Sipah Sahaba, which led to a major break-down of law and order in certain areas of Karachi for some days.

Musharraf, the commando, believes in achieving his objective by hook or by crook without worrying about the means used. In his anxiety to bring Sindh under control and to weaken the PPP, the MQM and the Sindhi nationalists, he has, through the ISI, created new Frankensteins which might one day lead to the Talibanisation of Sindh, a province always known for its sufi traditions of religious tolerance and for its empathy with India.

Musharraf is under pressure from sections of senior army officers concerned over these developments to suppress the Sipah Sahaba and the Lashkar-e-Jhangvi. He and Lt.Gen.Haider have been making the pretence of planning to do so. It is to be seen whether they really would and, even if they did, whether they would or could effectively enforce the ban on them.

In India, there is a point of view in some circles that the only way of effectively countering the ISI activities against India is to have an Indian version of the ISI, with extensive powers for clandestine intelligence collection, technology procurement and covert actions and that the proposed Defence Intelligence Agency (DIA) should be patterned after Pakistan's ISI rather than after the DIA of the US and the Defence Intelligence Staff (DIS) of the UK, which are essentially agencies for the analysis and assessment of military intelligence in a holistic manner, with powers for clandestine collection only during times of war or when deployed in areas of conflict and with no powers for covert action.

The principle of civilian primacy in the intelligence community is widely accepted in all successful democracies and the discarding of this principle in Pakistan sowed the seeds for the present state of affairs there. In our anxiety for quick results against the ISI, we should not sacrifice time-tested principles as to how intelligence agencies should function in a democratic society.

In the 1970s,Indian policy-makers wisely decided that the Indian intelligence should not get involved in clandestine procurement of denied technologies since the exposure of any such procurement could damage the credibility and trustworthiness of the Indian scientific and technological community in the eyes of other countries.

This is what has happened to Pakistan. Its intelligence community did some spectacular work in clandestine procurement and theft of technologies abroad. But, once the details of this network were exposed, post-graduate students of Pakistan in scientific subjects, its academics, research scholars and scientists are looked upon with suspicion in Western countries and find it difficult to enter universities and research laboratories for higher studies and research and get jobs in establishments dealing in sensitive technologies and are less frequently invited to seminars etc than in the past. In its anxiety to catch up with India in the short term, Pakistan has damaged its long-term potential in science and technology.

PAKISTAN'S ISI 'FULLY INVOLVED' IN 9/11

The Sept. 11 Commission has found troubling new evidence that Iran was closer to al-Qaida than was Iraq. More importantly, and through no fault of its own, the commission missed the biggest prize of all: Former Pakistani intelligence officers knew beforehand all about the September 11 attacks. They even advised Osama bin Laden and his cohorts how to attack key targets in the United States with hijacked civilian aircraft. And bin Laden has been undergoing periodic dialysis treatment in a military hospital in Peshawar, capital of Pakistan's Northwest Frontier Province adjacent to the Afghan border.

The information came to the commission's attention in a confidential report from Pakistan as the commission's own report was coming off the presses. The information was supplied with the understanding that the unimpeachable source would remain anonymous.

Pakistan still denies that President Pervez Musharraf knew anything about the activities of A.Q. Khan, the country's top nuclear engineer who spent the last 10 years building and running a one-stop global Wal-Mart for "rogue" nations. North Korea, Iran and Libya shopped for nuclear weapons at Mr. Khan's underground black market. Pakistan has also denied the allegations by a leading Pakistani in the confidential addendum to the September 11 Commission report.

After U.S. and British intelligence painstakingly pieced together Mr. Khan's global nuclear proliferation endeavors, Deputy Secretary of State Rich Armitage was assigned last fall to convey the devastating news to Mr. Musharraf. Mr. Khan, a national icon for giving Pakistan its nuclear arsenal, was not arrested. Instead, Mr. Musharraf pardoned him in exchange for an abject apology on national television in English.

No one in Pakistan believed Mr. Musharraf's claim he was totally in the dark about Mr. Khan's operation. Prior to seizing power in 1999, Mr. Musharraf was — and still is — army chief of staff. For the past five years, Pakistan's Inter-Services Intelligence chief has reported directly to Mr. Musharraf.

Osama bin Laden's principal Pakistani adviser before Sept. 11, 2001, was retired Gen. Hamid Gul, a former ISI chief who, since the 2001 attacks, is "strategic adviser" to the coalition of six politico-religious parties that governs two of Pakistan's four provinces. Known as MMA, the coalition also occupies 20 percent of the seats in the federal assembly in Islamabad. Hours after Sept. 11, Gen. Gul publicly accused Israel's Mossad of fomenting the plot. Later, he said the U.S. Air Force must have been in on it since no warplanes were scrambled to shoot down the hijacked airliners.

Gen. Gul spent two weeks in Afghanistan immediately before Sept. 11. He denied meeting bin Laden on that trip, but has always said he was an "admirer" of the al-Qaida leader. However, he did meet several times with Mullah Mohammed Omar, the Taliban leader.

Since Sept. 11, hardly a week goes by without Gen. Gul denouncing the United States in both the Urdu and English-language media. In a conversation with this reporter in October 2001, Gen. Gul forecast a future Islamist nuclear power that would form a greater Islamic state with a fundamentalist Saudi Arabia after the monarchy falls.

Gen. Gul worked closely with the CIA during the Soviet occupation of Afghanistan when he was ISI chief. He was "mildly" fundamentalist in those days, he explained after Sept. 11, and indifferent to the United States. But he became passionately anti-American after the United States turned its back on Afghanistan following the 1989 Soviet withdrawal and began punishing Pakistan with economic and military sanctions for its secret nuclear buildup.

A ranking CIA official, speaking anonymously, said the agency considered Gen. Gul "the most dangerous man" in Pakistan. A senior Pakistani political leader, also on condition of anonymity, said, "I have reason to believe Hamid Gul was Osama bin Laden's master planner."

The report received by the Sept. 11 Commission from the anonymous, well-connected Pakistani source, said: "The core issue of instability and violence in South Asia is the character, activities and persistence of the militarized Islamist fundamentalist state in Pakistan. No cure for this canker can be arrived at through any strategy of negotiations, support and financial aid to the military regime, or by a 'regulated' transition to 'democracy.'"

The confidential report continued: "The imprints of every major act of international Islamist terrorism invariably passes through Pakistan, right from September 11 — where virtually all the participants had trained, resided or met in, coordinated with, or received funding from or through Pakistan — to major acts of terrorism across South Asia and Southeast Asia, as well as major networks of terror that have been discovered in Europe.

"Pakistan has harvested an enormous price for its apparent 'cooperation' with the U.S., and in this it has combined deception and blackmail — including nuclear blackmail — to secure a continuous stream of concessions. Its conduct is little different from that of North Korea, which has in the past chosen the nuclear path to secure incremental aid from Western donors. A pattern of sustained nuclear blackmail has consistently been at the heart of Pakistan's case for concessions, aid and a heightened threshold of international tolerance for its sponsorship and support of Islamist terrorism.

"To understand how this works, it is useful to conceive of Pakistan's ISI as a state acting as terrorist traffickers, complaining that, if it does not receive the extraordinary dispensations and indulgences that it seeks, it will, in effect, 'implode,' and in the process do extraordinary harm.

"Part of the threat of this 'explosion' is also the specter of the transfer of its nuclear arsenal and capabilities to more intransigent and irrational elements of the Islamist far right in Pakistan, who would not be amenable to the logic that its present rulers — whose interests in terrorism are strategic, and consequently, subject to considerations of strategic advantage — are willing to listen to....

"It is crucial to note that if the Islamist terrorist groups gain access to nuclear devices, ISI will almost certainly be the source.... At least six Pakistani scientists connected with the country's nuclear program were in contact with al-Qaida and Osama bin Laden with the thorough instructions of ISI.

"Pakistan has projected the electoral victory of the fundamentalist and pro-Taliban, pro-al Qaeda Muttahida Majlis-e-Amal (MMA) in the November elections as 'proof' the military is the only 'barrier' against the country passing into the hands of the extremists. The fact, however, is that the elections were widely rigged, and this was a fact acknowledged by the European Union observers, as well as by some of the MMA's constituents themselves. The MMA victory was, in fact, substantially engineered by the Musharraf regime, as are the various anti-U.S. 'mass demonstrations' around the country.

"Pakistan has made a big case out of the fact that some of the top-line leadership of al Qaeda has been arrested in the country with the 'cooperation' of the Pakistani security forces and intelligence. However, the fact is that each such arrest only took place after the FBI and U.S. investigators had effectively gathered evidence to force Pakistani collaboration, but little of this evidence had come from Pakistani intelligence agencies. Indeed, ISI has consistently sought to deny the presence of al Qaeda elements in Pakistan, and to mislead U.S. investigators.... This deception has been at the very highest level, and Musharraf himself, for instance, initially insisted he was 'certain' bin Laden was dead....

"ISI has been actively facilitating the relocation of the al Qaeda from Afghanistan to Pakistan, and the conspiracy of substantial segments of serving Army and intelligence officers is visible...."

"The Pakistan army consistently denies giving the militants anything more than moral, diplomatic and political support. The reality is quite different. ISI issues money and directions to militant groups, specially the Arab hijackers of September 11 from al Qaeda. ISI was fully involved in devising and helping the entire affair. And that is why people like Hamid Gul and others very quickly stated the propaganda that CIA and Mossad did it...."

"The dilemma for Musharraf is that many of his army officers are still deeply sympathetic to al Qaeda, Taliban militants and the Kashmir cause.... Many retired and present ISI officers retain close links to al Qaeda militants hiding in various state-sponsored places in Pakistan and Kashmir as well as leaders from the defeated Taliban regime. They regard the fight against Americans and Jews and Indians in different parts of the world as legitimate jihad."

The report also says, "According to a senior tribal leader in Peshawar, bin Laden, who suffers from renal deficiency, has been periodically undergoing dialysis in a Peshawar military hospital with the knowledge and approval of ISI if not of Gen. Pervez Musharraf himself."

The same source, though not in the report, speculated that Mr. Musharraf may plan to turn over bin Laden to President Bush in time to clinch Mr. Bush's re-election in November.

PAKISTAN'S POLITICAL LEADERSHIP AND THE ISI

Experts say Musharraf exercises firm control over his intelligence agency. "I do not accept the thesis that the ISI is a rogue organization," Milam says. "It's a disciplined army unit that does what it's told, though it may push the envelope sometimes." With a reported staff of 10,000, ISI is hardly monolithic: "Like in any secret service, there are rogue elements," says Frederic Grare, a South Asia expert and visiting scholar at the Carnegie Endowment. He points out that many of the ISI's agents have ethnic and cultural ties to Afghan insurgents, and naturally sympathize with them.

President Musharraf's admission that retired ISI agents may be helping Taliban fighters suggests his government knows of at least some unsanctioned Pakistani support for the Afghan insurgency. Experts note Musharraf's acknowledgement also gives him plausible deniability of any sanctioned assistance Pakistan may also be providing. Marvin G. Weinbaum, an expert on Afghanistan and Pakistan at the Middle East Institute, says Pakistan has sent "retired" ISI agents on missions the government could not officially endorse. Some observers believe Pakistan's duplicity is deliberate: "Musharraf's been playing with us since day one," Grare says.

What has Pakistan done to Combat Terrorism?

Pakistan has arrested scores of al-Qaeda affiliates, including Khalid Sheikh Mohammed, the alleged mastermind of the 9/11 attacks. The ISI and the Pakistani military have worked effectively with the United States to pursue the remnants of al-Qaeda. Pakistan also stationed 80,000 troops in the troubled province of Waziristan near the Afghan border. Hundreds of Pakistani soldiers died there in resulting clashes with militants, which Musharraf told a recent

CFR meeting "broke the al-Qaeda network's back in Pakistan." Though Pakistan has effectively battled al-Qaeda, Weinbaum says it has largely ignored Taliban fighters on its soil. "There are extremist groups that are beyond the pale with which the ISI has no influence at all," he says. "Those are the ones they go after."

What is Pakistan's Interest in aiding the Taliban?

Pakistan does not enjoy good relations with the current leadership of Afghanistan, partly because of rhetorical clashes with Afghan President Hamid Karzai, and partly because Karzai has made strong ties to India. Some experts say Pakistan wants to see a stable, friendlier government emerge in Afghanistan. Though the raging insurgency certainly doesn't serve this goal, increased Taliban influence, especially in the government, might. Supporting the Taliban also allows Pakistan to hedge its bets should the NATO coalition pull out of Afghanistan. Not everyone agrees with this analysis. According to Weinbaum, Pakistan has two policies. One is an official policy of promoting stability in Afghanistan; the other is an unofficial policy of supporting jihadis in order to appease political forces within Pakistan. "The second [policy] undermines the first one," he says.

Pakistan's interest in aiding Kashmiri Militants

Throughout its existence, Pakistan has viewed India as its enemy. Though Islamabad has a real interest in fostering better relations with New Delhi, little love is lost between the nations. Some experts say the Kashmiri militants keep pressure on the Indian government, though others point out the militants' actions have sparked tense showdowns between the two nuclear-armed states in the past. While Pakistan has a formidable military presence near the Indian border, Gannon says the militant groups there serve as "their second line of defense and offence."

British and Indian Charges against Pakistan

Experts are skeptical. Indian officials claim to have evidence that the ISI planned the July bombing of the Mumbai commuter trains, but the charges seem unlikely to some observers of the long, difficult India-Pakistan relationship. The two nations have a history of finger-pointing, and while some of the allegations hold water, there is a tendency to exaggerate. Furthermore, endorsing an attack on India would undermine Musharraf's own policy. "Pakistan is genuinely trying to open up relations with India," Gannon says.

In Weinbaum's view, the British report—which London insists is not a statement of policy—makes "too broad a statement." Though Pakistan does offer safe haven to Kashmiri groups, and perhaps some Taliban fighters, the suggestion that the ISI is responsible for the 7/7 bombings of London's mass transit system is "a real stretch," Gannon says.

Pakistan's Relationship with the Tribal Leaders in its Northwestern Provinces

Despite President Musharraf's claims of success in Pakistan's three-year military incursion into Waziristan, the region remains problematic. Local tribesmen are the traditional power brokers, and over the last two decades, they have earned large sums of money offering safe haven to Taliban and foreign fighters. At the outset of the U.S.-led war in Afghanistan, many militants fled across the border into Waziristan, putting pressure on the Pakistani government to address the situation. ISI officials met resistance when they asked local leaders to hand over foreign militants. Pakistan deployed troops to the area, though reports suggest that they took as many casualties as their adversaries. Unable to make military progress, Pakistani officials negotiated a peace deal with the local tribesmen, which was seen by many as a capitualtion to tribal influence in the area.

FUTURE ENGAGEMENT WITH THE ISI

When interviewed about the relationship between the West and Pakistan and the ongoing conflict in Afghanistan, the bestselling author Steven Coll stated:

This could not be a more complicated war. If you think about it, the United States is essentially waging a war against its own ally. The Taliban are a proxy of the government of Pakistan [orchestrated by the ISI]. We are an ally of the government of

Pakistan. We are fighting the Taliban. In the end, the Taliban will be defeated strategically when the government of Pakistan makes a strategic decision that its future does not lie in partnership with Islamic extremists. (2009)

Coll pinpoints the root of current and future problems in dealing with the ISI and their clandestine terrorist support networks. In 2009, the U.S. provided close to $6.5 billion dollars in aid to the Pakistani government; $300 million of that was dedicated to military spending (Mohammad). The West is figuratively caught between a rock and a hard place. It requires the assistance of Pakistan to successfully prosecute counter-terrorism campaigns in Southwest Asia. Yet, the ISI has infiltrated all ranks of Pakistan's military structure and leverages sympathizers and supporters throughout the Pakistani population. A large amount of that military aid is falling into the hands of the sponsors of the exact networks the West is attempting to defeat. On February 16, 2010 the Taliban's second in command, Mullah Baradar, was captured in a raid conducted jointly by the ISI and the U.S. Western leaders hoped that this would be a catalyst for strengthening the cooperation between the ISI and Western intelligence agencies and serve as an indication that the ISI would begin dismissing its historical involvement with militants. However, after a close examination into the raid, the New York Times provided: Relations between the intelligence services, [CIA and ISI], of the United States and Pakistan have long been marred by suspicions that Pakistan has sheltered the Afghan Taliban. The Pakistanis have long denied it. New details of the raid indicate that the arrest of the No. 2 Taliban leader was not necessarily the result of a new determination by Pakistan to go after the Taliban, or a bid to improve its strategic position in the region. Rather, it may be something more prosaic: "a lucky accident..." (Shane and Schmitt) Upon Baradar's capture, ISI officers delayed allowing U.S. intelligence officers to question him and were hesitant in sharing news and information about his detention with the Pakistani press (in fear of casting themselves in a pro-Western light).

The ISI will continue to act out of its own interest. It has grown in size from its inception and now forms a state within the Pakistani state. While it serves as an intelligence agency of the Pakistani government, the Pakistani government is largely unable to control its actions or relationships with terrorist organizations, both domestic and abroad. Ongoing operations to defeat extremists and terrorists places the ISI at a crossroads with Western intelligence agencies and irregular warfare personnel. Without a complete transformation of the ISI's motivations, allegiances, extremist slant, and structure, it will continue to exist as more of an enemy to the West than an ally.

Conclusion

The historic actions of the ISI in sponsoring organizations like al-Qaeda, JEM, LET and HUM, as well as their utilization of the Taliban as a proxy for foreign policy, signals that the ISI is a significant state sponsor of terrorism.

"Since Pakistan has terrorism, nuclear weapons, religious extremism, economic instability, and political volatility, easy [foreign policy] answers provide little guidance in a dangerous, fluid environment. If, due to ISI sins of omission or commission, terrorists acquire Pakistani nuclear weapons and there is a nuclear incident or nuclear war, the consequences will be unthinkable" (Roberts 109). These variables set the ISI's sponsorship apart from other international sponsors and make it definitively the most dangerous.

A careful policy of continued engagement with the ISI and accountability of Western funding to Pakistan will be essential to secure future stability in the region.

The ISI will continue to be a clandestine sponsor of worldwide extremism and transnational terrorism. The fragile nature of Pakistani politics, the existence of deeply entrenched Islamic foundations, and insecurity surrounding the Pakistani nuclear arsenal make the ISI the foremost terrorist threat and non-state sponsor of terrorism in the international community. The ISI masquerades as a controllable tool of the Pakistani government while covertly supporting enemies of the international community – conclusively acting as a threat to international stability and as a fifth column within the Pakistani state.

PAKISTAN'S INTELLIGENCE AGENCIES

There are three main intelligence agencies in Pakistan: Inter-Services Intelligence (ISI), Military Intelligence (MI), and the Intelligence Bureau (IB), although smaller organizations such as the National Accountability Bureau (NAB), abolished in 2008, have also played a role. The MI is a purely military institution, while the ISI is sometimes characterized as "semimilitary." The IB is a civilian agency. For the purposes of this study we will focus mainly, although not exclusively, on the ISI.

Inter-Services Intelligence. The Inter-Services Intelligence (ISI) is the best known of the intelligence agencies. Charged with coordinating intelligence among the three military services, the ISI is tasked with collecting foreign and domestic intelligence and conducting covert offensive operations. In this capacity, it is famous for its role in the Afghan conflict through its support of the mujahideen and, later, the Taliban as well as for its involvement in the Kashmir conflict. Its domestic political activities, which range from managing to suppressing political opposition, are, however, less known. Also important is its role in the surveillance of its cadre, foreigners, the media, foreign diplomats accredited to Pakistan, Pakistani diplomats serving outside the country, and the interception and monitoring of communications.

Located in Islamabad, the ISI is reportedly organized into eight divisions:

- Joint Intelligence X (JIX) serves as the secretariat that coordinates and provides administrative support to the other ISI wings and field organizations. It also prepares intelligence estimates and threat assessments.
- The Joint Intelligence Bureau (JIB), also called the "internal wing," responsible for political intelligence, is the largest division of the organization. Its main responsibility is to gather intelligence on political parties. It also has three subsections that manage operations in India, conduct antiterrorism operations (counterterrorism became an autonomous directorate in the fall of 2007), and provide security to visiting dignitaries. It was supposedly dismantled in November 2008.

- The Joint Counter Intelligence Bureau (JCIB) is responsible for field surveillance of Pakistani diplomats stationed abroad as well as for conducting intelligence operations in the Middle East, South Asia, China, Afghanistan, and the Muslim republics of the former Soviet Union.
- Joint Intelligence/North (JIN) is responsible for Jammu and Kashmir operations, including infiltration, exfiltration, propaganda, and other clandestine operations.
- Joint Intelligence Miscellaneous (JIM) conducts espionage in foreign countries, including offensive intelligence operations.
- The Joint Signal Intelligence Bureau (JSIB), which includes deputy directors for wireless, monitoring, and photos, operates a chain of signal intelligence collection posts along the border with India and provides communications support to militants operating in Kashmir.
- Joint Intelligence Technical (JIT) deals with the collection of all technical intelligence other than communications; with gadgetry; and, possibly, with the subsections involved with explosives, chemical weapons, and monitoring personnel with nuclear weapons roles in Pakistan.
- The Special Wing is responsible for intelligence training for the Pakistan armed forces at the Defence Services Intelligence Academy and possibly for liaison with foreign intelligence and security agencies.

Over the years, the ISI has assumed greater prominence among the Pakistani intelligence agencies. The agency's importance was recognized owing to its role in the Afghan conflict, but it was deeply involved in domestic political affairs long before.

Conflicts between intelligence agencies have, however, occurred during military regimes. They do not necessarily reflect differences on matters of policy—although these may eventually occur—but essentially of personality, turf battles, or both. The reform of the intelligence apparatus carried out by Pervez Musharraf aimed partly at improving the coordination and sharing of burdens among the various agencies.

The ISI was for a long time essentially a federal agency. Because Ayub Khan was reluctant to increase the military budget, neither the ISI nor the MI could post its officers in the districts. The domestic activities of the agencies therefore remained limited. The ISI now has a lieutenant colonel heading a unit in every district of the country and a brigadier, who is in charge of five to six districts, in every major city. A major general heads the ISI's political wing. General Musharraf also created a new body, an intelligence corps, whose officers, after training at the newly created intelligence academy, are meant to serve in the MI, ISI, or both. The idea of the intelligence corps emerged in 1998–1999, and the corps itself became operational in 2000–2001.

Short history of ISI involvement in politics. Created in 1948 to focus essentially on India, the ISI comprises the three branches of Pakistan's military: the army, navy, and air force. It originally had no active role in conducting domestic intelligence activities except in Pakistan-controlled Kashmir and the Northern Areas.

The ISI's political role was a direct result of the coup d'état led by the then-COAS, General Ayub Khan, in 1958. The agency at that time became responsible for monitoring Pakistani politicians. Monitoring the media and politically active segments of society also became part of the ISI mission. As a result, "social organizations with potential political influence, such as student groups, trade organizations, and unions [were warned] not to become involved in the political arena" and were kept under tight surveillance. Compared with the situation that developed under and after Zia ul-Haq, who launched an Islamization policy aimed at uniting Pakistan and pressuring the opposition, clerics during Ayub's time were instructed "to leave political rhetoric out of their exhortations."

Relations among the various Pakistani intelligence agencies also changed after Ayub's coup. Although the ISI, MI, and IB each has its own sphere of duty, all have a common goal—preserving national security— a situation that inevitably generates some overlap in their work. In the early years of Pakistan's existence, however, the IB concentrated on domestic political activities while the ISI and MI concerned themselves essentially with military matters. The director of the IB "reported directly to the Prime Minister and the two military agencies to the Commander in Chief of the Army. It was left to the Commander in Chief to bring all matters of interest to the notice of the Prime Minister through the Ministry of Defense."

When martial law was promulgated in 1958, all the intelligence agencies were placed under the direct control of Ayub Khan, who had become president and chief administrator of martial law. In practice, the intelligence agencies became instruments of consolidation for Ayub's regime, which saw any criticism as a threat to national security. Keen to demonstrate their loyalty to the president, the three agencies began to compete with each other.

This competition did not necessarily improve their effectiveness. The MI and ISI became particularly active on the domestic scene during the 1964 presidential election. They started providing the president with assessments of trends in public opinion. Too eager to please and lacking professionalism, they systematically underestimated the popularity of Fatima Jinnah, sister of Muhammad Ali Jinnah.

The intelligence agencies became even more deeply involved in domestic politics under General Yahya Khan. ISI activities at that time were directed more specifically at ethnic separatists, who were to become a nightmare for successive Pakistani regimes. East Pakistan politicians were among the ISI's first victims, and several were assassinated. A National Security Council was created under the chairmanship of General Yahya Khan himself to control an intelligence operation to ensure that no political party won an overall majority in the 1970 general election. The ISI tried unsuccessfully to infiltrate the inner circles of Sheikh Mujibur Rahman's Awami League, the leading nationalist party in East Pakistan, but the overall operation proved disastrous and the agencies failed to eliminate the Bengali resistance movement.

ISI was also employed by civilian Prime Minister Zulfikar Ali Bhutto against Balochi nationalists and was on occasion no less ruthless than it had been under Bhutto's military predecessors. But in order to counterbalance the ISI, Bhutto also created the Federal Security Force (FSF), a group parallel with the regular police, which operated as a private army "to force his opponents and former allies into submission." More important, however, through an executive order in 1975, Bhutto created the Political Cell of the ISI, which he used unnecessarily to rig the 1977 elections. Bhutto also tried to increase control over the ISI by appointing Lieutenant General Ghulam Jilani Khan, a general he thought loyal to him but who later paved the way for Zia ul-Haq's military coup. These two decisions ultimately brought about Bhutto's downfall.

The FSF was disbanded under Zia ul-Haq, who further expanded the ISI's powers to collect domestic intelligence on political and religious organizations that opposed his regime. The ISI was responsible for collecting intelligence about Sindhi nationalist activities and monitoring the leadership of the Pakistan People's Party (PPP) of Benazir Bhutto, which had launched the Movement for the Restoration of Democracy in the early 1980s. Dissident political leaders were constantly monitored and harassed by the intelligence agencies, in particular the IB and the ISI, but also the Criminal Investigation Agency and the Criminal Investigation Department.

After the success of the Islamic revolution in Iran, the ISI also took on responsibility for controlling the activities of Pakistan's Shi'i organizations. It was also during Zia's reign that the MI, although focused on military and security-related affairs, became involved in domestic political activities. The MI later played an important role in implementing orders to dismiss the two Bhutto-led governments in August 1990 and November 1996.

Intelligence agencies in Pakistani politics under Pervez Musharraf. One of the most important and most difficult tasks General Musharraf faced after his coup was to tame the ISI. After September 11, 2001, Musharraf's replacement of General Mahmood Ahmed with Lieutenant General Ehsan ul-Haq as head of the ISI was generally interpreted as a strong signal that he intended to regain control of an agency he thought was too close to the radicals he now intended to fight alongside the Americans. But the timing of General Mahmood's retirement, on October 7, 2001, was coincidental, corresponding with the natural end of his tenure as head of the ISI. Moreover, according to some in Pakistan, Musharraf himself had in the past sent General Mahmood to tell Taliban leader Mullah Omar not to accede to Nawaz Sharif's demand that the Taliban hand over Osama bin Laden, a request expressed through the then–ISI chief, Ziauddin. Several authors, however, argue that General Mahmood made a major mistake when, during a visit to Washington on September 12, 2001, he accepted the "non-negotiable" demands of the U.S. Department of State, demands that would ordinarily have been accepted by Musharraf himself. When Musharraf learned that Mahmood had accepted the demands before he had even been informed of them, Musharraf probably became more suspicious of the ambitions of his subordinate.

Reforms did come to the intelligence agencies. These reforms, however, had much less to do with the ideological convictions of agency leaders than with their willingness to make the entire intelligence apparatus more effective by clarifying the role of each agency, improving their coordination, and optimizing their capabilities. In no way did the reforms reduce the agencies' involvement in domestic politics. All through the campaign leading up to the October 2002 national elections, Benazir Bhutto complained about pre-election rigging by the ISI and coercion against PPP workers. On the other side of the political spectrum, Tehmina Daultana, vice president of the Pakistan Muslim League (Nawaz Group) once described as "a routine practice that the intelligence agencies, which should strengthen national solidarity, are now getting more powers and playing a major role in national politics."

All political parties, not just the opposition, blame the ISI for its interference in Pakistani politics, before and during the time of Pervez Musharraf. Senator Mushahid Hussain, who held the post of minister of information under Nawaz Sharif but by 2002 was very close to Musharraf, felt the need to reform intelligence, asking in particular for a clearer demarcation of each agency's responsibilities and stating that "ISI and MI should be freed from domestic politics, since this is not their job or their mandate." The situation was ironic because Hussain's own party, the Pakistan Muslim League–Quaid-i-Azam Group (PML-Q), had been literally midwifed by the agencies, with the aid of the NAB. Musharraf's subsequent reform of the intelligence agencies partially answered Hussain's first demand, but answering the second remains as unlikely as ever.

The ISI was no stranger during the constitution of the PML-Q, and it openly twisted politicians' arms to join the newly formed "King's party." The agency again played an open role in cobbling together the government of Mir Zafarullah Khan Jamali in 2002, and it rapidly became clear that it would be central to the implementation of the general's political agenda. So even more than it had been under Jamali's predecessors, the agency was given the task, the funds, and the freedom to operate however it wanted.

The agency undertook political engineering to weaken the major parties on the one hand and to ensure the complete loyalty of the ruling coalition on the other. Bribes and blackmail were used extensively in both cases. The role of the ISI was particularly obvious in convincing the Muttahida Majlis-e-Amal (MMA) leaders to accept General Musharraf as president in uniform.

Under Musharraf, the ISI also lost a great deal of its secrecy, and its political role became more visible. In March 2003, for example, the *Nation* reported that a dinner had been organized by the ISI at its headquarters for senators of the PML-Q (many of whom it had selected and helped get elected), reportedly "to provide them orientation and get introduced to each other." If the practice was not necessarily new, publicizing it certainly was. In a more formal manner, ISI officials appeared for the first time before the Senate Standing Committee on Defence to brief the committee members about the agency's functions and covert operations. But this did not make the ISI accountable to the Senate.

Although the relationship between the intelligence agencies and Musharraf was sometimes close, it was not without periods of unease. The main intelligence agency especially disliked the free hand Musharraf gave the U.S. Federal Bureau of Investigation to operate within Pakistan. The South Asia Tribune, an online news site, reported at the end of 2002 that the ISI had launched a "whispering campaign" against General Musharraf in the army barracks.

At the end of 2007, despite a deteriorating security situation in parts of the country, monitoring the political opposition seemed to be the main task of the intelligence agencies. Quoting Pakistani security sources, the French newspaper *Le Monde* opined on November 10, 2007, that the military intelligence chief, Nadeem Ejaz (a nephew of Pervez Musharraf's wife), spent more time harassing Musharraf's political opponents than taking care of the security situation in the western provinces of Pakistan.

HOW THE ISI SUBVERTS THE POLITICAL SYSTEM

The Soviet withdrawal from Afghanistan in 1989 marked the beginning of a new period of intense political activity for the Pakistani intelligence agencies. Both the MI and the ISI worked hard to implement the military's political agenda, and they have played an active role in every general election since. They have been used to support, oppose, or eventually suppress particular political groups and to aid domestic adversaries of civilian governments with which the military had grown dissatisfied. Intelligence quickly became and remains central for senior commanders pursuing behind-the-scenes political interventions.

The army chief brings information collected by the agencies to the president and the prime minister in a discretionary manner. The president has in the past relied on political intelligence gathered by the agencies to formulate the charges against governments he wanted to dismiss. The army chief therefore controls a very powerful instrument—an instrument that can be used indirectly through the president when civilians are in power, or directly when the military is in power. The latter was the case under Musharraf, to whom the army chief reported.

Funding political parties. The military ultimately managed to have Prime Minister Benazir Bhutto dismissed in 1990, and the ISI again became active in the general elections, during which it supported a number of her political opponents.

Allegations of the ISI's interference in domestic politics went public on March 24, 1994, when Mehran Bank president Yunus Habib was arrested for siphoning money from the bank. On April 20, the issue was brought to the floor of the National Assembly by Interior Minister Nasrullah Babar. In 1997, retired air marshal Asghar Khan, former chief of the Pakistan Air Force, filed a Supreme Court petition challenging the legality of a "donation" by the Mehran Bank, a nationalized institution, of some approximately $6.5 million to the then-COAS, General Mirza Aslam Beg, in 1990. The chief justice, Sajjad Ali Shah, called a hearing on ISI's role in domestic politics.

General Aslam Beg, who admitted he had put the money at the disposal of the ISI and MI through a secret service account, had earlier declared that "it was a practice with the ISI to support candidates during the elections under the direction of the chief executive." The money was then used by the MI and ISI for "duly authorized purposes." It was used in particular to fund the Islami Jamhoori Ittehad (IJI), which received a little less than half the total sum. Beneficiaries also included the future prime minister, Nawaz Sharif. A substantial part of the money was also used as "special funds," destined to finance covert operations.

The 1990 election was not the first instance of ISI involvement in Pakistani politics. Manipulation of elections has been the norm since the creation of the country, particularly under military regimes trying to compensate for their lack of legitimacy. Millions of rupees were embezzled from secret funds for that purpose in 1970 by General Umar, a close associate of Ayub Khan, and N. A. Rizvi, who directed the IB at that time.

Besides the PPP, the only victim of the scandal was the banker, Yunus Habib, who was arrested and jailed. The COAS suffered no judicial consequences and went on the offensive, demanding that legal action be taken against the former chief of the Pakistan Air Force and General Nasrullah Babar for violating the provision of the Official Secrets Act and bringing the armed forces into disrepute.

Although technically still pending before the Supreme Court, the case was de facto suspended by the October 1999 coup d'état of Pervez Musharraf. Almost eight years later, in February 2007, Asghar Khan, one of the main protagonists of the scandal, was still asking the Supreme Court to "determine the role of Inter-Services Intelligence (ISI) in national politics."

Support for particular political groups or parties is not primarily the result of ideological sympathies. Like all individuals, intelligence agents have their own ideological inclinations and political preferences, but these pale in comparison with the military's institutional interest in its own domination of the political landscape. Therefore, support or opposition to any given organization varies over time, the latter being eventually as vicious as the former can be generous.

Setting up alliances. In 1988, the ISI, led by Lieutenant General Hamid Gul, set up the IJI, an alliance of right-wing and religious political parties, to prevent Benazir Bhutto's PPP from sweeping the polls. The ISI arranged the reunification of Pakistan's two Pakistan Muslim League factions, which were then joined by smaller organizations, and helped them campaign against the PPP. Imtiaz Ahmed, who was then additional director general of national security at the ISI and as such was involved in all ISI political dealings, launched a campaign to discredit Benazir Bhutto for allegedly working against Punjabi interests. The military opposition failed to prevent a PPP victory in the elections, but ISI manipulations led to greater electoral success for the religious parties, which obtained, collectively, 12 percent of the vote in the 1988 national election, a score they never again reached, including in 2002.

Bibliography

Alam, Aftab : *US Policy Towards South Asia: Special Reference to Indo-Pak Relations,* Raj, Delhi, 1998.

Allana, G.: *Pakistan Movement: Historic Documents,* Karachi, Department of International Relations, University of Karachi, 1967.

Askari Rizvi: *Military, State, and Society in Pakistan,* New York: St. Martin's Press, 2000.

Ayesha Siddiqa-Agha: *Military Inc.: Inside Pakistan's Military Economy,* London: Pluto, 2007.

Benjamin, Joseph : *Indo-Pak Relations : Prospect and Retrospect,* Reference Press, Delhi, 2004.

Bernard Wood: *Development Dimension of Conflict Prevention and Peace-building,* New York: UNDP,. 2003.

Brian Cloughley: *War, Coups, and Terror: Pakistan's Army in Years of Turmoil,* New York: Skyhorse, 2008.

Bruce, Hoffman: *Inside Terrorism,* New York: Columbia University Press, 1998.

Buzan, Barry & Eric Herring: *The Arms Dynamic in World Politics,* London: Lynne Rienner Publishers, 1998.

Choudhury, Golam W: *Pakistan: Transition from Military to Civilian Rule,* Scorpion, 1988.

Choueiri, Y.M. : *Islamic Fundamentalism,* London: Pinter Publishers; Delhi, 1990.

Cohen, Stephen P., *The Pakistan Army,* University of California Press, 1989.

Daniel Pipes : *In the Path of God: Islam and Political Power,* New York: Basic Books Inc., 1983.

Das. P.K.: *Jihad : Terrorist Strategies Against the West,* Sumit Enterprises, Delhi, 2009.

Dilip H. Mohite : *Rise of Islamic Fundamentalism and the Grand American Strategy* : Kalinga, Delhi, 2002.

Duscha, Julius. *Arms, Money and Politics.* New York, 1965.

Graham, Allison: *Nuclear Terrorism: The Ultimate Preventable Catastrophe,* New York: Times Books, 2004.

Greene, Mott : *Natural Knowledge in Preclassical Antiquity,* Baltimore, Johns Hopkins University Press, 1992.

Hassan, Lt Gen Gul, *Memoirs of Lt Gen Gul Hassan,* Oxford University Press, 1993.

Hiro, Dilip : *Holy Wars: The Rise of Islamic Fundamentalism* New York: Routledge, Chapman and Hall, Inc., 1989.

Hussain Mushahid: *Pakistan: Problems of Governance,* Vanguard 1993.

Juvale, R.P. : *Military Strategy and Diplomacy,* Cyber Tech Publications, Delhi, 2010.

Laquer, Walter, *The New Terrorism: Fanaticism and the Arms of Mass Destruction,* Oxford: Oxford University Press, 1999.

Mahmood Suhail : *Islamic Fundamentalism in Pakistan, Egypt and Iran,* Vanguard Books Ltd., Lahore, 1995.

Mazhar Aziz: *Military Control in Pakistan: The Parallel State,* London: Routledge, 2008.

Multani, R K P : *Islamic Fundamentalism in South Asia* : Sumit Enterprises, Delhi, 2007.

Noorani, A.G.: *Islam and Jihad,* Leftword, Delhi, 2002.

Posen, B.R.: *The Sources of Indian Military Doctrine,* Ithaca, 1984, Cornell Univ. Press.

Rizvi, Hassan Askari: *The Military and Politics in Pakistan: 1947 - 86,* Progressive Publishers 1986.

Roxanne L. Euben, *Enemy in the Mirror : Islamic Fundamentalism and the Limits of Modern Rationalism : A Work of Comparative Political Theory* : Oxford University Press, 2001.

Shahid Javed: *Pakistan: The Continuing Search for Nationhood,* Westview Press, 1991.

Sharma, Rajeev: *Global Jihad : Current Patterns and Future Trends,* Kaveri Books, Delhi, 2006.

Thomas Arnold: *The Spread of Islam in the World, A History of Peaceful Preaching,* Goodword Books, 2001.

Thomas R. Metcalf : *A Concise History of India and Pakistan,* New York: Cambridge University Press, 2002).

William R. Thompson: *The Grievances of Military Coup-makers,* Beverly Hills: Sage Publications, 1973.

Index

R

T

W

❑❑❑